MICHAEL STAUNTON

THE VOICE
OF THE
IRISH

THE STORY OF
CHRISTIAN IRELAND

HiddenSpring

Cover design by Stefan Killen Design

Cover photo: © Getty Images, 2002

Cover art: Chi Rho initial from the Book of Kells © Art Resource, NY

Text design by Stefan Killen

Library of Congress Cataloging-in-Publication Data

Staunton, Michael, 1967–
    The voice of the Irish : the story of Christian Ireland / Michael Staunton.
        p. cm.
    Includes bibliographical references and index.
    ISBN 1-58768-022-X
    1. Ireland—Church history. 2. Ireland—Civilization. I. Title.
    BR792 .S73 2003
    274.15—dc21

                                                                2002154625

Published in North America by
HiddenSpring
An imprint of Paulist Press
997 Macarthur Boulevard
Mahwah, New Jersey 07430

www.hiddenspringbooks.com

Printed and bound in the United States of America

CONTENTS

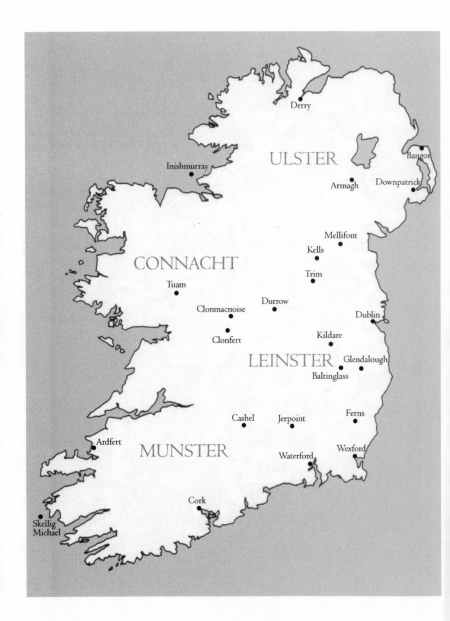

Medieval Ireland

Modern Ireland

Cross of the Scriptures, Clonmacnoise, County Offaly

INTRODUCTION

Sometime in the middle of the fifth century A.D., a young man from the west coast of Britain dreamed that a man approached him bearing a letter with the heading, "The Voice of the Irish." Reading the letter, he imagined that he heard a chorus of voices calling on him to walk among them in Ireland. These are the words of St. Patrick, known as the Apostle of the Irish and famous worldwide as the symbol of Irish identity. Irish history does not begin with St. Patrick's mission to Ireland: People lived in Ireland for thousands of years before that. But the coming of Christianity marks a crucial point in Ireland's development, for it is only from this point that we can know anything about individual Irish people or comment with any authority on the major events which marked their history. It is only with the coming of Christianity that Ireland was brought fully within the mainstream of European culture and Irish culture came to be known abroad. Christianity more than any other single human force has helped to shape political identity on the island, to bring people together and to divide them. It also brought literacy and the culture of the book to the Irish people, something which over time they have made very much their own. In other words, it gave the Irish a voice.

A visitor to Ireland today might find this picture incongruous. He or she will encounter a bustling, prosperous and secularized society much like that of Ireland's European neighbors, a far cry from the slow-moving, rural and overwhelmingly Christian society that it once was. North and south, Christian churches are no longer the social focal points that they have been for centuries, and indeed one might be as likely to hear criticism of the churches and their leaders as praise. Nor does religion play such a prominent role in the political life of Ireland. But look closer and you will see all around you the enduring legacy of Ireland's Christian past.

At the southwestern extremity of Ireland, the last piece of European land before America, is the island of Skellig Michael. On this sheer rock off the Kerry coast, extending six hundred feet above the sea, so exposed to the elements that it is no longer inhabited, remain some of the earliest signs of Christianity in Ireland. There, in the tiny stone huts which still stand, early Christians found a counterpart to the deserts of Egypt where the first Christian monks had sought to retreat from the world. As one moves inland, past the rocky Irish coastline to the more fertile soil of the midland plains, one finds relics of the medieval "Golden Age" of the Irish church, when it grew in confidence and influence: in the ruins of the monastery of Clonmacnoise in County Offaly, the round tower at Glendalough in County Wicklow and in St. Cormac's Chapel on the Rock of Cashel, County Tipperary.

The towns and cities also bear testimony to Ireland's Christian past. They were mainly foundations of the Vikings, an invading people who once destroyed churches but came to embrace Christianity. Dublin's Christ Church Cathedral, where thousands gather annually to ring in the new year, is a Viking foundation. The Normans who came to Ireland in the twelfth century revitalized urban life but also reformed religious practice. Scattered over the country are not only the stone castles which bear testimony to their rule, but the monasteries and friaries which prospered under it.

Many of these houses were suppressed as a consequence of the Reformation, but that movement produced a new and lasting force in the shape of the Protestant churches. The elegant Georgian streets and squares of Dublin are witness to the eighteenth-century heyday of the Anglican tradition in Ireland. Likewise, the industrial landscape and Victorian halls of Belfast are the product of Ulster's Presbyterian heritage. The resilience of Catholicism is evident in the rural sites where Mass was celebrated in the Penal Era and the Marian shrines which cropped up in the aftermath of the Great Famine of the 1840s. Throughout Ireland, too, is the evidence of conflicts waged in the name of religion: from the rural monuments to battles won and lost, and the commemorative statues on Dublin's O'Connell Street to the republican and loyalist murals of Belfast and Derry. And everywhere, less conspicuous but perhaps more important, are the places where Christian worship continues every day.

These are the physical symbols of Christian Ireland, but it is also present in the word. The *Book of Kells,* one of the greatest works of art of the European Middle Ages, is an elaborate ornamental and pictorial celebration of the word. From religious hymns and poems to the polemic writings of religious partisans, Christianity has provided a central theme in Irish writing through the ages. It is also there in the modern literature of Yeats, Joyce and Heaney—writers who are ambiguous about or critical of Ireland's Christian legacy, but know that they cannot escape it or ignore it. And this legacy continues to have a hold on the lives of Irish people today, at home and abroad.

Newgrange passage tomb, County Meath, on the morning of the winter solstice

I

BEFORE CHRISTIANITY

When Christians first came to Ireland, around A.D. 400, they found a place different from any other where their faith had been established. A distant and forbidding island on the periphery of the European continent, surrounded by rough seas and covered by woodland and bog, the Romans referred to it as Hibernia—the Winter Land. Not only was it distant from the core of the Christian world, it was also markedly different in culture. Christianity had spread from the Holy Land to Greece, Italy and North Africa through the Roman Empire, where centralized institutions, urban society and the written word prevailed. It had spread west and north to the Roman provinces of Spain and Gaul, and to the furthermost outpost of the empire, Britain. But Ireland never experienced Roman rule and remained untouched by the features of Roman life which came with it. Instead, well established on the island were its own patterns of social organization, its own customs and beliefs. Christianity has had a profound impact on Ireland, but Christianity has also been shaped by Ireland. There, Christian culture found a fertile soil in which it could develop at a time when it faced threat throughout Europe, and a base from which its faith and traditions could be exported back to the Continent in a new and vital form. The distinctive character of Irish Christianity which has lasted through the ages owes much to the particular circumstances which it found when it began to take root in the fifth century.

PREHISTORIC IRELAND

We think of the Irish as the quintessentially Celtic people. The words *Celtic* or *Gaelic* are often used as blanket terms to describe Irish traditions and characteristics. But many different peoples have lived in Ireland both before and after the Celts. For seven thousand years before the coming of Christianity, Ireland was home to a succession of civilizations as various peoples crossed from the west coast of Britain or from the European continent. None of these early Irish men and women have left a written record to us, but traces of their way of life, their culture and their beliefs have not entirely perished. In addition to archaeological evidence, we can find in the writings of Ireland's early Christians intriguing echoes of the pre-Christian world. From the ninth century at least, Irish monks began to put in writing oral traditions which dated back to pagan times: mythological stories describing the origins of the Irish people, and epic tales of Cú Chullain, Finn mac Cumhail and other warrior-heroes. These are secondhand glimpses of the pagan past, obscured by the writers' confusion and by deliberate distortion and interpolation: Noah and St. Patrick make incongruous appearances alongside pagan gods and heroes, and the influence of Christian and classical literature is often evident. Nevertheless, there remains at the core of these writings an invaluable insight into an ancient world.

A collection of poems and legends compiled by monks in the eleventh century called the *Lebor Gabála* or *Book of Invasions* provides a mythological explanation of Ireland's past based on a series of invasions by magical peoples. The first were the Partholonians, a tribe of twenty-five men and twenty-five women who came to

Ireland from the west. They thrived for 5,000 years until they were wiped out by plague. Their successors, the tribe of Nemed, were shipwrecked near Ireland after a journey from the Caspian Sea, and made Ireland their home, but that people too was eventually wiped out by plague. Nevertheless, during the reign of the Partholonians and Nemedians, the island came to grow in size, beauty and fertility, land was cleared and lakes appeared. Next, the four tribes of the Fir Bolg settled in Ireland and formed an alliance with the Fomorians, a tribe of warlike giants who had contended with the earliest settlers. The Fir Bolg were said to have divided Ireland amongst them and to have instituted kingship. The fourth invaders, the most colorful of all, were the Tuatha Dé Danann, or "Tribe of the Goddess Danu." Among them were Lug, whose spear ensured victory in battle, Nuada, whose sword could not be resisted, and the Daghdha, whose cauldron satisfied any company. Falling to Ireland in the form of a mist, they went on to defeat the Fir Bolg in a great battle of magical powers and established their sway over the island. The fifth and final invaders were not gods but mortals: the Milesians—sons of Mil—who arrived from Spain. Despite their mortality, they triumphed in battle over the Tuatha Dé Danann by engaging the support of Ireland's goddess of sovereignty, Eriú. The Milesians took their place as rulers of Ireland, but the Tuatha Dé Danann were not fully banished. Instead, after an agreement with the Milesians, they retreated to the "Otherworld": the bogs, lakes and stones of Ireland.

This of course is a fanciful confection which, as we can see (see p. 14–15), tells us more about pagan beliefs than it does about history. Nevertheless, the image of a series of settlers, if not "invaders" is a valid one, as archaeological study testifies. Over time, too, land was cleared, and new technologies, if not magical powers, helped certain cultures to establish their dominance. Around 7000 B.C. people first crossed to Ireland from Scotland and settled along the coasts and the waterways. Further numbers of these hunters and fishers crossed from England and came to be found all over Ireland, but they have left little trace to posterity. The next wave of settlers, however, left a mark on the landscape which still inspires awe. All around Ireland there stand great stone constructions, older than the Pyramids, and just as mysterious. These are the megalithic (large stone) tombs, cairns and standing-stones erected by the Neolithic peoples who had come to dominate Ireland by 4000 B.C. Exactly why they were built we do not know, but their construction involved tremendous effort and precision. In a bend of the River Boyne in County Meath* stand the most impressive cluster of megalithic creations in Europe. The passage-graves of Newgrange, Knowth and Dowth must have taken decades to build, and involved whole communities carrying stones for miles and helping in the intricate construction. They consist of large mounds, each with one or two passages leading to a central chamber. That people were buried there is certain, as evidenced by the cremated bone discovered there, but the chamber's significance seems to be greater. On the morning of the winter solstice, the sun beams down the sixty-foot passage of Newgrange, illuminating the chamber within. The twin passages of Knowth are similarly aligned with the spring and summer equinoxes. The spiral symbols carved on the stone, the quartz-covered roof of Newgrange designed to reflect the sun, and the map of the moon recently discovered on the chamber wall of Knowth—the oldest known in the world—all provide clues but do not solve the mystery. The most obvious explanation is that these were places of ceremony, connected to the natural elements, but beyond that we cannot come close to the people who built these remarkable structures and who once dominated Ireland.

The Neolithic peoples were Ireland's first farmers, and from their arrival the island became increasingly prosperous and technologically advanced. From the inception of Ireland's Bronze Age, around 2200

---

* References to counties throughout are to the present-day counties, which derive from the Norman division of Ireland in the late twelfth century.

B.C., metal weapons and tools began to be made, and some spectacular works of gold jewelry survive from the first millennium B.C.

Then, around 500 B.C., a new people began to appear in Ireland. They came not as invaders but as settlers in a number of waves from Britain, Gaul and Spain. The indigenous population was not displaced—indeed it is thought that Ireland's present-day gene pool is still dominated by its Bronze Age ancestors. But by the time St. Patrick arrived in Ireland, the language and culture of the people were those of the Celts, the Gaels, or the Milesians as they are called in the *Lebor Gabála*. It was their ideas of social organization, kingship and law which the first Christians encountered, and their ideas of the gods ever present in the "Otherworld."

THE CELTS

The Celts were not a race, still less an empire, rather a group of tribes of Asian origins which were similar in language and culture. By around 700 B.C. they had settled in central Europe, and impressed themselves upon their neighbors. The Greeks called them *Keltoi,* or *Galatae,* and the Romans called them *Celtae* or *Galli*—hence our terms *Celt, Celtic, Gaul* and *Gaelic.* Although much of Europe has a Celtic past and the Celts were relative latecomers to Ireland, it is here that this civilization has been best preserved. The Celtic culture of Spain, Gaul and Britain came to be overlaid with Roman institutions and customs as the empire extended its sway north and west, and survives mainly in archaeological artifacts, place-names and descriptions by classical writers. Ireland, untouched by Roman rule, preserved its Celtic civilization intact until it embraced Christian culture.

Unique as a testament to the Celtic world is the epic poem, the *Táin Bó Cuailigne (The Cattle Raid of Cooley),* Ireland's counterpart to Greece's *Iliad* and *Odyssey* and Rome's *Aeneid.* Written down by Christian monks and heavily influenced by the classical epics, it nonetheless reflects, in its description of chariots and weaponry, a society which archaeology tells us existed in Celtic Gaul of the second century B.C. It also provides an illustration of some of the primary features and concerns of pagan Celtic Ireland.

The *Táin* begins with an argument between Ailill, king of the western province of Connacht and his wife Queen Medbh over which of them has the higher standing. They try to settle the argument by comparing their possessions, and Ailill claims victory by virtue of his white bull. Medbh, refusing to accept defeat, asks the Ulsterman Dáire to borrow his "brown bull of Cooley," but after this request is granted, Medbh's envoys insult Dáire's hospitality and he retracts his offer. The great cattle raid begins. In the face of Medbh's forces only one man, Cú Chullain, stands in defense of Ulster. The son of the God Lugh and a mortal mother, he alone was exempt from the dying curse of a pregnant woman, Macha, who was forced to race against the king's horses outside the royal palace: that the men of Ulster should suffer the pangs of childbirth for a time every year. Medbh is confident of victory, but when the men of Connacht advance they suffer heavy defeat at Cú Chullain's hands. Thereafter, it is arranged that the battle will proceed in the form of single combat between Cú Chullain and a series of Connacht's bravest warriors, and culminates with the prolonged hand-to-hand contest with his beloved foster-brother Fer Dia, now in Medbh's service. Cú Chullain is victorious and buries Fer Dia with great sorrow. Meanwhile Medbh's men had succeeded in capturing the brown bull of Cooley, though the bull's roars woke Ulster's warriors who drove the Connacht army back. The story ends with a contest between the brown bull and Ailill's white bull, in which Dáire's bull kills his opponent. The brown bull then charges back to Cooley in a frenzy, where his heart bursts and he dies.

The *Táin* is about cattle, and cattle were at the heart of Irish life. In this primarily pastoral society, one's social standing could be determined by how many cattle one owned. A freeman bound himself to a lord, in a system known as clientage, by borrowing stock to be repaid with interest over time. Cattle also formed the basis of exchange: Law tracts record a slave woman valued at three cows or six heifers. Celtic society was a strictly hierarchical one, comprised of nobles, various ranks of freemen and women, then the unfree who were tied to the land, and finally slaves. The most important social bond, however, was the extended family, which was responsible in law for each of its members. Close links between families were forged through marriage and fosterage, as we can see in the tragic combat between Cú Chullain and Fer Dia. A group of families comprising around fifteen hundred individuals formed a *tuath* or tribe, and each tuath had its own king. The king was not a great landowner or a legislator, rather the symbolic embodiment of the tribe. Gerald of Wales, who visited Ireland in the twelfth century, described a royal inauguration ritual in which the king mated with a white mare and then, along with his kinsmen, bathed in the blood of the slaughtered horse. Intriguingly, this ceremony, symbolizing the union of the tribe with the natural world, bears close similarities with an ancient Hindu royal inauguration ritual. It was customary upon a king's inauguration for him and his warriors to launch a cattle raid against neighboring *tuatha*. And from the epics, warfare appears the principal activity of the early Irish aristocracy. We also have some descriptions of more peaceful activities. The *Táin* describes how Conchubar, the king of Ulster, spent his days:

> As soon as he arises, settling the cares and business of the province, thereafter dividing the day into three, the first third of the day spent watching the youths playing games and hurling [a field game], the second third playing *brandub* and *fidchell* [board games] and the last third in consuming food and drink until sleep comes on them all, while minstrels and musicians are meanwhile lulling him to sleep.[1]

Great attention is paid in these stories to feasting, and the duty of hospitality was a vitally important one. As we have seen, it was an insult to Dáire's hospitality which set off the war between Ulster and Connacht.

In the *Táin*, Ireland is conceived of in terms of five provinces: Ulster, Connacht, Leinster, Munster—names which are still used— and the middle province, Mide, or Meath, which came to be swallowed up by the others. It describes a great victory for Ulster at a time when that province was in the ascendancy. But ironically, by the time Christianity came to Ireland, the Connacht dynasty of the Uí Néill had begun to dominate the northern half of Ireland and would continue to do so for centuries thereafter. The peoples of Ireland shared a common language and law and common customs and beliefs, but they were not united politically. In the pagan era there was no concept of a high king of Ireland, and it is clear that at no time did one ruler or dynasty hold sway over the whole island. The essentially decentralized nature of power in Ireland did much to influence the pattern which Christian evangelization followed, and the shape that the Irish church took thereafter. Conversion had to work through the tuath, and when the church became established it did so on a local basis. Whereas in continental Europe, ecclesiastical provinces and dioceses mirrored the Roman administrative structures, in Ireland, monasteries attached to tuatha formed the basis of ecclesiastical organization. The structures of royal overlordship were mirrored in the monastic federations which developed from the seventh century. And the Christian clergy took their place within the social hierarchies of Celtic Ireland, with bishops and abbots, for instance, granted the same rank as kings or senior nobles.

One group in pagan Celtic Ireland existed beyond the normal social hierarchies. These were the *aés dána*, a creative, intellectual and priestly caste, which included the *filidh,* or poets, the *breitheamh,* who memorized the law, and the *druid.* The popular image of the Celtic druid derives from the comments of classical writers about the continental Celts: Pliny describes a white-robed, bearded figure, performing rituals with a sprig of mistletoe in hand. Irish literary and legal works also use the word *druí* (plural: *druid*) to describe a priestly class, though their functions often seem to overlap with those of poets, jurists and visionaries. Druids are mentioned among the earliest settlers in the *Lebor Gabála,* and are particularly prominent among the Tuatha Dé Danann. In the *Táin* the druid Cadhbad is an important character, though he is portrayed more as a prophet than as a priest. It is possible that Christian writers deliberately obscured or diminished the druids' power, but they were

A Celtic cult idol on Boa Island, Lough Erne, County Fermanagh

clearly aware of their importance: The earliest biography of St. Patrick has at its center a battle of mystical powers between the saint and the pagan druids. It is also likely that many of the aés dána, including druids, became monks or priests with the establishment of Christianity.

THE GODS OF THE CELTS

Who, then, were the gods whom the pagan Celtic Irish worshiped? The gods described in Irish mythology show many similarities with those described by classical writers of the British and Continental Celts, and certain features are found in all pagan cultures. But in certain ways these beliefs are distinctively Irish, particularly in the importance attributed to the natural world.

According to the *Lebor Gabála,* the chief priest of the invading Milesians spoke these mysterious words as he placed his right foot on Irish soil:

> I am Wind On The Sea
> I am Ocean-Wave
> I am Roar Of Sea
> I am Bull Of Seven Fights
> I am Vulture On Cliff
> I am Dewdrop
> I am Fairest Of Flowers
> I am Salmon In Pool
> I am Lake On Plain
> I am Mountain In A Man[2]

The Milesians, mortal though they were, triumphed over the Tuatha Dé Danann because they won the support of the goddess of sovereignty, Eriú. In return, they promised that she would rule for all time and that her name would be given to the whole island. Today's Gaelic name for Ireland, Éire, derives from her legend. There are many other cases throughout Irish history of the land's identification with a woman. In the early modern period, for example, a popular form of poem envisaged the apparition of a beautiful woman who appealed to the bard to save her from the English.

All around the country, ancient local traditions identify aspects of the landscape, particularly mounds, rivers and lakes, with female power. The Tuatha Dé Danann means "the people of the goddess Danu," a name which means in Sanskrit "the flowing one." The River Danube, the basin of which was settled by some of the earliest Celtic peoples in Europe, has the same derivation. Just as significant in Irish history is the River Boyne, which flows through the valley where Newgrange stands. The goddess Boinn was said to dwell in Newgrange, one of many divine spirits who retreated to the megalithic sites after the victory of the Milesians. Two of the most important sites in early Ireland are Emain Macha (or Navan Fort), County Armagh, the royal seat of Ulster, and the nearby Ard Macha (Armagh), which became Ireland's principal ecclesiastical center. Both take their name from Macha who, as we have seen, was forced to race the king's horses when pregnant and laid a dying curse on the men of Ulster. Her cult is associated with agriculture, childbirth and war. Similarly, the royal site of Tara in County Meath is said to be the burial ground of the goddess Tea. Tailltiu (Teltown), a Celtic center for great annual festivities, is named after a woman of that name who cut down a wood to create a plain of blossoming clover and whose heart burst in the effort. Most important for later history was Brigid, goddess of fertility and poetry, whose attributes came to be associated with the Christian saint of the same name.

If goddesses tend to dominate local tradition, male figures are also prominent in Irish mythology. Particularly notable is the Daghdha, often called "the Great Good God." An inhabitant of Newgrange and consort to the goddess Boinn, he was characterized as a figure of enormous size and great appetite, the possessor of a cauldron so great that his ladle was "big enough for a married couple to sit in its middle." Although the Daghdha, like many other of the gods, appears to have had many functions, he is perhaps principally a god of plenty. Also notable is Lugh, whose name is associated with light, and Mananann mac Lir, a sea god who gave his name to the Isle of Man.

Archaeology tells us much of pagan practices. An important element was deposition: the burial of precious possessions such as weapons, bridle bits or jewelry as gifts to the gods. It could also take the form of sacrifice, both animal and human: the position of a woman's body, found in the Curragh, County Kildare, suggests that she was buried alive. Also notable is the importance given to the human head as a trophy and source of power. There are shrines made for human heads and many references to their powers in the heroic epics. After Finn mac Cumhail was decapitated, he is said to have demanded a piece of fish to eat from his murderers.

To the early Christians many of these beliefs and practices were repellent, and writers such as St. Patrick explicitly contrasted pagan spirituality with the message of the Gospel. When Christianity became established in Ireland, efforts were made to root out paganism and certain of their social practices, such as slavery. But many of the early missionaries saw that certain aspects of pagan tradition were worthy of preservation and that a widespread shift to Christianity demanded an appreciation of the society and customs of their hosts. Much of the reason for the success of the Christian mission was its ability to integrate Christian life with that which had existed before the arrival of the faith.

In the year 601, Pope Gregory I wrote a letter of advice to some Christian missionaries who were attempting to reintroduce Christianity to England, which had reverted to paganism under the Anglo-Saxons:

> The temples of idols in that nation should not be destroyed, but…the idols themselves that are in them should be. Let blessed water be prepared, and sprinkled in these temples, and altars constructed, and relics deposited, since, if these same temples are well built, it is needful that they should be transferred from the worship of idols to the service of the true God; that, when the people themselves see that these temples are not destroyed, they may put away error from their heart, and, knowing and adoring the true God, may have recourse with the more familiarity to the places they have been accustomed to.[3]

By the time Gregory wrote, Ireland had become a Christian country, but the life of the Christian people of Ireland was determined by the same forces which dominated the concerns of their pagan forebears: the natural elements, the success of crops and cattle breeding. It is no surprise, then, that Christian practices should be linked to nature's cycles, just as pagan practices had.

In pagan times, the year began at the start of November with the feast of Samhain. This, the end of one pastoral season and the beginning of another, was seen as the time when the gods of the Otherworld walked among mortals. With the coming of Christianity, this time of year was marked by the feasts of All Saints (November 1) and All Souls (November 2). When the ewes first came into milk at the start of February, pagans celebrated the feast of Imbolc, which centered around the goddess of fertility, Brigid. The Christian saint of the same name, also associated with fertility, came to be celebrated on February 1. The feast of Bealtaine at the start of May was aimed at the encouragement of cattle and crops, and marked by the lighting of bonfires. In Christian times, the bonfires lit at this time were dedicated to St. John. The harvest festival of Lughnasa, which was marked by celebrations and games around August 1 came to be associated with St. Patrick, so that whereas earlier people climbed hills in honor of the God Lugh, now it became a central part of St. Patrick's veneration.

Since the revival of interest in all things Celtic at the end of the nineteenth century and the present-day recurrence of that interest, the Celtic world has often been prone to idealization and overromanticization. Also, the role of the Celts in Irish life may be exaggerated at the expense of other traditions. Nevertheless, the character which Irish life, and in particular Irish Christianity, took over the past millennium and a half has been determined to a great extent by the Celtic civilization which flourished in the pre-Christian era. The survival and development of that civilization, free from Roman influence, meant that Ireland was different from its European neighbors, and this difference came to be mirrored in its church.

Seventh-century crucifixion plaque at St. John's, Rinnangan, County Roscommon

II

ST. PATRICK AND THE COMING OF CHRISTIANITY

On March 17, from Dublin to New York to Sydney, people celebrate the feast of St. Patrick. In Ireland, so often riven by religious differences, St. Patrick is claimed by all Christian traditions, Catholic and Protestant, as the founder of Christianity on the island, and the patron saint of their church. We know more about Patrick than any other person from fifth-century Ireland, yet he remains a baffling figure. There exists a historical Patrick, whose story we can read in his own words. But there also exists a legendary Patrick, which began to develop two hundred years after his death. The story of the legendary Patrick tells us just as much, if not more, about the early Irish church as does the Patrick of history.

PATRICK THE BRITON

Patrick, patron saint and symbol of Irish identity, was not an Irishman, but a Briton. He came from a place he called Banna Venta

Skellig Michael, or "The Great Skellig," off the west coast of County Kerry

Berniae, probably near Carlisle. Born into a Christian family around A.D. 415, he was the son of a deacon who was himself the son of a priest. By that time, Christianity had been established in Britain for more than two hundred years. An outpost of Roman rule, its garrisons were filled with men from different corners of the empire, some of whom had taken on the Christian religion. An organized church, though still small in numbers, existed by the early fourth century, and we know that three British bishops traveled to Gaul to attend a church council at Arles in A.D. 318. However, in the intervening centuries the church in Britain had faced serious challenges, and Patrick grew up in an atmosphere of decline and danger. The fourth century had witnessed a revival of paganism, and the first decades of the fifth century saw the British church tainted by a heretical movement known as Pelagianism. More dangerous still was the political situation. Roman rule had acted as a stabilizing influence and when Emperor Constantine made Christianity the state religion in 313, the empire became all the more important for the fate of Christian communities. As the empire began to crumble, the Roman legions were unable to support their position in this remote province. The rebellion of the Britons in A.D. 409 inflicted great damage and by A.D. 442 the last of the Roman legions had left. This was the cue for a series of invasions by northern European pagan peoples—Angles, Saxons and Jutes—who eventually settled and made a distinctive imprint on the country. Likewise, the Picts of Scotland, formerly contained by the Romans' border fortification, Hadrian's Wall, poured across and pillaged the northern lands of the Britons.

For Patrick and his family, the greatest threat came from Ireland. The west coast of Britain provided easy pickings for Irish pirates and adventurers in the early fifth century. The short distance across the Irish Sea afforded easy opportunities for snatch-and-grab raids on coastal areas, similar to those carried out by the Vikings on Britain and Ireland centuries later. Slaves were an especially common form of booty: In fact, seven and a half centuries later the bishops of Ireland were to attribute the recent invasion from England [see p. 85] to divine punishment of the Irish for centuries of enslaving that nation. Most of these slaves left no trace on history—the exception is Patrick.

Years later, at an advanced age, Patrick wrote down the story of his capture and how he came to Ireland. "I was then barely sixteen. I had neglected the true God, and when I was carried off into captivity, along with a great number of people, it was well deserved." He was taken to a place in County Mayo, where he worked as a shepherd for six years and turned to Christ:

I found myself pasturing flocks daily, and I prayed a number of times each day. More and more the love and fear of God came to me, and faith grew and my spirit was exercised, until I was praying up to a hundred times every day—and in the night nearly as often. So that I would even remain in the woods and on the mountain in snow, frost and rain, waking to pray before first light. And I felt no ill effect, nor was I in any way sluggish—because, as I now realize, the Spirit was seething within me.[1]

One night, he heard a voice in his sleep, saying: "It is good that you fast, who will go soon to your homeland." And after a short time he heard the words: "Look! Your ship is ready." According to Patrick, he walked for two hundred miles, guided by God, before he found the ship with its crew ready to sail. His refusal to take part in pagan ritual and his efforts to convert them to Christianity angered the captain, who initially refused Patrick's request to travel. However, as Patrick was departing from them, praying as he went, one of the sailors came after him and called on him to return. The ship set sail and after three days landed at an unnamed place. Thereupon they wandered in a wilderness for twenty-eight days, hungry and weak. "What's this, Christian?" mocked the captain. "You say your God is great and all-powerful. Then why can't you pray for us?" Patrick assured the sailors that they would be provided for abundantly if only they would trust in God—and straight away a herd of pigs appeared before them. God continued to provide for them in the following days, until they finally met with people who gave them help.

After a number of years, Patrick returned from this unnamed land to his family in Britain. They pleaded with him never to depart from them again, but one night he received a vision which prompted him to leave his family and go back to the land where he had tended the herds for six years:

I saw a man coming, as it were from Ireland. His name was Victoricus, and he carried many letters, and he gave me one of them. I read the heading: "The Voice of the Irish." As I began the letter, I imagined in that moment that I heard the voice of those very people who were near the wood of Foclut, which is beside the western sea…and they cried out, as with one voice: "We appeal to you, holy servant boy, to come and walk among us."

I was pierced by great emotion and could not read on, and so I woke. Thank God that after many years the Lord answered them according to their cry.[2]

We are very fortunate in having Patrick's story in his own words. This autobiographical work, the *Confession,* is one of the few documents (along with Patrick's letter to the pagan king Coroticus) to cast light on a very obscure century in Irish history. Not only does it give us an insight into Patrick's life and character but it is also one of the few firsthand accounts of the conversion of a barbarian people. The *Confession* is a response to charges made against him by an unidentified group of British "seniors." It appears that Patrick was originally condemned in his absence, and although this condemnation was subsequently overturned, it is clear that the accusations continued to rankle. "Although I am imperfect in many ways," he wrote, "nevertheless I

Sculpture of St. Patrick in County Limerick

wish my brethren and kin to know what sort of person I am, so that they may understand my motives." What the charges against Patrick were is never made clear. He claims that they "found a pretext from thirty years earlier, bringing against me words of a confession I made before I was a deacon. Because, in an anxious and melancholy state of mind, I had privately told my dearest friend about something I had done one day—indeed, in one hour—when I was a boy, before I had strength of character." But if this youthful misdemeanor was the pretext, it appears from the nature of Patrick's declaration that the substance of the allegations concerned his mission to the pagans in the more remote areas of Ireland. He describes how many attempted to hinder his mission, talking behind his back, saying: "Who is this fellow going into danger among enemies who do not know God?" Patrick insists that this mission was proposed to him by God and guided by His will. Furthermore, he is at pains to make clear that he did not profit in any way from his mission:

> Perhaps when I baptized so many thousands of people I was hoping for as much as a ha'penny from any of them? Tell me and I will return it to them. Or when the Lord, through my very ordinary person, ordained clergy everywhere and I assigned his ministry to each of them free of charge—if I asked any of them for as much as the price of my shoe, speak out against me and I will return it to you.[3]

At the close of his work Patrick summarizes the main thrust of his argument:

> See: again and again, I would reiterate what I wish to express in my declaration. I testify, in truth and in joy of heart, before God and His angels, that I never had any reason beyond the Gospel and its promises, ever to return to that people from whom I had formerly barely escaped.[4]

What kind of picture of Patrick emerges from the *Confession*? He characterizes himself throughout in most humble terms. "I, Patrick," he begins, "a sinner, am a most uncultivated man, and the least of all the faithful, and I am greatly despised by many." He frequently refers to his rusticity and ignorance. Such statements have been given credence by many who have seen his language as clumsy, though recent analysis of his Latin has suggested that the *Confession* is a more sophisticated literary work than many have realized. It was commonplace for medieval writers to make statements of humility, but, that said, the Patrick of the *Confession* comes across as a genuinely unassuming figure. The justifications of his actions are defensive, not self-aggrandizing. Most importantly, nowhere in Patrick's own words are found many of the claims later made for him, which became central to the Patrick legend. Although he refers to his mission among the people "in the ends of the earth" and his baptism of "so many thousands of people," at no stage does he suggest either that he brought Christianity to Ireland or that he was responsible for the conversion of the whole country.

Patrick was evidently a very remarkable man. That a captured slave would return to the land of his captivity and sustain danger and persecution from the heathens and opprobrium from his colleagues within the church shows extraordinary strength of character. That Ireland, a Celtic country at the fringes of Europe, should accept Christianity more than a century before the Anglo-Saxons and long before many of the people of northern Europe is a great achievement. Patrick's role in it was clearly a significant one: His mission came at a crucial time, and it evidently met with success. But, at the same time, Patrick was not the only person to play a part in the conversion of the Irish people. Others certainly played a role, one which was later diminished by those who sought to portray Patrick as the Apostle of Ireland.

PALLADIUS THE DEACON

It is likely that a full century before Patrick's time there were Christians living in Ireland. Though remote from Christian Europe, Ireland was never entirely isolated. We have already seen how Irish pirates plundered the west coast of Britain. More peaceful interaction also existed, particularly through trade. Irish artifacts found in Britain, as well as place-names there which seem to derive from the Irish language suggest that in the late fourth and early fifth centuries there was much migration from Ireland to Wales, Cornwall and western Scotland. These settlements meant more sustained contacts between the two islands. Contacts also existed with Gaul—in the wine trade, for example—where the Christian church was more firmly established than in Britain. Though Gaul was by no means fully Christian at that time, it had a developed episcopal structure based on the Roman administrative provinces, and in Martin of Tours had one of the great figures of the early church. All this points to the existence of Christian communities in Ireland before Patrick and also ties in with Patrick's own testimony. Though the island that he came to was obviously overwhelmingly pagan, the implication throughout the *Confession* is that Patrick did not come as a bishop to the heathens, but rather to an existing Christian community. It was his decision to go on an evangelizing mission to the pagans on the west coast, presumably those amongst whom he had lived as a slave, that seems to have caused problems with his superiors.

None of the Christians living in Ireland before the arrival of Patrick has left so much as a name to posterity, except for one. Although this individual left little more than a record of his name, his role has exercised historians ever since. "Palladius was ordained by Pope Celestine and sent to the Irish believers in Christ as their first bishop": So reads the entry for the year A.D. 431 in the *Chronicle* of Prosper of Aquitaine. Prosper, a resident of Marseilles, was in close contact with Rome and is a reliable source. This one-line entry in a chronicle which deals with the church and state in the eastern and western parts of the empire in the age of the barbarian invasions is generally regarded as the first reliable piece of information about the Irish church. First, it provides us with evidence that a community of "Irish believers in Christ" already existed by A.D. 431. Secondly, it introduces the mysterious figure of Bishop Palladius. There is another reference to this man in Prosper's entry for A.D. 429, in which he refers to the corruption of British churches with the Pelagian heresy: "But, through the negotiation of the deacon Palladius, Pope Celestine sent Germanus, Bishop of Auxerre, to act on his behalf." However, if Palladius was appointed bishop and reached Ireland, we have no evidence of the success or otherwise of his mission. Perhaps his ministry did not prosper and he returned to Gaul. It is also possible that he did have a degree of success but that a record of his achievements has not reached us. Or could it be that Palladius, the first bishop to minister to the Irish, came to be confused with Patrick, the writer of the *Confession*, and was subsumed within the legend of the "Apostle of Ireland"?

Although we know the year of the inception of Palladius's mission, we are on more shaky ground when we try to date Patrick's efforts. Not a single date is mentioned in Patrick's own writings, and the first sources to give a year are the less reliable Irish annals. These are chronicles with year-by-year entries, in the same style as Prosper of Aquitaine. There is a crucial difference, however. While Prosper was writing about events which happened in his own time, the annalists were writing of the fifth century retrospectively, from the vantage point of the seventh century or later. In addition to doubts about the reliability of the annals, we are faced with the fact that they mention a number of different dates for Patrick's death. So, while they may have their basis in a reliable earlier tradition, they must be examined with caution. The relevant entries for the *Annals of Ulster* state:

[431] In the year 431 of the Incarnation of the Lord, Palladius was ordained bishop for the Irish by Celestine, bishop of Rome, and was sent to Ireland so that they might believe in Christ—in the eighth year of Theodosius.

[432] Patrick reached Ireland in the ninth year of Theodosius Minor, and the first year of the episcopate of Xistus, forty-second bishop of the church of Rome....

[461] Here some place the death of Patrick....

[492] The Irish say that Patrick the archbishop died....

[493] Patrick, arch-apostle of the Irish, rested on the 17th of March, in his sixtieth year since he had come to Ireland to baptize the Irish.[5]

Nowadays, most historians would agree that we do not know anything for certain about Patrick's mission, apart from what we can learn from his own words. Few would now accept the theory, once widely held, that a brief, unsuccessful mission by Palladius was followed by Patrick's sixty-year ministry. It has been argued that the later date is a mistake and that a failed mission of Palladius was followed immediately by Patrick's more successful venture, and that Patrick died in 461. An alternative argument is that there were "two Patricks": that is, two important missionaries with similar names who became confused by later writers, whether by accident or design. According to this theory, "Patrick the Elder," that is, Palladius, a deacon from Auxerre, was ordained bishop and sent to Ireland by Pope Celestine in 431. He died in 461 and was succeeded by "Patrick the Younger," that is, Patrick the Briton, the author of the *Confession*, who died in 492 or 493. This theory has gained widespread currency and is supported by reference in eighth-century documents to an older and younger Patrick, and to Palladius also being known as Patrick. One troubling question remains: If Patrick the Briton followed Palladius, why does he make no mention of the earlier missionary in his *Confession*? Was it because they moved in different spheres—Palladius in the south, Patrick in the north? Or was it a deliberate slight by the author of the *Confession*?[6]

Though we know little of Patrick apart from what he tells us himself, he undoubtedly had an important impact on the development of Christianity in Ireland. But just as important as the real St. Patrick is the legend which grew up around him: the stories of Patrick and the paschal fire, his battle with the druids at the hill of Tara, his connection with the see of Armagh and later associations with shamrocks and snakes. These legends are the product of the Irish church of the seventh century and beyond, and tell us a great deal about the ideas and aspirations of the church which emerge as such a force in the history of Christianity. Before we turn to the legendary Patrick, it is necessary to explain how the church which gave us that legend emerged and developed.

THE BEGINNINGS OF THE IRISH CHURCH

We know little about how Christianity spread throughout Ireland, but we can catch some glimpses and make some assumptions based on what we know of the experience of conversion elsewhere in Europe. It was one thing to convert individuals, but to have any real impact the early evangelists needed to connect with the existing social structures. In Ireland, the most important bonds were those of the family and the tribe [see p. 11]. It seems that while some were converted and then found it necessary to leave their families, it often happened that whole families were baptized together. The best way to bring Christianity to a tribe was to win the confidence of the king. Patrick tells us that "at times I gave presents to chiefs, apart from the stipend I paid their sons who traveled with me." Another way of winning over the people was through a display of supernatural power. The "Lives" of the first Irish saints are filled with accounts of the early Christians traveling through the country performing miracles: bringing fertility to the lands, curing illnesses and taking vengeance on those who stood in the way of God's work. In later legend Patrick is portrayed primarily as a won-der-worker whose miraculous power is shown to be greater than that of the pagan druids. The work of evangelization required charisma, but also dedication. The early Christians faced many dangers: Patrick described how at one point during his mission he had his possessions stolen and was imprisoned for two weeks. Despite the great success of many missionaries, the conversion of the Irish proved to be a very slow process. We can see this in an early set of decrees called *The First Synod of St. Patrick* that were attributed to Patrick and his fellow bishops Auxilius and Iserninus but probably date from a century or so after Patrick's mission. At the time the decrees were written, paganism was still very much present and the danger of apostasy constant. Christians were prohibited from swearing before seers in the way that the pagans did, and those who declared their belief in witches were to be excommunicated. There was an emphasis on Christians distancing themselves from communion with pagans. Churches could not accept alms from pagans and clerics were prohibited from entering into armed combat against a pagan who had defaulted on a loan.[7]

For a church to survive and prosper in an environment that was still strongly pagan required not only Christian communities but organization. In the fifth century, the rulers of the Irish church were, as elsewhere, bishops. Patrick was one, and the other names associated with his—Secundinus, Auxilius and Iserninus—were, according to the annals, bishops sent to help him. The evangelists who came to Ireland from Britain and Gaul brought with them a church government which was well established in their homelands: a system based on the authority of bishops, each with jurisdiction over a territorially defined diocese. This system was based on the Roman administrative structure, the bishop mirroring the rule of the imperial governor, based in a *civitas*, an urban center with a

The Gallarus Oratory, on the Dingle Peninsula of County Kerry, built between the ninth and twelfth centuries

hinterland about the size of a modern Irish county. These bishops were in turn subject to an archbishop who ruled his province from a major city or *metropolis*, as the Roman provincial governors had done—hence the term "metropolitan see." We can see this system in practice in Ireland in *The First Synod of St. Patrick:* A priest was only permitted to say Mass in a church he had built after a bishop had consecrated it; a stranger who entered a community could not baptize, offer a Mass or build a church without the bishop's permission; and a bishop who traveled into another jurisdiction had to obtain permission before ordaining there.[8] The church in Ireland was initially organized along the same lines as the church in Britain and Gaul, with bishops wielding jurisdictional powers in a diocese probably corresponding to the tuath. However, whereas the Roman organizational structure had proved to be a convenient framework in the territories which had experienced Roman rule, it was entirely artificial when applied to Ireland. The system which flourished elsewhere in the Christian west foundered in Ireland, but it was not just the alien nature of this structure which undermined the dominance of bishops. Another powerful force found itself ideally suited to the Irish situation: monasticism.

Christian monasticism has its origins in the east, primarily in Egypt and Syria. As the Roman Empire began to experience crisis and Christianity began to expand, many people chose to reject wealth, power and family, to leave the city and retreat to deserted places, and there devote their lives fully to Christ. The earliest of these individuals, such as St. Antony (A.D. 251–356), tended to dwell in complete solitude, living a harsh and frugal life, the better to focus the mind on God. However, such hermits rapidly attracted followers, and soon communities of like-minded Christians grew up in remote places. The pioneer of community monasticism was St. Pachomius (d. A.D. 346), who established a rule for resident communities which involved asceticism, physical work and obedience to superiors. Early monasticism took on many forms. St. Basil (c. A.D. 330–79), for example, promoted the combination of an inner spiritual purpose with acts of charity for one's neighbor. As monasticism spread west it continued to change, with a greater emphasis on learning being found in the monasteries of southern Gaul and the orderly communal life established in the Rule of St. Benedict (c. A.D. 480–550) becoming very influential. In Ireland, too, monasticism followed these different paths, but, more so than anywhere else in the west, it stayed true to its eastern roots.

To those who sought to flee the crumbling Roman Empire in the sixth century, the rocky coasts of Ireland and Scotland's Atlantic seaboard proved as much a desert as the parched wildernesses of Egypt and Syria. It was there that the most demanding, and perhaps purest, form of monasticism first took root in the west and then spread to the former Roman provinces of Britain and Gaul and beyond. One of the earliest monastic settlements was Candida Casa

Bee-hive huts, Skellig Michael, County Kerry

at Whithorn in the southwest of Scotland, supposedly founded by St. Ninian. The harsh and simple life attracted Christians from the newly converted lands of the Picts in northeast Scotland and from Ireland. One of these was a native of Meath, a former soldier called Enda (d. c. A.D. 530). After a spell of training at Candida Casa he returned to Ireland, where he founded a number of monasteries, most notably on Inismore, one of the Aran Islands, where he built a stone church surrounded by huts. The story goes that when he asked the king of Munster for permission, the king replied: "The place is all rock. I promised St. Patrick a gift of land for the church, but it was to be the best land in the kingdom. Why go to Aran? You can have much better land near Cashel." Enda's impulse to found a monastery in the wildest and most remote place possible was followed by many others. Perhaps the most spectacular example of such a retreat is the monastic site at Skellig Michael (or the Great Skellig), off the coast of Kerry. To this day it is possible to see the traces of the settlement consisting of six stone huts and two tiny oratories six hundred feet above the Atlantic Ocean on a crag of rock buffeted by fierce winds and lashed by stormy waters. Influence on the Irish monastic life came not only from Galloway but from Wales, where a Leinsterman, Finnian (d. A.D. 549), trained at St. David's. His most famous foundation was Clonard (County Meath) which quickly attracted many novices. In contrast to the monastic tradition of Candida Casa, which emphasized physical work and paid little attention to learning, Finnian promoted intellectual life, and Clonard soon became a monastic school of some note. Many other foundations were to follow this tradition, and soon the monasteries of Ireland became synonymous with learning and culture. Finnian encouraged his monks to found houses of their own. One of these was Ciaran (c. A.D. 512–45), the son of a carpenter, who studied first under Finnian at Clonard and then under Enda at Inismore. In contrast to Enda's monastery, Ciaran's most important foundation, Clonmacnoise (County Offaly), was built on good land in close proximity to secular powers, under whose patronage it became a center of some note. Armagh, Kildare, Glendalough and Lismore were also monasteries in this mold, that

Clonmacnoise, County Offaly. A sixth-century foundation, it became one of the most important monasteries in medieval Ireland.

is, important centers where trade prospered and social contacts were strong.

As is clear from the examples of Enda, Finnian and Ciaran, there was a great degree of interconnection between the early monasteries. As a monastery became successful, it was likely to spawn daughter houses and it was natural that such houses would maintain close links. By the second half of the sixth century monasteries were forming themselves into federations, or *paruchiae*. Each community of monks would live as a family under the rule of an abbot, who in turn owed obedience to the abbot of the motherhouse, in much the same way as a tribal king would accept the authority of an overlord. Most significantly, this system was not a territorial one. Monasteries might be scattered throughout distant provinces, or even overseas. Through the travels of Colmcille and Columbanus (see pp. 53–57), Derry was joined in federation not only to Durrow (County Offaly), but also to Iona off the coast of Scotland, while Bangor was joined to the continental monasteries of Annegray and Luxeuil in the eastern part of Gaul, and Bobbio in northern Italy. As the system of paruchia began to gain strength it had serious repercussions for the episcopal structure introduced in the fifth century. Bishops never disappeared from the Irish scene—their role in performing the sacraments could not be dispensed with—but their jurisdictional authority came to be increasingly eclipsed by the powers of the abbots. An illustration of this is the fact that while far more bishops than abbots are mentioned in the Irish annals before the middle of the sixth century, and the numbers are roughly equal until the year A.D. 600, thereafter abbots come to be mentioned far more frequently than bishops. In fact, the most powerful bishops were those who, as often happened, also held the office of abbot. So, between the seventh and the twelfth centuries, it was abbots and monasteries, rather than bishops and dioceses, which dominated the Irish church.

This system of monastic federations did not simply mirror the overlordship of the kings; it became intertwined with it. Many of the most important foundations, such as Clonmacnoise, were under the patronage of a royal house. It was a mutually beneficial relationship. The churches gained patronage, wealth and protection. Kings and their families gained the blessing of an educated and influential force in society. In fact, in very many cases, the office of abbot was passed down through a royal family. Furthermore, the expansion of monastic communities into paruchiae corresponded with an expansion of power by certain royal dynasties. In the seventh century Armagh emerged as the principal ecclesiastical center in the northern half of Ireland. At the same time, the Uí Néill dynasty emerged as the greatest power in that region. Both church and dynasty had further ambitions—to claim authority over all of Ireland—and in doing so they coopted the figure of St. Patrick.

ARMAGH AND THE LEGEND OF ST. PATRICK

Armagh has held a central position in the Irish church from the early Middle Ages to the present, and much of the story of the Irish church can be told through the history of that see and its vicissitudes throughout the ages. However, its origins are obscure. No written evidence exists before the seventh century, but recent excavations have uncovered a cemetery which may date back to the time of Patrick. It was well placed as an ecclesiastical center, built on a hill overlooking good land within two miles of the ancient royal center of Emain Macha. Armagh's rise to prominence coincides with the expansion of the monastic paruchiae, and it tells us much about the growing maturity of the Irish church.

It was the church of Armagh in the late seventh and early eighth centuries that gave us the legend of St. Patrick.

Armagh was originally a diocesan church, that is, the seat of a bishop who presided over a defined territorial unit, roughly corresponding to the local kingdom. However, as monasteries emerged in greater numbers, began to build up monastic federations and came to take on an increasingly important role within the church, Armagh too converted to a monastic church. It did not lose its status as a diocesan church but instead its bishops took on the additional office of abbot and attracted monks. Soon Armagh developed its own paruchia, with daughter houses scattered over the northern half of Ireland, and even as far south as Sletty in present-day County Laois. So, by around the year 700, the abbot-bishops of Armagh not only held direct authority over a diocese but also exercised looser control over a large number of far-flung monasteries. Along with this expansion came riches, power and further ambition.

The extent of the paruchia corresponded roughly to the overlordship of the Uí Néill dynasty, the most powerful royal house in the northern half of Ireland, and the expansion of Armagh mirrored the growing authority of the Uí Néill. In the Middle Ages authority was inextricably bound up with legitimation. For a royal dynasty or a monastic house to claim to rule over another kingdom or monastery, it was essential that it backed up its claim with evidence that it was a rightful one. So, a royal house wishing to rule over a certain people would present evidence that its family had ruled over them for centuries. Sometimes, of course, this was pure fabrication: One party would conquer another by military force, and then legitimize its position by claiming that it had held a similar position in the distant past. This was precisely what occurred in the case of the Uí Néill dynasty, as they extended their authority by military might over most of the northern and central kingdoms of Ireland. Soon there emerged stories of an ancient high-kingship of all Ireland to whom the Uí Néill were the rightful heirs. The same occurred as Armagh came to extend its authority beyond its territorial diocese over far-flung monasteries. In the late seventh and early eighth century Armagh propagandists began to advance their church's claim to authority over the entire Irish church. They did so by building up the legend of St. Patrick as the Apostle of Ireland and presenting the rulers of their church as his rightful successors.

Much of the popular legend and image of St. Patrick, which has remained current to this day, derives from the first biography of the saint, written by Muirchú, one of the clergy of Armagh, toward the end of the seventh century. Muirchú's *Life of St. Patrick* provided a very different picture to that which had emerged from Patrick's own writings. Whereas the *Confession* showed a humble human figure struggling against the difficult circumstances of pagan Ireland and with his own church, Muirchú described a powerful, all-conquering hero. Though Patrick himself did not claim to have converted the whole island, his biographer set him up categorically as the Apostle of Ireland. Also, Patrick made no mention of Armagh, but Muirchú made it clear that that place was the center of his mission and remained heir to his founding of the Irish church.

Muirchú had evidently read the *Confession*; he began his *Life* by telling the story of Patrick's captivity and deliverance, much as Patrick had done himself. However, while Patrick was silent about the period between his return to his family in Britain and his call to minister to the Irish, Muirchú provided intriguing details. According to this account, as Patrick was approaching the age of thirty he decided to set out for Rome, so as to learn the divine mysteries and prepare himself for preaching. But, as he was traveling through Gaul on his way, "he found a very holy man of approved faith and doctrine, bishop of the city of Auxerre, leader of almost all Gaul, the great lord Germanus."[9] There he remained for thirty or forty years, under the tutelage of Germanus, until he received a vision urging him to return to minister to the Irish people. He visited a bishop nearby called Amathorex, who consecrated him bishop, and then he made his way to Ireland.

What are we to make of this new information about Patrick? It could well be that Patrick was educated in Gaul and made bishop after his return to Britain, for it certainly seems that he had some degree of education and training before he began his mission in Ireland. But a more convincing explanation is provided by the connections Palladius had with Auxerre. Before his mission to Ireland, he had acted as an intermediary between the pope and Germanus. Furthermore, Germanus's predecessor as bishop of Auxerre, and perhaps the man who consecrated Palladius bishop, was called Amator, a name very similar to that of the man credited by Muirchú with consecrating Patrick. Muirchú makes a brief mention of Palladius, saying that he had failed in his mission to Ireland and ended his days in Britain, but in all likelihood his information on Patrick's education and consecration is derived from the career of Palladius. Here we get the clearest picture of how Palladius's life was incorporated into the legend of St. Patrick, and subsumed by it. We may wonder how many other acts and achievements attributed to St. Patrick were in fact the work of his more obscure predecessor.

The centerpiece of Muirchú's *Life of St. Patrick* is the account of the saint lighting the paschal fire and his subsequent contest with the druids at the hill of Tara. The story goes that, shortly after his return to Ireland, Patrick chose to celebrate the feast of Easter on the great plain of Brega in Meath. He and his companions pitched their tents and celebrated the festival by lighting a great fire and blessing it. However, at that same time a great pagan festival was being held on the hill of Tara, "the capital of the realm of the Irish," which towered above the plain. There were gathered the kings, leaders and nobles of the kingdom, and also the druids, fortune-tellers and sorcerers, all under the leadership of King Loiguire, leader of the Uí Néill royal family. According to custom, on that night everyone, far or near, was prohibited from lighting a fire before it was lit in the king's household. When Loiguire saw

The ancient royal site of Tara, County Meath

Patrick's fire he was enraged, but his druids gave him more worrying news:

> Unless this fire which we see, and which has been lit on this night before the fire was lit in your house, is extinguished on this same night on which it has been lit, it will never be extinguished at all; it will even rise above all the fires of our customs, and he who has kindled it and the kingdom that has been brought upon us by him who has kindled it will overpower us all and you, and will seduce all the people of your kingdom, and all kingdoms will yield to it, and it will spread over the whole country and will reign in all eternity.[10]

Alarmed by this, the king sent his men to summon whoever was responsible for this deed, and Patrick was brought to Tara.

Muirchú's account of the encounter between Patrick and the druids which followed showed him more as a hero from an old Irish saga, Cú Chulainn or Finn mac Cumhail, than as a churchman.

When a druid uttered blasphemies against the Christian God, Patrick caused him to be lifted into the air and his head dashed on a rock. When the king's men tried to arrest him, he caused an earthquake to erupt, whereupon "seven times seven men perished through the curse of Patrick." Then Patrick succeeded in proving his miraculous powers greater than those of druids. The druids dropped poison into Patrick's goblet but, when the saint blessed it, the goblet froze over and the poison dropped out. A druid covered the land with snow, but when he admitted he was unable to remove it, Patrick blessed the plain and the snow disappeared at once. Eventually, convinced of Patrick's superior powers and fearful for his life, King Loiguire converted to Christianity. Patrick left in peace and continued with his mission.[11]

Muirchú went on to describe how Patrick, "the bishop of all Ireland," preached to and baptized all peoples, and related a number of miracles. On one occasion Patrick saw a vision of heaven; on another he made a field barren by his curse; and on yet another his fingers provided light to search for missing horses. On the subject of Patrick's connection with Armagh, he described how Patrick asked for the hill of Armagh as his place to settle and worship, but the owner of the land, a man called Dáire, was reluctant to grant it to him and instead gave the saint and his followers some land at the bottom of the hill. However, after Patrick saved Dáire from certain death, the man offered him the hilltop:

> And they went out together, holy Patrick and Dáire, to inspect the marvellous and pleasing gift that he had offered, and they climbed to the top of that hill and found there a doe with its little fawn lying in the place where there is now the altar of the northern church at Armagh.[12]

In Muirchú's *Life*, then, the humble Patrick of the *Confession* was transformed into the Apostle of Ireland. He was given sole credit for the conversion of the Irish, and the Irish church was his foundation. Furthermore, he was seen to have chosen Armagh as the center of his ministry. Further elaboration of the Patrick legend may be found in other works produced in Armagh around the same time. *The Book of the Angel* begins by telling how Patrick went out one day from Armagh to preach to the people. That night he was awoken from his sleep by an angel, who praised his work with the Irish people before turning to the subject of Armagh: "The Lord your God knows that your present place which we see before us, placed high on the hill, is narrow and has (only) a small church, and is also hemmed in by some inhabitants of the region, and the surrounding territory is not sufficient to give shelter to all." Therefore, he reported, God had granted Armagh a vast area, extended over much of the northern half of Ireland, over which it was to have direct rule. "And further," added the angel, "the Lord God has given all the tribes of the Irish as a *paruchia* to you and to this city."[13] Another work of this type was the *Account of St. Patrick's Journey* by Bishop Tírechán, written in the second half of the seventh century. He explained that he was prompted to write because "my heart within me is perturbed with love for Patrick, since I see disputants and bombasts and warriors of Ireland who hate Patrick's ecclesiastical jurisdiction—because they have stolen from him what was his." Patrick, he insisted, was given the whole island by God; he was responsible for baptizing the people of Ireland and "all the primitive churches of Ireland are his."[14] He related Patrick's travels throughout Ulster and Connacht and showed how these churches owed obedience to Armagh.

The efforts of Muirchú, Tírechán and the other Armagh propagandists were remarkably successful. Though by no means all the churches in Ireland accepted the claims of Armagh, that church, with the support of the Uí Néill dynasty, won a special reputation as the see of St. Patrick, the Apostle of Ireland. Furthermore, the stories of St. Patrick's exploits and his prime role in bringing

Christianity to Ireland became a matter of fact to most people in Ireland, and remain so even in the twenty-first century despite the fact that there is no reliable evidence that Patrick founded Armagh, or even visited it.

The legend of St. Patrick is the product of a firmly established Irish church. It shows that by the seventh century the early foundations laid by Patrick and others had been built upon. Success brought with it power and riches, greater secularization, and in some cases corruption, but it also meant that Christianity was able to flourish in Ireland and spread its gospel abroad. The structures which had developed by the seventh century were to withstand invasion, conquest, schism and war over the following centuries. We should not regard the propaganda of this period as conflicting with the genuine piety of those involved; such endeavors on behalf of one's church were commonplace throughout Europe during the Middle Ages, and the people involved believed that to exalt their church was to exalt God. Perhaps we owe them a debt of gratitude, as none of the principal authorities on the Irish church in the seventh century even mention Patrick. Had it not been for the Armagh propagandists, Patrick might have slipped into obscurity and we might never have learned the story of the slave-boy who returned to convert the Irish.

The Book of Kells: *the incarnation initial from St. Matthew's Gospel*

III

SAINTS AND SCHOLARS

The early Irish church was an oddity. While other churches were governed by bishops, the Irish church was run by abbots; elsewhere the city was the focus for Christian life, but the devout Christians of Ireland sought out the fringes and the wastelands. As long as the Roman Empire remained strong, the centralized, urban ecclesiastical system flourished in continental Europe, but as the empire collapsed and the vacuum it left was filled by dangerous forces, the Christian world and the literate Roman culture which it had adopted faced destruction. It was the idiosyncratic world of Irish Christianity which proved capable of withstanding the threat of anarchy and of fostering Christian thought, practice and the arts which the faith had brought with it from the Roman world. This period, from around the seventh to the ninth century, is the fabled "Golden Age" of Irish monasticism, when Ireland was the "Land of Saints and Scholars." The land which had never experienced Roman rule now became a sanctuary for classical culture. In the scriptoria of the Irish monasteries, monks copied the precious Latin volumes that had come to them from the Mediterranean world. There they found the Latin language and the learning of the church fathers—Augustine, Ambrose and Jerome.

There they could also inspect the art of manuscript illumination which had flourished as the Roman Empire was waning. The Irish monks took these influences and made them their own, creating writings and art which fused classical learning with the Celtic culture which they found around them. As Irish monasticism flourished, it began to look further afield, to Britain and to continental Europe, and in this way it was able to export to a troubled Europe a vibrant form of Christian life and culture.

BRIGID AND BRENDAN

The achievement of the early Irish church was in part due to its success in adapting to Celtic society and its resilience in the face of primitive conditions, but it was also to do with people. It is in the Christian era that we truly discover individual Irish people for the first time. Though they are partly hidden behind legendary material and the pious sentiments of their hagiographers, we can still discern something of the remarkable figures who helped to make the Golden Age. Two of the most colorful are St. Brigid and St. Brendan. Their stories, written down by churchmen, also tell us something about the times in which they lived.

The Christian church has always been dominated by men and Ireland is no exception. Most of the famous figures of the early church—Patrick, Finnian,

The round tower at the sixth-century monastic site of Glendalough, County Wicklow

Brendan, Colmcille, Columbanus—are men. Nevertheless, women played an important role from the start in spreading the faith and building up the fledgling church. In fact, it is likely that the monastic movement which was to define Irish Christianity in the early Middle Ages was pioneered not by men but by women. No evidence exists of a monastery for men before the second quarter of the sixth century; until then, it seems, the men of the church were bishops, deacons and priests. Women, on the other hand, who were excluded from these positions, instead joined together in communities of virgins. Patrick tells us how he baptized a certain noblewoman, who soon after chose to become a "virgin of Christ." Such women, he writes, "endure harassment and false accusation from their parents. And nonetheless their numbers increase…the Lord has given grace to many of His handmaids, so that they can bravely imitate Him in spite of all prohibitions."[1] We know nothing of most of these women, but one is second amongst Irish saints only to Patrick: St. Brigid of Kildare.

The earliest surviving "Life" of an Irish saint is the *Life of St. Brigid* by Cogitosus. Cogitosus was an Irishman, in all likelihood a religious of Kildare, who wrote in the seventh century. His *Life* is far from a biography in our sense of the word, but we gain some biographical detail along the way. He tells us that she was born of noble Christian parents of the tribe of Eochu (since traced to the Louth-Armagh-Down area). From the earliest days she showed herself to be of sober and modest character, and her miraculous powers also appeared in her youth. As a young woman she was sent by her mother to churn butter, but when she had done so her generous nature led her to give away all the milk and butter to the poor. Fearing the wrath of her mother she prayed to God, and immediately a plentiful supply of butter was miraculously provided for her. Soon after, Cogitosus tells us, her parents wished Brigid to be married, but the girl instead sought out a bishop and took the veil of a virgin. Most of the rest of Cogitosus's book is made up of a series of miracle stories, much in the same vein as the story of the butter: Brigid's crops remained dry in a rainstorm; she hung her cloak on a sunbeam; she turned water into beer; she made salt from a rock and divined a supply of honey; she miraculously moved a river.

These miracle stories have their roots in the pre-Christian mythical tradition. As we have seen, the pagan gods were linked to natural phenomena—the sun, the air, water and land—and the rural society of the Celts looked to them for their prosperity. The Brigid who emerges from Cogitosus's pages is essentially a pagan fertility goddess disguised by a thin veneer of Christianity, and the success of her cult is bound up with pagan tradition. A pagan goddess of the same name was widely revered not only in Ireland but in the other Celtic lands. She was the daughter of the Daghdha, the father of the Gods, and was a fertility goddess who also presided over learning and literature. It seems that the popularity of St. Brigid's cult throughout Ireland was largely thanks to her confusion with the

Glendalough, County Wicklow

pagan Brigid. There are other pre-Christian elements in her legend. The name of the monastery that she founded, Kildare or Cell-Dara, means "church of the oak" and was probably a former pagan sanctuary centered around a sacred tree. Indeed, Brigid is said to have built her cell under an oak tree. Furthermore, her feast day, the first day of February, corresponds to the important pagan festival of Imbolc, when the new fertility of spring was welcomed (see page 17). By the time Cogitosus was writing, Christianity had penetrated most corners of Ireland, but the old beliefs did not die easily. Many of them lived on, as in Brigid's case, by developing a Christian framework.

But if the legend of Brigid is essentially a transposition of pagan folklore, that is not to deny that the real Brigid of Kildare existed, and if we look beneath the legend we can, as with Patrick, make out something of the historical figure. It is likely that she was born around the middle of the fifth century and died at an advanced age, and that all of her life was spent in or around Kildare. There she founded a monastery for women and became its first abbess. In doing so she called on a certain distinguished hermit to join her as bishop and coruler of the church of Kildare, and for him to consecrate other churches and confer orders on clergy. The foundation of that monastery was Brigid's lasting achievement. It was originally, as Cogitosus puts it, an "episcopal and feminine see"—a monastery for women linked to a diocesan church. But with the growing popularity of male monasticism, Kildare became a double monastery, with men and women living separate religious lives under the same roof. Cogitosus described its structure in his time:

> ...The church is spacious in its floor area, and it rises to an extreme height. It is adorned with painted boards and has on the inside three wide chapels, all under the roof of the large building and separated by wooden partitions....

The church has many windows, and an ornamented door on the right side through which the priests and the faithful of [the] male sex enter the building. There is another door on the left through which the virgins and the congregation of the female faithful are accustomed to enter. And so, in one great basilica, a large number of people, arranged by rank and sex, in orderly division separated by partitions, offers prayers with a single spirit to the almighty Lord.[2]

The centerpiece of the church was the shrine of Brigid under the altar, covered in gold, silver and precious gems. Cogitosus also described how Kildare had become a great ecclesiastical center:

But who could convey in words the supreme beauty of her church and the countless wonders of her city, of which we would speak? "City" is the right word for it: that so many people are living there justifies the title. It is a great metropolis, within whose outskirts—which St. Brigid marked out with a clearly defined boundary—no earthly adversary is feared, nor any incursion of enemies. For the city is the safest place of refuge among all the towns of the whole land of the Irish, with all their fugitives. It is a place where the treasures of kings are looked after, and it is reckoned to be supreme in good order.

And who could number the varied crowds and countless people who gather in from all territories? Some come for the abundance of festivals; others come to watch the crowds go by; others come with great gifts to the celebration of the birth into heaven of St. Brigid.[3]

Kildare was not a city or a metropolis in the sense of the term the Romans had used or that we would use today. Rather, Cogitosus is using the term applied first in continental Europe to the major ecclesiastical centers (see p. 30–31). And, allowing for exaggeration, Cogitosus's description of Brigid's church rings true. By the seventh century it was unquestionably one of the most important churches in the land. In this it was aided by its favorable location and the patronage of the Leinster kings. It was also aided by the spread of Brigid's cult. The existence of many sites with connections to Brigid gave Kildare an opportunity to claim authority over them and build up an extensive paruchia. Cogitosus claimed that Kildare "is the head of virtually all the Irish churches and occupies the first place, excelling all the monasteries of the Irish. Its jurisdiction extends over the whole land of Ireland from sea to sea."[4] The church of Armagh did not quite agree, but its propagandists, while exalting its own claims over the whole island, did accept that the church of St. Brigid held a special place.

If some of Ireland's early saints carry with them traces of the

A carving on the doorway of Clonfert Cathedral, County Galway

Celtic pagan divinities, others echo the exploits of the heroes of pre-Christian legend. One such is St. Brendan the Navigator, whose story has similarities not only to the sagas of the Celtic world, but even to the works of Homer and Virgil. Brendan was born around the year A.D. 489 in or around Tralee (County Kerry) and is said to have founded a number of monasteries, most notably Clonfert (County Galway) on the Shannon. It was at Clonfert, the legend goes, that Brendan was told by a monk called Barinthus of a magical island far away. It was known as "the Land of Promise."

Fired by this story, Brendan gathered fourteen companions and sailed out into the Atlantic. The account of Brendan's voyages, which dates from around the ninth century but is based on an earlier legend, tells of the dangers and wonders which the monks encountered. They came upon "the soporific well," from which they drank too much and slept for days, and "the coagulated sea," which carried them around for twenty days, and they fought off various fearsome beasts. They came to an island where they were greeted by choirs of boys, youths and elders, and another where birds chanted "salvation belongs to our Lord who sits upon the throne, and to the Lamb," and spoke to Brendan in prophecy. References to a gigantic crystal pillar in the sea and a mountain spouting flames suggest that the stories originate in real travels in the North Atlantic; places described have been identified with Iceland, Greenland and the Faroe Islands. It has even been claimed that Brendan and his companions reached America. Eventually the travelers came across an island surrounded by fog. They were greeted by a youth who told them: "There before you lies the land which you have sought for a long time. You could not find it immediately because God wanted to show you his varied secrets in the ocean." They set foot on the island, where they were given fruit and precious stones, and then they returned to Ireland.[5]

One gets the impression from the story that it was at least as important for Brendan to travel as to arrive, and this idea was close to the hearts of many of the early Irish saints. Irish monks were known for their love of *peregrinatio pro Christo*—pilgrimage for Christ. Men and women would remove themselves from their friends and families and travel to remote places, their outward traveling expressing an inward spiritual journey. Sometimes this was a penance for specific sins, but often it was a general acceptance of hardship as an attempt to get closer to God. Though the purpose was usually purely spiritual, the practical consequences could be far-reaching, and the wanderings of two men in particular—

Colmcille and Columbanus—changed the face of Christianity in western Europe.

COLMCILLE AND COLUMBANUS

The Irish church knew no borders. Its formation had resulted from various foreign influences, such as Patrick and Palladius, the monks of Candida Casa and St. David's, and other visitors to Ireland who have left no record to posterity. The spread of Christianity to Ireland was the product of more than evangelical zeal. It was occasioned by trade links, by political factors and by family connections. Similarly, when the distinctively Irish brand of Christianity began to spread out to Britain and the Continent, it was facilitated by such connections. One of the oldest and most enduring of Irish connections is that with northwest Scotland. In every generation people have traveled back and forth across the twenty-mile strait between Kintyre on Scotland's western coast and the coast of Antrim. The Celtic peoples of northeast Ulster had much in common in terms of culture and language with their fellow Celts, the British of Strathclyde in the west and the Picts of northeastern Scotland. The people of Dalriata in Antrim had been colonizing lands in eastern Scotland since the third century A.D., and by the seventh century they held sway over large parts of Galloway. In the year A.D. 561 a monk called Colmcille sailed from Derry with twelve companions to western Scotland. Off the coast of Galloway, on the island of Iona, they built a monastery which was to form the key link between Irish monasticism and the outside world.

Colmcille (c. 521–97) was of aristocratic birth, a descendent of the Uí Néill kings on his father's side and the kings of Leinster on his mother's. Known also as "Columba," meaning "dove," he was born in Gartan, County Donegal, where he was fostered by a priest. He trained as a monk, first with Finnian of Moville, and then Finnian of Clonard. There are tales of his early devotion to scholarship, and he is said to have written a number of scholarly works, though none survive. Before he left Ireland he had already founded a number of monasteries, including Derry, Durrow, Clanmore, Swords, Lambay and Drumcliffe. His reasons for leaving Ireland remain mysterious. His biographer Adomnán (627–704), a monk of Iona who wrote around a century after the saint's death, simply stated: "In the second year after the battle of Cúl-drebene, the forty-second year of his age, Columba sailed away from Ireland to Britain, wishing to be a pilgrim for Christ." While there was a powerful urge in Irish spirituality to turn away from the world and travel far from home, it has been argued that Colmcille's exile was an act of penance imposed by the church hierarchy, or by Colmcille himself, for his part in the battle that Adomnán mentions.

The monastery which the exiles established at Iona became a bridgehead between the Christian Irish and the neighboring pagan Picts. Adomnán and, later, the English historian Bede claim that Colmcille was personally responsible for the conversion of the Pictish King Bridei and for the evangelization of his people. On these grounds, Colmcille has sometimes been hailed as the national apostle of the Scots. As with the role of St. Patrick in Ireland, it seems likely that his significant but limited involvement in this exercise came to be exaggerated. Christians had already existed in Pictland, and Colmcille himself was not solely responsible for their conversion. His successors consolidated the Scottish mission, and within a century there were perhaps ninety monasteries in Scotland linked to Iona. The abbots of Iona were also careful to retain their contacts with the Irish houses of their paruchia, thereby cementing the close relationship between the Irish and the Scottish churches.

Colmcille died in his church at Iona in A.D. 597. That same year a group of monks landed on the coast of Kent, in southeast England, sent from Italy by Pope Gregory the Great with a mission to convert the English. Led by a man called Augustine, they succeeded in gaining the confidence of the local king and were allowed to set up a church at Canterbury. Though they faced many reverses, they managed to build up a Christian community amongst the pagan Anglo-Saxons of southern England, and established a church with close links to Rome. England at this time was divided into a number of kingdoms, most of which remained pagan. Though Christians existed beyond the southeast, they were a marginalized few. It was the fledgling mission from Iona to the Picts, in combination with the efforts of Augustine's successors, which is responsible for making the English a Christian people. In the year A.D. 616 the claimant to the throne of Northumbria in northeast England, Oswald, was forced to flee into exile in Scotland. There he encountered the monks of Iona and was baptized a Christian. In A.D. 633 he returned to Northumbria to reclaim his throne and, once established as king, he sent to Iona requesting an evangelizing mission. The first mission apparently foundered, but a second, led by a monk called Aidan, took root. Aidan was granted the island of Lindisfarne where he established a monastery which acted as a base for the conversion of the northern part of Northumbria. That monastery went on to produce one of the masterpieces of medieval art, the *Book of Lindisfarne*. Aidan's successor as abbot of Lindisfarne, Finan, sent Northumbrian and Irish missionaries south to the kingdoms of Mercia and Essex. From there, one of these missionaries, Cedd, went on to establish Christianity in the kingdom of the East Angles.

If the driving force behind the extension of Irish monasticism to Britain was Colmcille, the pioneering figure in its application to Europe was Columbanus (c. 543–53). Until Columbanus, the luminaries of the Irish church are sketchy figures, shrouded in hagiographical distortion. With Columbanus we have extensive biographical details, and his own writings, to illuminate his life and character. Columbanus was born around A.D. 543 to a noble family of Leinster, and it was in Leinster that he was first educated in the liberal arts and in religious studies. Deciding to become a monk, he entered the monastery of Bangor (County Down), where he remained for a number of years. When first he spoke to his abbot about his desire to go abroad, he was rebuked, but eventually he was granted permission to sail for Gaul with twelve companions. They made their way for the mountains of the Vosges, where they built a monastery at Annegray. Soon the Irishmen attracted local followers and, as the numbers of monks expanded, they founded other houses nearby at Luxeuil and Fontaine. These monasteries operated in the same manner as those in Ireland, with an emphasis on asceticism, learning and the authority of the abbot. Though admired by many for bringing a breath of fresh air to the increasingly degenerate Gaulish church, Columbanus's endeavors brought him into conflict with the local church hierarchy and the secular powers. In the year A.D. 600 he appealed to the pope above the heads of the Frankish bishops, arguing that his community ought to be allowed to carry on their own traditions without disturbance. Soon afterward, he fell foul of the local royal family and he and his monks were escorted to Nantes for expulsion from the country. However, the boat was forced back in a storm and Columbanus was allowed to continue his mission in the Frankish lands, albeit more precariously. He traveled first through central Gaul and then up the Rhine to present-day Switzerland, facing dangers along the way, but also, according to his biographer, gaining converts and performing miracles. After around three years of wandering, he crossed the Alps into Italy and was granted land to found a monastery at Bobbio, where he died in A.D. 615.

As a young man, even before he became a monk, Columbanus had written a commentary on the Psalms and some poetry, and throughout his life he continued to be a prolific writer of letters, sermons, poems and law codes. These writings survived, and they give us not only a valuable insight into the man, but also the monastic life of the time, and the difficulties his monks faced. Life in an Irish monastery on the Continent was a harsh one, and was expected to be so. Columbanus wrote three guides to monastic life. The *Regula Monachorum* (Rule of the Monks) provides a statement of principles on monasticism, emphasizing obedience, poverty, mortification, fasting and prayer. The *Regula Coenobialis* (Community Rule) gives a commentary on the minutiae of monastic life and lists punishments for breaches of the Rule, many of which seem very harsh to modern eyes. For example: "The monk who through coughing goes wrong in the chant at the beginning of a psalm—it is laid down to correct him with six blows. Likewise, the one who bites the cup of salvation with his teeth—with six blows."[6] The *Penitential* provides penalties not only for the sins of the clergy but also the laity: "If any laymen becomes drunk, or eats or drinks to the point of vomiting, let him do penance for a week on bread and water."[7]

The guidelines which Columbanus laid down for his monks, coming as they did from a particular tradition, did not find favor with all. Many of his letters reflect the antagonism that he and his monks found amongst foreigners. To a French bishop he wrote: "Don't look on us as aliens from you. For we are all fellow members of one body, whether Franks or Britons or Irish or whatever our race." He wrote similar words to Pope Boniface IV: "We are disciples of Saints Peter and Paul and of all the disciples who by the Holy Spirit wrote the divine canon—we, all the Irish, dwellers at the ends of the earth, who accept nothing beyond the evangelical and apostolic teaching. No one of has been a heretic, no one a Jew, no one a schismatic." But Columbanus was still determined to cling to his native traditions. Elsewhere he declared: "It is clear that we are in our native land as long as we accept no rules of these Franks."[8] This was the dilemma that the Irish monks faced: how to work amongst other peoples while retaining their own way of life.

There were a number of matters of discrepancy between Irish practice and that generally favored elsewhere. There were differences in the rite of baptism and in the monastic tonsure (the shaved part at the top of the head), and in various matters of liturgy and discipline. But the most important difference was over the date of Easter. The methods of calculating the date of Easter had gone through many changes over the centuries, but the Irish church held to one of the older methods. This was not an academic matter; it was essential to Christian unity that all churches should celebrate the principal Christian festival on the same day. In the late 620s the southern churches of Ireland, after a visit to Rome, had agreed to follow the Roman usage, but other Irish communities, at home and abroad, continued to hold to the old ways. The two sides clashed at the Synod of Whitby, in Northumbria, in A.D. 664. There the Romanists won the day by appealing to the higher authority of St. Peter. Their representative, Bishop Wilfrid, argued:

> For although your Fathers were holy men, do you imagine that they, a few men in a corner of a remote island, are to be preferred before the universal Church of Christ throughout the world? And even if your Columba—or may I say, ours also if he was the servant of Christ—was a Saint of potent virtues, can he take precedence before the most blessed Prince of the Apostles, to whom our Lord said: "Thou art Peter, and upon this rock will I build my church"?[9]

In the aftermath of the synod, many Irish monks in Britain, led by Colman of Lindisfarne who had made their case at Whitby, returned to Ireland. The monasteries of Ireland, some of which had already adopted the Roman dating of Easter, gradually came fully into line with their neighbors.

Whitby could be seen as the beginning of the end of the Golden Age of Ireland. No longer could Irish missionaries export their own brand of Christianity to Europe while still resolutely holding to their own traditions. Nevertheless, Irish monks continued to go abroad and influenced the development of European civilization. When Charlemagne, toward the end of the eighth century, sought to renew Christian life and learning within the kingdom of the Franks, he did so with the aid of Irish monks. And when, a century later, Alfred the Great embarked upon a similar programme in his kingdom of Wessex, he made use of Irish learning. Although the year 664 marked a defeat for the distinctively Irish monastic practices, the culture fostered by these practices had only just begun to flourish.

MONASTIC LIFE AND LEARNING

The image that usually springs to mind of a medieval monastery is that of a complex of stone buildings around a cloister where monks lived, worked and prayed together. The Irish monastery was somewhat different. Although the monks worked together in tilling the fields and engaged in a daily round of communal prayers, they lived in separate cells within a compound surrounded by a ditch. In their austere cells of wood or wattle, each monk spent much of his day

The eighth-century Derrynaflan chalice, discovered in 1980 in County Tipperary

in prayer and contemplation, a harking back to the ideals of the early hermits of the Egyptian desert. Monasteries served a number of purposes. They could act as centers of pilgrimage or of trade and were often used as places for storage of wealth. But they were also centers of learning and of literary and artistic production, and in this respect the Irish differed from the desert monks. By the eighth century, all of the major monasteries of Ireland had a scriptorium, where classical Mediterranean culture was preserved and new works were produced.

Though the people of Ireland had not experienced Roman rule, they took to Roman culture with great enthusiasm. This formerly nonliterate people developed a fascination with the written word, and soon made it their own. Found scribbled on the side of a ninth-century manuscript is a poem in Irish in which a monk describes his quest for words:

> I and Pangur Bán, my cat
> 'Tis a like task we are at;
> Hunting mice is his delight,
> Hunting words I sit all night.
>
> Better far than praise of men
> 'Tis to sit with book and pen;
> Pangur bears me no ill will,
> He too plies his simple skill.
>
> ....
>
> Practice every day had made
> Pangur perfect in his trade;
> I get wisdom day and night
> Turning darkness into light.[10]

Some of the earliest Christians came to Ireland with knowledge of the Latin language, but native-born Irish monks had to learn it in the monasteries. Their texts were the works of late Roman grammatists, principally those of the North African writer Donatus. The Irish monks adapted classical Latin and gave it certain special features, so that a specific form of the language, Hiberno-Latin, emerged. They took delight in the display of linguistic ability, introducing obscure words from Greek and Hebrew, and in engaging in complex wordplay.

The fostering of learning in Ireland depended on the dissemination of books, and much of the work of the scriptorium involved the copying of the precious codices which had come to them from all over Europe and beyond. Such works were very valuable, the product of visits to Rome and other parts of Europe, and it is reported that St. Colmcille's refusal to return a book to a monastery from which he had borrowed it provoked a battle in which many people lost their lives. Biblical texts were the most frequently copied, but many monastic libraries also had the works of the church fathers (Augustine, Ambrose, Jerome and Gregory the Great), canon law texts, histories and liturgical works. While the majority were Christian writings—saints' "Lives," works of theology, hymns and monastic rules, calendars, commentaries on the Bible and service books—the monks also recorded secular law and in the annals provided a chronicle of yearly events. Also, for the first time, the pre-Christian legends of the Celts were written down, though they were often given a Christian slant.

The scriptoria of the golden age produced a fusion between Irish Celtic culture and that of Rome, northern Europe and even the Asian world. Nowhere is this seen as clearly as in such illuminated manuscripts as the *Book of Durrow*, the *Book of Lindisfarne* and, most famously, the *Book of Kells*. *Kells* is one of the latest of such works, produced in the eighth or ninth century, and marks the artistic high point of Irish medieval art. Painted on vellum and measuring only thirteen by nine-and-a-half inches, it consists of the four gospels, plus preliminaries. Its extraordinary visual craft and inventiveness quickly won it fame. The very form of the book, a codex in Latin script, betrays Roman influence. Such influence is also present in the representation of people and objects. The illustration of the Virgin and Child, for example, shows a high-backed throne and a classical architectural frame, both of which must have been copied from a Roman manuscript. The folds in the clothing and the shapes of the faces recall icons from the Byzantine world. Yet, within panels in the frame, we see a group of monks wearing the distinctive Irish tonsure. Irish influence is also evident in the ornament. The medallions, whorls, scrolls and spirals evident in the illustration of the arrest of Christ echo early Celtic stone and metal work. The interlacing birds and animals reflect not only the local environment but can also be seen in manuscripts from Assyria to Northumbria. The more geometric lozenges and step patterns, similar to the jewelry designs found in the Sutton-Hoo hoard, show the influence of Germanic art. The *Book of Kells* illustrates the Irish fascination with the word. Every page contains decoration, and at every turn one can see letters becoming entangled, or transmuting into animals or humans. The first mention of Christ in St. Matthew's Gospel is marked by a whole page taken up with the symbol of Christ: *XPI*. Around the letters swirl intricate ornamentation which has been likened to a cloud of incense.

Gerald of Wales, who visited Ireland in the twelfth century, wrote:

> Among all the miracles of Kildare nothing seems to me more miraculous than that wonderful book which they say was written at the dictation of an angel during the lifetime of the VIRGIN.
>
> This book contains the concordance of the four gospels according to Saint Jerome, with almost as many drawings as pages, and all of them in marvellous colours....If you look at them carelessly and casually and not too closely, you may judge them to be mere daubs rather than careful compositions. You will see nothing subtle where everything is subtle. But if you take the trouble to look very closely, and penetrate with your eyes to the secrets of the artistry, you will notice such intricacies, so

delicate and subtle, so close together and well-knitted, so involved and bound together, and so fresh still in their colourings that you will not hesitate to declare that all these things must have been the result of the work, not of men, but of angels.[11]

The *Book of Kells* is the greatest achievement of the Golden Age. But even as it was being produced, new threats were emerging, from within and without, which would bring that age to a close.

THE VIKINGS

Bitter is the wind tonight,
It tosses the ocean's white hair:
To-night I fear not the fierce warriors of Norway
Coursing on the Irish Sea.[12]

These are the words of an Irish monk, scribbled on the margins of a manuscript he was working on in a scriptorium. Though safe that night, he knew that when the wind died down he and his fellow monks could be the victims of Viking attack.

The first recorded attack by the Vikings on Ireland was in A.D. 795 on "the island of Rethru," possibly Rathlin Island, off the Antrim coast. Others followed in quick succession and by the 820s they had circled the country. A number of factors prompted the Viking attacks on Ireland. It is thought that the large-scale movement of people out of Scandinavia was precipitated by a growth in population and a dearth of resources. To the south and west lay richer lands, easily reached and easy prey to these skilled seafarers and warriors in their longships. Their approach to Ireland was a natural progression: They had already attacked the Orkneys and northern Scotland; they had traveled along the east coast of

England and were threatening the northwestern coasts of the Frankish kingdom.

The eighth-century Ardagh Chalice: detail of the handle and escutcheon, engraved with the names of the twelve apostles

The Irish monasteries were especially vulnerable. Their exposure might have insulated them from the pressures of the world, the better to concentrate on divine contemplation, but it left them open to attacks from the sea. They were obvious targets as centers of wealth, holding valuables and cattle. To these pagan raiders, ideas of sanctuary or respect for clergy meant nothing. A few examples from the *Annals of Ulster* from the second quarter of the ninth century provide ample evidence of the destruction wrought by the Vikings on the Irish churches:

[824] The heathens plundered Bennchor at Airtriu, and destroyed the oratory, and shook the relics of Comgall from their shrine.

[825] Dun Lethglaise was plundered by the heathens. Mag Bile with its oratories was plundered by the heathens.

[828] Diarmait, abbot of I [Iona], went to Scotland with the halidoms of Colum Cille.

[832] The first plundering of Ard Macha [Armagh] by the heathens three times in one month.

[836] Cell Daire [Kildare] was plundered by the heathens from Inber Dea, and half of the church was burned.[13]

It has been said that the advent of the Vikings marked "the passing of the old order": The arrival of the first new peoples since the coming of the Celts shattered the existing institutions and way of life, destroying the great churches and introducing a harsher world in which Irish monasticism could no longer flourish.[14] The Vikings were a warlike people, and much of their impact was indeed destructive. And not only were they alien invaders, but they were pagans.

At the same time, it would be unjust to attribute the end of the Golden Age solely to the destructiveness of the Vikings. Although the annals persistently report church burnings and plunder, these sources must be viewed with a degree of caution. Telescoping the centuries-long era of the Vikings into a picture of incessant raiding disregards the many periods of calm that also occurred, as well as Viking settlement and peaceful coexistence with the Irish. It must also be remembered that the annals were written by churchmen. In a short entry detailing the events of the year, an attack on a church merited particular attention, just as a violent attack seemed more worthy of record than a peaceful exchange between Irish and Norse. Furthermore, an examination of these sources shows that the Irish themselves were not averse to attacking and endangering the churches. In the same period we read:

[831] The fair of Tailtiu was disturbed at the platforms owing to [dissension over] the shrine of MacCuilinn and the halidoms of Patrick, and many died as a result.
[833] Feidlimid, king of Cashel, put to death [members of] the community of Cluain Moccu Nois [Clonmacnoise] and burned their church-lands to the very door of their church. The community of Dairmag were treated likewise—to the very door of their church.[15]

This King Feidlimid struck terror into the hearts of many, just as the Vikings did. The annalist says of him in verse:

Feidlimid is the king
For whom a single day's work is
[To take] the hostages of Connacht without battle
And to spoil Mide[16]

Not only was he a king, but also a bishop and abbot. The annalist refers to his diverse offices in recording a defeat at the hands of a certain Niall:

The crozier of devout Feidlimid
Was abandoned in the blackthorns;
Niall, mighty in combat, took it
By right of victory in battle with swords[17]

Feidlimid was indeed devout. He was the champion of a new reformist movement in the Irish church, the Célí Dé or Culdees, an ascetic group which emphasized prayer, physical works, strict observance of Sundays and feast days, and distrust of women. The burning of Clonmacnoise was Feidlimid's punishment for the refusal of that community to adopt the ways of the reformers. Feidlimid may be an extreme example, but he was a reflection of a feature of Irish life that had existed for some time: the involvement of the monasteries in secular political rivalries. By the time the Vikings first struck, most monasteries were the possessions of ruling dynasties, which held the office of abbot by hereditary succession. Various pitched battles are recorded between the clergy of different communities. In A.D. 760 for example, a battle was fought between the monastic communities of Clonmacnoise and Birr, followed four years later by a major battle between Clonmacnoise and Durrow in which two hundred from the Durrow side perished. Though they certainly raised the temperature of violence, the Vikings were not responsible for initiating it.

Along with the image of the Vikings destroying the monastic life of Ireland goes the image of Brian Boru saving Celtic Christian

The early-tenth-century Cross of St. Muirdeach, Monasterboice, County Louth, and a detail showing the arrest of Christ

A carving of a figure carrying a crozier and a bell at White Island monastery, County Fermanagh

Ireland from the marauding pagan outsiders at the Battle of Clontarf in 1014. As with the first image, the second consists of a grain of truth enveloped in a great degree of legend. Brian Boru (or Bóruma) was a great king, the man who first came close to establishing his authority over all the Irish people. He helped to extend the authority of his dynasty, the Dál Cais, beyond present-day County Clare to the whole of Munster before challenging the authority of the Uí Néill powers over the northern part of the island. His biographer, the anonymous author of the *Cogadh Gaedhel re Gallibh* ("The War of the Irish against the Foreigners"), depicts him as the ideal Christian king: He was not only the Irish Caesar or Alexander the Great, but Solomon, David and Moses rolled into one. Like Charlemagne and Alfred the Great, "[H]e sent professors and masters to teach wisdom and knowledge; and to buy books beyond the sea, and the great ocean; because their writings and their books, in every church and in every sanctuary where they were, were burned and thrown into water by the plunderers." He paid a visit to Armagh, where he confirmed the right of that see to primacy over the Irish church and laid twenty pounds of gold on the altar. The *Cogadh* culminates with the description of the battle of Clontarf on Good Friday, 1014, when Brian's forces defeated the Vikings of Dublin, though Brian himself fell. It was written a century later in an attempt to boost the fortunes of Brian's successors, and it is a skilful panegyric of the ideal Christian king, but it has also helped to distort many perceptions of the time. The wars in which Brian was involved were never really between the Irish and the foreigners—alliances were made all the time between Vikings and Irish, and each was represented on both sides at Clontarf. Nor was Clontarf the defining point as it has often been depicted. The Vikings were not defeated; they continued to live in Dublin and the other towns that they had founded, to intermarry and to influence Irish life. Well before Clontarf they had been turning to Christianity. In fact, the Viking connection was crucial to the next step in the development of Irish Christianity.

The Rock of Cashel, County Tipperary. St. Cormac's chapel, on the rock, is Ireland's earliest example of Romanesque architecture.

IV

THE ANGLO-NORMAN
CHURCH

At the beginning of the second millennium A.D., the Irish church was still a world unto itself. Irish monks continued with their own forms of organization and practice, untouched by the patterns of monasticism which had become established in England and Europe. And while amongst other peoples the churches were organized under the authority of bishops and archbishops, the Irish church remained under the control of monasteries and their abbots. All this was soon to change. Western Europe was on the verge of revolutionary developments which would take it out of the darkness that had descended with the fall of the Roman Empire and inspire some of the greatest achievements of medieval civilization. The church, under a series of energetic and imaginative popes, was about to become a truly universal, transnational institution, no longer simply the possession of local princes. Growing stability and prosperity would soon be reflected in architecture, art and literature. New political powers were emerging, too, most notably the Normans, who were soon to hold sway over England. Though on the fringe of these movements, the

A scribe from Gerald of Wales's Topograpy of Ireland, *written in the 1180s*

consequences for Ireland were great. The year 1169 is sometimes seen as the date when Ireland's splendid isolation was shattered in the face of Norman invaders, but for more than a century before that the Irish church had been drawn ever more closely into the ecclesiastical world of England and Europe. The Norman invasion cemented that bond, and Ireland was allowed to share in the flowering of medieval civilization. Later, when the western church and English authority went on to suffer from corruption, conflict and natural disasters, the Irish church was forced to share in that decline.

TWELFTH-CENTURY REFORM

In the eleventh and twelfth centuries a new wind was blowing through the national churches of western Europe, a movement of reform which sought to turn its back on the ravages of previous centuries and to establish the Christian church on a stronger footing. At the center of this reform was the position of the papacy. Prior to the eleventh century the papacy had been increasingly undermined by corruption in Rome and disorder beyond, so that the office had become little more than a focus for the political ambitions of Italian families and an irrelevancy to many in northern Europe. During the eleventh century, however, the election of the pope was taken out of the hands of laymen and entrusted to a college of cardinals. Popes began to raise their voices against abuses within the church, the most prominent being clerical marriage, the buying and selling of church offices (simony) and the holding of more than one church office (pluralism). At the same time, through the codification of canon law (the law of the church), the extension of papal jurisdiction, the growth of papal administration and the efforts of some individuals of great quality, the church in western Europe began to look less parochial and more international. Conflicts did ensue—most seriously that between the pope and the German emperor, which centered on the imperial role in the appointment of ecclesiastics—but, nevertheless, the eleventh and twelfth centuries were times of opening up to the exchange of ideas among churches in different parts of Europe, and also periods when national churches were increasingly brought into line with Roman thinking. At the same time, new religious movements emerged—the Cistercians, Augustinians, Carthusians and others— which rejected luxury and secularity and sought to return to the ideals of the apostles and the desert fathers.

The Irish involvement in the reform movement gained much of its impetus from a seemingly unlikely quarter—the descendants of the Norse invaders. From the ninth century onward Scandinavians had settled in Ireland, primarily in coastal regions, and had, for the first time on the island, initiated urban life. The towns of Dublin, Limerick and Waterford, in particular, prospered on the basis of trade with other Viking colonies in Ireland and abroad and, increasingly, with the native Irish. Along with settlement came intermarriage and integration, and the adoption of Christianity. By the end of the tenth century, the Vikings of the towns—the Ostmen, as they were called—were mostly Christian, though adherence to their Scandinavian gods persisted for some time. Dublin, which had as yet played no role in the story of Irish Christianity, was soon to come to the forefront. In 1028 Sitric Silkbeard, king of Dublin, along with other notables, paid a visit to Rome. The end of the Viking, Muslim and Magyar invasions and the establishment of greater stability throughout western Europe meant that in the eleventh century it was possible, as it had not been before, for Irish people to visit the Holy See. Over the succeeding decades many kings and nobles made such a pilgrimage, and contacts were maintained by the existence of a community of Irish monks in Rome. Inevitably, those who traveled to Rome returned with ideas and ambitions which were to transform the Irish church. On Sitric's return, most likely in 1038, he granted a site for the foundation of a new cathedral church in Dublin— Christ Church, known as Holy Trinity in the Middle Ages—and established the new diocese of Dublin.

It was natural for the Christians of Dublin to look not to the native Irish church but to the Scandinavians of northwestern Europe, and particularly to England. The English crown was held by Danes during the first half of the eleventh century and the Danes had established extensive settlements in northern England. It seems likely that from the start the bishops of Dublin were consecrated by members of the English hierarchy, and these links continued with the conquest of England by the Normans in 1066, themselves of Scandinavian origins and enthusiastic church reformers. Our first firm evidence of such a link comes in 1074 when the clergy and people of Dublin wrote to Lanfranc, archbishop of Canterbury, asking him to consecrate their bishop, reminding him how "we have always gladly submitted to the government of your predecessors from whom we remember that we received ecclesiastical dignity."[1] Lanfranc's letter, written shortly after to the king of Dublin, acknowledges this custom. "Dearest son," he wrote, "we received with honour our venerable brother and fellow bishop Patrick, whom your excellency sent to us to be consecrated; with the grace of the Holy Ghost to help us we consecrated him in due form to his appointed duties; after his consecration we sent him back to his own see with our letter of commendation, as was the custom of our predecessors."[2] So, from the eleventh century, the diocese of Dublin considered itself bound to the archdiocese of Canterbury, owing it obedience as its superior. Waterford and Limerick, also Viking towns, soon followed suit. This was a matter of convenience for Canterbury, as it added to its claim, disputed by York, to hold a position of primacy within the English church. For the clergy of Dublin, Waterford and Limerick, it meant not having to seek the approval of the Irish hierarchy, of whom they were suspicious. Furthermore, it opened the door to rich contacts between the Irish church and its English counterpart, and thereby to the continental reform movement.

If the diocese of Dublin acted as one of the earliest conduits of reform ideas, Munster was even more significant. The descendants of Brian Boru took an interest in the state of the church and communicated with reformers from abroad. In 1076 the greatest of these, Pope Gregory VII, wrote to Toirdelbach Ua Briain (whom the pope addressed as "illustrious king of Ireland") and "the archbishops, bishops, noblemen and all Christians who dwell in Ireland." In this short letter the pope urged the Irish people toward unity and obedience to Rome:

Thus we exhort you as most dear sons to perform righteousness, to keep and love the catholic peace of the church, and loving it to bind it to you with the arms of charity. Should any matters of business arise amongst you which seem to call for our aid, be sure straightaway to have recourse to us, and whatever you rightly ask you will with God's help obtain.[3]

The kings and clergy of Munster were also recipients of letters from Lanfranc and his successor Anselm criticizing the state of the Irish church and urging reform. Around 1074 Lanfranc wrote to Toirdelbach Ua Briain:

But among many things which are commendable certain reports have reached us which are quite the opposite: namely that in your kingdom a man abandons at his own discretion and without any grounds in canon law the wife who is lawfully married to him, not hesitating to form a criminal alliance—by the law of marriage or rather by the law of fornication—with any woman he pleases, either a relative of his own or of his deserted wife or a woman whom someone else has abandoned in an equally disgraceful way. Bishops are consecrated by a single bishop; many are ordained to villages or small towns; infants are baptised without the use of consecrated chrism; holy orders are conferred by bishops for money. No one who has the least familiarity with Christian learning is unaware that all these abuses and others like them are contrary to the Gospels and to apostolic teaching, that they are prohibited by canon law and are contrary to what has been established by all the orthodox Fathers who have gone before us.[4]

Lanfranc's solution was that the king of Munster should "order the bishops and all men of religion to assemble together, attend their holy assembly in person with your chief advisers, and strive to banish from your kingdom these evil customs and all others that are similarly condemned by canon law." Such a programme was instituted by Toirdelbach's successors. The synods of Cashel (1101), Rathbreasail (1111) and Kells (1152) were to create a truly national church and transform its organization.

We know little about what happened at Cashel, but it was clearly a great occasion. It was presided over by King Muirchertach O'Briain, along with the bishop of Munster, Máel Muire Ua Dunáin, who it has been claimed acted as papal legate. A program of reform was decreed and the great hill of Cashel, formerly the site of the kings of Munster, was granted to the church. The Synod of Rathbreasail in 1111 had a more far-reaching impact. At its center was Gilbert of Limerick, a friend of Anselm of Canterbury, papal legate for twenty years and the great theoretician of Irish church reform. Faced with the existence of too many bishops with powers too weak and subordinate to abbots who were often laymen, Gilbert attempted in his work *De Statu Ecclesiae* (Concerning Church Order) to make a clear separation between diocese and monastery. Monks were to abandon all worldly pursuits and leave ecclesiastical government to bishops. The bishops would rule over clearly defined territorial dioceses which would be ultimately subject to the pope. The synod put these plans into effect, creating two provinces, Armagh and Cashel, each with twelve dioceses. The Synod of Kells in 1152 completed this process. It legislated against such abuses as simony, usury and marital irregularity, and enforced the payment of tithes. Also, while Rathbreasail had made no mention of Dublin, Kells made it its business to bring Dublin within a single structure. Under the authority of the papal legate, Cardinal John Paparo, the two provinces of Dublin and Tuam were added, and Armagh was granted primacy over the Irish church. With only a few changes, this is the structure that stands in Ireland to this day.

ST. MALACHY AND THE
NEW RELIGIOUS ORDERS

Although he died four years before it was held, the inspiration for the Synod of Kells and the greatest figure in the twelfth-century reform movement in Ireland was St. Malachy of Armagh. Malachy was by instinct a recluse from the world, and nothing was dearer to him than monastic life. To his misfortune, but to the benefit of the Irish church, he was drawn out of the cloister again and again to minister to the needs of his people. In this respect he resembles his friend and admirer, the dominant figure in the European church of the twelfth century, Bernard of Clairvaux. Though Bernard sought nothing but a life of asceticism and contemplation, he became one of the central figures in the church, preaching the Second Crusade, condemning heresy and dispensing advice to popes. He came to know Malachy and, after the Irishman's death, wrote his friend's biography, praising Malachy's spiritual qualities and his role in the reform of what Bernard viewed as a barbarous and corrupt church.

Malachy was born into the deepest traditions of the Irish church. He trained as a monk at Armagh, where his father had taught in the monastic school. He became a priest at the age of twenty-five, and in his early years he hoped to devote himself to the monastic life at Bangor. However, against his will he was made, first, bishop of Connor and, later, archbishop of Armagh. Though reluctant to become involved in practical affairs, Malachy was a staunch reformer in these positions and suffered the antipathy of many, both clergy and lay, who sought to retain the old practices. Bernard describes the situation that Malachy faced in the following fashion:

> Once he had begun to exercise his office the man of God realised that he had been sent not to men but to beasts. Never had he known such men, so steeped in barbarism; never had he found people so wanton in their way of life,

so cruel in superstition, so heedless of faith, lawless, dead set against discipline, so foul in their lifestyle; Christians in name, yet pagans at heart.[5]

Yet, according to Bernard, Malachy's efforts softened his people's hearts and he established correct ecclesiastical practice, removed barbarous customs, ordained suitable clergy and reformed the sacraments. He was often inhibited, however, by the existing political situation. Though elected archbishop of Armagh in 1132, he was prevented from taking up his position until 1134 by local powers, and was never accepted there. After two years he resigned his office and retired to the smaller diocese of Down to lead a monastic life. He never abandoned his ambitions to reform the church, though, and in 1139 he went on foot to Rome to seek the pallium—a vestment symbolizing episcopal office—for the bishops of Cashel and Armagh. Along the way Malachy stopped at the Cistercian monastery of Clairvaux, a visit which was to change his life and that of the Irish church.

For an Irish monk to visit a Cistercian house was to experience an entirely different way of approaching the religious life. Malachy's concept of a monastery would have been that which had existed in Ireland, largely unchanged, for centuries, that is, an enclosure comprising a scattered group of oratories, each occupied by one monk, devoting himself to private prayer. In this respect Ireland had remained almost untouched by the changes in monasticism influenced by the sixth-century Rule of St. Benedict of Nursia, which laid down a common life based on uniform duty, brotherhood and obedience. The Cistercians, who first emerged in Cîteaux, Burgundy, in 1098, saw themselves as leading the most perfect form of the Benedictine life. Sometimes known as the "white monks" because they wore habits of undyed wool, theirs was a harsh existence, based on a daily round of communal prayer and manual labor, along with private contemplation. They were self-sufficient communities, the monks being supported by *conversi* or lay brothers who worked the fields. Their monasteries included workshops, barns and stables, as well as a chapter house, library and scriptorium; all plain buildings, but impressive to an Irish eye.

Mellifont Abbey, County Louth, Ireland's first Cistercian monastery

Inspired by what he saw and by his meeting with Bernard, Malachy traveled on to Rome. There he asked the pope to allow him to retire from his responsibilities as bishop and to become a Cistercian monk, but the pope, recognizing Malachy's importance as a reformer of the church, refused his request. Malachy managed to stop at Clairvaux again on the return journey and left four of his men there to be trained in the Cistercian life. In 1142 the first Irish Cistercian monastery was founded at Mellifont (County Louth), staffed by a combination of Irish and French monks. In 1147 a daughter house of Mellifont was founded at Bective; the following year four more were founded, including Baltinglas, and others, notably Jerpoint (County Kilkenny), soon followed. By

1171 there were fifteen Cistercian abbeys in the country, most of them derived from Malachy's foundation of Mellifont, which by that time was said to have a hundred monks and three hundred lay brothers. The Cistercian movement was one of the defining phenomena of the mid–twelfth century throughout Europe—more than three hundred monasteries were founded between 1125 and 1161—but its growth in Ireland was particularly remarkable. It fitted in well; the austerity of the order appealed to the Irish tradition of desert monasticism, and its self-sufficiency meant that the monks could adapt to uncultivated land in remote areas. The order also introduced much that was new. Though a communal form of monasticism on a European model had been seen in Ireland before (in 1127 a monastery for Benedictine monks of the congregation of Savigny was founded at Erenagh in Down), the Cistercians made the Benedictine life the norm. In addition, the Cistercian form of government, which involved a federal structure and the visitation of houses by senior figures from sister houses, meant that Irish monasticism was brought further into the reformed mainstream.

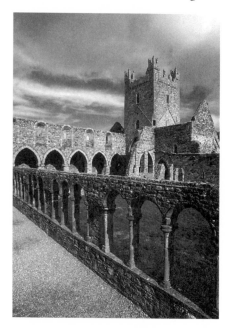

Jerpoint Abbey, County Kilkenny

The Cistercians were perhaps the most important of the new religious movements of the twelfth century, but they were by no means the only ones. Also very influential were the Canons Regular of St. Augustine, a group who followed the monastic rule of St. Augustine of Hippo (A.D. 354–430). Here again Malachy played a central role in their introduction to Ireland, building contacts with the canons of Guisborough in Yorkshire and visiting the Augustinian house of Arrouaise in Flanders. This prompted the foundation of houses in Ireland from the 1140s onward, the first perhaps being St. Mary's Abbey in Louth. The Augustinian canons followed a more flexible rule than the Cistercians. Some concentrated on the contemplative life, while others involved themselves in charity, education and tending to the sick, and in Ireland women tended to play a prominent role. By 1171 Ireland had more than sixty Augustinian houses, some of those conversions of older foundations.

The new religious movements literally transformed the Irish landscape. Up to this point, Irish architecture had been virtually untouched by the Romanesque style, based on Roman principles of rounded arches, heavy pillars and large basilicas. In 1134, however, St. Cormac's chapel, with its Romanesque high stone roof, was consecrated on the Rock of Cashel. The Cistercians gave this new architecture its greatest impetus, introducing continental styles and adapting them to the Irish environment. In 1157 the abbey church of Mellifont was completed and consecrated in the presence of seventeen bishops and numerous kings. There King Muircheartach Mac Lochlainn presented one hundred and forty cows and sixty ounces of gold to the church "as an offering for the health of his soul." In the following decade Irish Romanesque architecture was to be found throughout the country, reaching its artistic high point with the cathedral of St. Brendan at Clonfert.

In 1148 Malachy again visited the pope and again stopped at Clairvaux. There he died, surrounded by the community, with his friend and inspiration, Bernard, at his side. His life had summed up the best of the Irish reform movement. His outlook was rooted in the old traditions of Irish monasticism and learning, but he nonetheless looked beyond them to the dynamic forces which were emerging on the Continent.

THE COMING OF THE NORMANS

Despite the efforts of Malachy and the other reformers, many still regarded the Irish as inferior in Christian living. "This is a filthy people, wallowing in vice. Of all peoples it is the least instructed in the rudiments of the Faith." So wrote Gerald of Wales, a churchman of Welsh-Norman origins, who first visited Ireland in the 1180s. Gerald's comments on Ireland often tell us more about himself than they do about Ireland, but such a view was evidently shared by Pope Adrian IV, the only Englishman ever to hold that office. In 1155, only three years after the Synod of Kells, he gave authority to the new king of England, Henry II, to conquer Ireland "to proclaim the truths of the Christian religion to a rude and ignorant people, and to root out the growth of vice from the field of the Lord." The king's clerk, John of Salisbury, himself one of the foremost churchmen of the era, records how he obtained this papal bull, known as *Laudabiliter*:

> In response to my petition the pope granted and donated Ireland to the illustrious king of England, Henry, to be held by him and his successors, as his letters, still extant, testify. He did this in virtue of the long-established right, reputed to derive from the Donation of Constantine [the first Christian Roman Emperor], whereby all islands are considered to belong to the Roman church. Moreover, through me the pope sent a gold ring, set with a magnificent emerald, as a sign that he had invested the king with the right to rule Ireland.[6]

Henry II was not interested in a religious crusade to Ireland, but he *was* interested in extending his authority westward as a way of consolidating and expanding his inheritance. Already king of England, duke of Normandy, count of Anjou, Maine, Touraine and Aquitaine, and claimant to overlordship in Wales and Scotland, it was said by a contemporary that he was "impatient of repose, and did not hesitate to disturb half of Christendom." But even a man of such ambition and energy was too fully occupied in the early years of his reign with the problems of controlling his vast dominions to turn his attention to Ireland. If *Laudabiliter* provided the legal pretext for invasion, the occasion, a combination of necessity and opportunity, was offered by the turbulent world of Irish politics in the 1160s.

In 1166 the enemies and former allies of Diarmait MacMurchada, king of Leinster, joined together and drove him out of his kingdom. This event might have stood as little more than a footnote to the ebb and flow of the Irish powers were it not for the man to whom Diarmait turned to regain his kingdom. Instead of looking for help in Ireland, he made his way to Henry II, then occupied with his French dominions, and gained license to recruit amongst the king's vassals. Those most eager to take up the challenge were disaffected knights on the fringes of the Anglo-Norman Empire, especially on the marches of Wales, who saw in Ireland opportunities for glory, lands and prosperity. The most famous of these Norman adventurers was Richard FitzGilbert de Clare, earl of Pembroke, better known as "Strongbow," to whom Diarmait granted his daughter Aoife in marriage and whom he designated as the successor to his kingdom. The kings of Leinster and the Norse towns of Wexford, Waterford and Dublin quickly fell to the superior armory and tactics of the Norman knights, and by 1169 Diarmait had been restored to his throne. Two years later, Diarmait died and Strongbow succeeded him as king of Leinster. This was a source of concern to Henry II. On his western flank he saw the establishment of a new power which might come to threaten his own position. Furthermore, the Christian world at the time was outraged at Henry's role in the murder of his archbishop Thomas Becket in December 1170, and Ireland provided a suitable diversion. In the winter of 1171–72 Henry went there and demanded the submission of the Norman knights. They quickly submitted, as did many of the Irish kings. English rule in Ireland had begun.

Though later characterized as "the beginning of the woes of Ireland," the coming of the Normans did not at the time present itself as such. To most Irish kings and nobles, the Normans constituted one other player in a fragmented political scene, albeit a very strong one. To the leaders of the church, the Normans must have seemed allies in reform. Gerald of Wales describes how, on hearing of the fall of Dublin, a synod of Irish bishops was held, where:

> At length it was unanimously resolved, that it appeared to the synod that the Divine vengeance had brought upon them this severe judgment for the sins of the people, and especially for this, that they had long been wont to purchase natives of England as well from traders as from robbers and pirates, and reduce them to slavery; and that now they also, by reciprocal justice, were reduced to servitude by that very nation.[7]

At the Synod of Cashel in 1172 the leaders of the church were quick to acknowledge Henry's authority, and there, in the words of Gerald, they made enquiry into "the enormous offences and foul lives of the people of that land."

The Normans were great warriors, as well as efficient and innovative rulers. In the seventy years after King Henry's visit they managed to consolidate their authority in Leinster and extend it over three-quarters of the island. Only central and western Ulster and parts of Connacht remained untouched by the Normans, though the rich lands of the east and south constituted the heartland of their rule. By the mid–thirteenth century Ireland had become accustomed to the feudal institutions which were the hallmark of the civilization of the central Middle Ages. The most visible signs of Norman influence were the castles which dotted the land, the towns which sprang up everywhere, and the manorial economy which regulated rural life. But the Normans also introduced other novelties: the subdivision of the country into counties administered by sheriffs; the establishment of royal justices; the exchequer; and eventually an Irish parliament. The same process was at work in the church. After 1172 the church was brought fully into conformity with the English church. Soon new clergy of Norman stock was introduced to the

A carving of the Virgin and Child under the south arch of the tower at the Franciscan friary, Ennis, County Clare

episcopate and these men sought to advance the reforms which had been begun by the Irish, subdividing the newly created dioceses into parishes. The advance of the new religious orders continued, and by 1230 there were around two hundred houses for men, eighty of these Norman foundations. Between 1180 and 1222, for example, ten new Cistercian monasteries were founded, including Dunbrody and Tintern, rivaling the Mellifont family, and by 1272 there were forty Cistercian houses in the country. The Normans also introduced such new orders as Hospitallers and Templars. The advances in church architecture continued as well. The transition from the heavy Romanesque to the lighter Gothic style, with its pointed arches and stained-glass windows, is evident in such churches as Baltinglas, Jerpoint and Boyle. By around 1230 Gothic had fully displaced Romanesque, with the aid of craftsmen introduced from England. The thirteenth century was the great age of the Gothic Irish cathedrals, from St. Patrick's and Christ Church in Dublin to St. Mary's in Limerick and St. Canice's in Kilkenny.

In the thirteenth century a new force emerged in the church: the mendicant orders. These orders, most notably the Franciscans and the Dominicans, marked a new departure in Christian life. They were founded respectively by St. Francis of Assisi (1182–1226), the son of a rich merchant who renounced his inheritance, and St. Dominic (1170–1221), an Augustinian canon from Castile who based his early movement in southern France. While they lived an ordered, communal life, they rejected one of the pillars of the monastic life—the principle of stability within the monastery. Instead, they saw their duty as one of preaching, often wandering from town to town. They rejected property and relied instead on the generosity of the communities to whom they ministered. In this they believed they were imitating Christ as depicted in the Gospels. In 1217, when both groups had gained a growing number of followers, they independently decided to scatter and launch a universal mission. The Dominicans reached England in 1221, the Franciscans in 1224, and it was not long before their influence was felt in Ireland.

Both orders tended to concentrate on towns and thus the Anglo-Norman settlements first gained their attention. They attracted the patronage of kings, nobles and burghers, and over time the number of friaries expanded. In 1224 the Dominicans made their first Irish foundations at Dublin and Drogheda. By 1250 there were twelve Dominican friaries in the country; by 1300 there were twenty-four, including Derry, Limerick and Athenry. The Franciscans arrived in Ireland around 1230 and laid their first foundation in Youghal. From there they went on to Cork, Waterford and Kilkenny, before moving to Dublin and further north. By 1290 there were thirty Franciscan foundations in the country. At the end of the thirteenth century Ireland was a prosperous and relatively orderly colony of the English crown, and its church had been reformed and revitalized on English and continental lines.

But already problems were emerging which would pose serious challenges to colony and church.

THE DECLINE OF THE NORMAN CHURCH

The Anglo-Norman advance of the twelfth and thirteenth centuries was spectacular, but it was not sufficient. Ireland as a whole remained unconquered and as soon as the Anglo-Norman advance began to falter, the colony began to fall apart. Whereas Anglo-Norman settlement and English rule were strong in Leinster and Munster, their influence weakened in the west and north. The rougher land of Connacht and Ulster was less inviting for Anglo-Norman adventurers, and there the Gaelic Irish—the native people—continued to live much as they had for centuries. Even in the southeastern half of the island, Anglo-Norman power was uneven and, especially in the uplands, Gaelic chieftains were waiting to prey on the colonists nearby. As Anglo-Norman expansion came to a halt, it quickly began to contract in the face of Gaelic resurgence. Furthermore, Ireland suffered from the same problems which afflicted the rest of Europe in the fourteenth and fifteenth centuries: war, plague, political crisis and the decline of the church.

From the beginning, the English crown had regarded the Gaelic Irish as a rough and barbarous people and, as tensions grew between the colonists and the colonized, royal policy became firmly racial in tone. In the Gaelic areas there was corresponding suspicion of the English. Though early on the Irish clergy and the newcomers from England and elsewhere had often cooperated, race soon became an issue in the episcopacy. In 1217 it was decreed that, as "the peace of Ireland has been frequently disturbed by the election of Irishmen," none should in future be elected or promoted in any cathedral. Under papal pressure this mandate was reversed, but in 1250 King Henry III tried once again to have Irishmen excluded from cathedral churches. By this time almost one-third of the bishops in Ireland were Anglo-Normans and the episcopacy was divided along the lines of existing settlement patterns and according to the strength or weakness of English rule in a particular area. While the provinces of Tuam and Armagh in the west and north were almost exclusively Irish, Dublin was English and Cashel mixed.

The same division was at work in the religious orders. The Cistercians became virtually two separate orders soon after the Norman invasions. The new Anglo-Norman foundations, filled with Englishmen, were considerably richer and closer to the rest of the order in England and on the Continent. The older houses tended to take on a local identity, with links to Gaelic society and politics, and a growing distance from the Cistercian chapter-general. Racial discrimination worked both ways, with monastic houses rejecting those who did not fit in. This division was often mirrored in individual houses, where an Anglo-Norman abbot might face opposition from his Irish monks and lay brothers. In 1227 a new Anglo-Norman abbot who had been imposed on Baltinglas was driven out of the monastery and knocked off his horse as he left. Such events soon reached the chapter-general. The next year Stephen of Lexington, abbot of Stanley in Wiltshire, was sent on a visitation of the Irish

Cistercian houses. He was appalled by what he saw, and in the letters he wrote to his superiors he related how he was met with armed resistance, his life threatened, and his party assaulted and robbed. His description of the scene at the abbey of Maigue shows how the Cistercian order had declined since Malachy first introduced it to Ireland not even a century earlier:

> They violently expelled and completely drove away from the monastery their abbot and monks and lay-brothers who had been sent there with the authority of the Order to teach the rule, which was completely reduced to nothing there, and to reform discipline. In addition, turning the monastery, the cloister as well as the church, into a fortress against God, they stored thirty head of cattle, slaughtered and salted down, under the dormitory; they strongly fortified the dormitories of the monks and lay-brothers with great stones, stakes, palings and weapons according to the custom of their people. They stored large amounts of grain, hay, flour and other necessities in the church and they placed vessels and containers adequate to hold water in the cloister...each one of the monks and lay-brothers equipped himself as best he could with weapons prepared especially for him, excepting the old monks and some of the more prudent ones who left the monastery lest they become involved in such crimes.[8]

With the aid of secular powers, Stephen arranged for many Irish monks to be transferred and newcomers introduced. Reform decrees were drawn up for the Cistercian houses as a whole, and detailed instructions were given to individual houses. Yet the two spheres continued, mirroring the political and social divide.

A similar situation was discernible amongst the Franciscans and Dominicans. Originally focused on the Anglo-Normans of the cities and towns, they soon mixed in with the Gaelic population, so much so that a report of the Royal Commission in 1284–85 complained that "the Dominicans and Franciscans make too much use of that language," the language in question being Irish. Two nations emerged, and the division was most bitterly played out at a meeting of the Franciscan chapter in Cork in 1291. There a dispute broke out between the Irish and English, and the townspeople soon joined in, leading to the killing of at least sixteen friars. After the great successes of the thirteenth century, no Franciscan house was founded for a quarter of a century after 1296, and no Dominican friary for half a century after 1305.

The friars were, however, prominent on both sides in the first major crisis to hit the colony. In 1315 Edward Bruce landed near Larne. His brother Robert had established himself as king of Scotland and the year before had defeated King Edward II of England at the Battle of Bannockburn. The Irish of Ulster hailed Edward Bruce as king, and he soon had control of the province. The Irish princes explained their rejection of English rule in the famous *Remonstrance* to Pope John XXII in 1317:

> For not only their laymen and secular clergy but some also of their regular clergy dogmatically assert the heresy that it is no more a sin to kill an Irishman than a dog or any other brute. And in maintaining this heretical position some monks of theirs affirm boldly that if it should happen to them, as it does often happen, to kill an Irishman, they would not on that account refrain from saying mass, not even for a day.[9]

And they pointed to the Franciscans in particular as holding this attitude. Meanwhile King Edward was warning his justiciars against the treacherous Irish friars, and complaining to the minister general of the Irish Franciscan order:

We have learned from numerous reports given by different subjects of yours that certain friars of your Order, unmindful of their profession and departing from the good conduct required of them, have by force of persuasion instigated and convinced some people of our allegiance in our kingdom of Ireland to make treaties with our enemies, the Scots. In that same country some of them have already been a loss and damage to ourselves and our subjects, and do not cease from daily inciting the Irish laity to rebel against us in every way possible and join up with the Scots who have illegally entered that country.[10]

Despite raids into Connacht and a march south, Edward Bruce was killed in 1318 and the revolt petered out. Nevertheless, it marked a turning point. Ravaged by war and famine, Ireland was now no longer a land of adventure or a prosperous resource for the English crown. Disaster struck again in 1348 when the Black Death arrived in the east and spread across the country the following year. A Franciscan friar left a record of the plague, and a few lines toward the end of his book sum up the terror it instilled:

And I, Brother John Clynn, of the Friars Minor of Kilkenny, have written in this book the notable events which befell in my time, which I saw for myself or have learnt from men worthy of belief. So that notable deeds should not perish with time, and be lost from the memory of future generations, I, seeing these many ills, and that the whole world is encompassed by evil, waiting among the dead for death to come, have committed to writing what I have truly heard and examined; and so that the writing does not perish with the writer, or the work fail with the workman, I leave parchment for continuing the work, in case anyone should still be alive in the future and any son of Adam can escape this pestilence and continue the work thus begun.[11]

At the end of the book a later hand added: "Here it seems the author died."

In the aftermath of the plague, the decline of the colony continued. Around one-third of the population had died, and the cramped and unsanitary towns under colonial rule were hit particularly badly. In the late fourteenth century a problem which had existed for some time became more pronounced: degeneracy. Over the generations, the descendants of the Anglo-Norman settlers had begun to take on the customs and manners of the Gaelic Irish. In the famous phrase, they became "more Irish than the Irish themselves." The Statutes of Kilkenny of 1366, which prohibited settlers and their descendants from speaking Irish, employing Irish harpists and minstrels, and playing Gaelic games such as hurling, was more a

A woodcut of 1483 illustrating the legend of St. Patrick's vision of hell at St. Patrick's Purgatory, Lough Derg, County Donegal

statement of the problem than the solution. By then there were three nations in Ireland: the native Gaelic Irish, those English who retained close links with England and kept to English customs, and the "degenerate English," descendants of settlers who had gone native. Sometimes it was difficult for outsiders to tell the difference. An Irish chaplain called Nicholas Hogonana made a visit to Rome, and on his way left his valuables with a cleric in Wales. When, on his return, he asked for his belongings, the Welsh clergyman raised the alarm, claiming that a "wild Irish rebel" was trying to steal from him. It took some time for Nicholas to establish his credentials as an Irishman of English stock.

By the fifteenth century, effective English authority had shrunk to an area encompassing Dublin and its environs known as the Pale. Beyond the Pale, the Gaelic areas were ruled by their ancient families—the O'Neills and O'Donnells in Ulster, the O'Briens in Munster—while much of what had been the heartland of the colony had become virtually independent states. The Fitzgeralds of Kildare, descendants of Anglo-Norman colonists, became the uncrowned kings of Ireland, treating with both the English authorities and the Irish chieftains.

In such circumstances, the clergy throughout most of Ireland resorted to practices thought to have been long rooted out by Malachy and the other reformers. Clerical celibacy had been virtually abandoned, especially in the west and the north, and monasteries were once again the hereditary possessions of leading local families. Clergy were reproved by successive synods for wearing lay dress, long hair and moustaches, and taking part in battle. In 1444, for example, Cormac McLoughlan, bishop of Clonmacnoise, was slain during a pitched battle between different factions of his family. Nor were murders amongst clerics uncommon. This situation was not helped by the condition of the papacy, which had degenerated into corruption. The papal curia was happy to condone abuses in the Irish church and to accommodate blatantly partisan appointments to ecclesiastical offices in return for payment. In English-controlled areas the situation was little better, with the colony presenting an increasingly unattractive prospect to incoming clergy. Only the friars seemed to merit any praise from contemporaries. The church was, then, clearly ripe for reform. But when that reform came, its consequences were greater than anyone could have imagined.

An angel waves a censer above the head of an abbot in a fifteenth-century carving at Kilcoole Abbey, County Tipperary.

V

REFORMATION
AND REVOLUTION

The Irish have always been a divided people. In addition to social divisions, there have existed differences of loyalty and ethnicity. But before the sixteenth century, religious difference had not played a prominent role. That century introduced the division between Catholic and Protestant which intensified in the seventeenth century and has endured to this day. This was never simply a religious divide; ethnic, political and social factors also continued to play an ever present part in the divisions and conflicts which came to plague Ireland. What changed was that religion became the most important flag of identity. The sixteenth and seventeenth centuries were times of conflict and confrontation, of rebellion, conquest and bloodshed. But, in addition to the dramatic upheavals of the era, there were more subtle developments. In particular, new religious identities emerged, not only in the shape of the Protestant congregations, but also amongst Catholics.

THE TUDOR REFORMATION

The decision by Henry VIII (r. 1509–47) to reject Roman authority had little to do with faith and less to do with Ireland, but it had profound consequences for both. Henry despised Martin Luther (1483–1546), the German monk whose resistance to the papacy had inaugurated the Reformation, and the pope had even granted Henry the title of "Defender of the Faith" for his actions against early Protestants. But the pope's refusal to dissolve Henry's marriage to Catherine of Aragon, who had failed to produce a male heir, prompted Henry to loosen and then fully sever his kingdom's ties with Rome. Appeals to papal jurisdiction were prohibited, certain dues formerly rendered to Rome were redirected to the Crown, and the first steps were taken to dissolve the monasteries. Henry's policy in Ireland was an extension of his English policy. The various measures passed by the Dublin parliament in 1536 and 1537 transferred authority over church matters from the pope to the king and established the Church of Ireland. First came the Act of Supremacy, which established Henry and his heirs as heads of the Irish church. Subsequent legislation established Dublin's court of chancery as the final court of appeal for ecclesiastical matters, gave the primate of Ireland, rather than the pope, power to grant ecclesiastical licenses and diverted certain church revenues to the crown instead of Rome. Finally, the Act Against the Authority of the Bishop of Rome affirmed these laws and summed up the spirit of the changes in the form of an oath.

The most visible manifestation of the early Reformation was the dissolution of the monasteries and friaries. By this time, many of these houses had fallen into decline, both physically and morally. The dilapidated buildings housed communities which were usually a shadow of their former selves, with dwindling numbers and often under the control of the local nobility. Already in the early 1530s some derelict monasteries had been dissolved, and from 1539 onward a concerted effort was made to suppress others. In the Pale and within the lordships of Leinster and Munster the majority of monasteries and friaries were suppressed, but beyond, in the Gaelic regions, these communities continued as before.

As regards the clergy, change was gradual, with bishops still in office continuing to be recognized, but all new appointments now made by the king's orders. Most notable amongst the reformed clergy introduced from England was George Browne, who was made archbishop of Dublin in 1536. A staunch supporter of Henrician policy, he exacted from the diocesan clergy an oath to recognize royal supremacy, enforced new ecclesiastical taxes and arranged for the public burning of all saintly images and relics. He also introduced guidelines for the clergy, which illustrated the new tone:

> Ye shall pray for the Universal Catholic Church, both quick and dead; and especially for the Church of England and Ireland. First, for Our Sovereign Lord the King, supreme head in earth immediate under God of the said Church of England and Ireland. And for the declaration of the truth thereof, ye shall understand, that the unlawful jurisdiction, power, and authority, of long time usurped by the bishop of Rome, in England and Ireland, who then was called Pope, is now by God's law...extinct and ceased for ever, as of no strength, value or effect in the Church of England or Ireland.[1]

In retrospect, the 1530s seem a turning point in Irish history. *The Annals of the Four Masters* describe the changes thus:

> They broke down the monasteries, and sold their roofs and bells, so that from Aran of the Saints to Muir nIocht [the English channel], there was not one monastery that was not broken and shattered, with the exception of a few in Ireland, of which the English took no notice or heed. They

afterwards burned the images, shrines and relics, of the saints of Ireland and England; they likewise burned the celebrated image of [the Blessed Virgin] Mary at Trim, which used to perform wonders and miracles, which used to heal the blind, the deaf, the crippled, the persons affected with all kinds of diseases: and [they also burned] the staff of Jesus, which was in Dublin, performing miracles, from the time of St. Patrick down to that time, and had been in the hands of Christ when he was among men.[2]

But this is a retrospective judgment, written a century later, when Gaelic power had been destroyed and the lasting impact of the Reformation had become clear. At the time it did not seem such a dramatic event to the English or the Gaelic Irish. Initially the innovations met with little resistance. The senior clergy conformed, at least in name, though the lower clergy were more resistant, as were many friars. For many people the changes were welcome, being seen as the beginning of a much needed reform movement. Nor did the dissolution of the monasteries arouse much regret. The monastic institutions had long been in decline, and many of the gentry benefited from their redistribution, whether as additions to their lands or as contributions to city life in the form of hospitals or inns of court. On the other hand, the Reformation was not met with any great enthusiasm. Of course, the central fact remained that Ireland was for the most part an unconquered land. Beyond the areas under English control religious life remained largely untouched, with traditional practices, monastic life and links with Rome continuing.

The short reigns of Henry's successors, Edward VI (1547–53) and Mary (1553–58), saw upheaval in England, but this was less pronounced in Ireland. During Edward's reign a more radical, "puritan" form of Protestantism came to the fore. Influenced by the teaching of John Calvin, it went further than Lutheran

Protestantism in the rejection of ritual and of the invocation of the saints, and in its hostility toward Catholicism. Mary, a Catholic, attempted to turn back the tide, removing the growing number of married clergy, including the archbishop of Dublin. Her persecutions of Protestants in England gained her the sobriquet "Bloody Mary," but her reign resulted in no Irish martyrs, proof that, as of yet, the Reformation in Ireland had had little of the impact of its counterpart in England. More significant was the reign of Elizabeth I (1558–1603). Elizabeth reasserted the Reformed Church and her authority over it. In 1560 parliament passed the Act of Supremacy, which established the queen as the supreme governor of the Church of Ireland. All senior lay and clerical figures were to take an oath to this effect, and as far as we know only two bishops refused to do so. The same year, the Act of Uniformity established the 1552 Book of Common Prayer as the basis of the liturgy and imposed fines for nonattendance at Protestant services. Now, with the force of the law behind it, the Protestant faith was less easy to ignore. This polarization was worsened by the pope's excommunication of Elizabeth in 1570. The Roman Catholic Church and the Reformed Church had become clearly divided, with Roman Catholics, the vast majority, as potential rebels.

Still, the contrast between Ireland and Britain at the end of the sixteenth century is striking. In 1600 England was a Protestant country in more than name. Though Catholics remained numerous, the established church had the support not only of authority but also of the majority of the people, practicing a distinctive "Anglican" brand of moderate Protestant Christianity. Scotland as well was firmly Protestant, though it had followed a different route, transmitted by John Calvin's followers, John Knox (1514–72) and Andrew Melville (1545–1622) (see p. 116). In Ireland, on the other hand, despite the official façade of Protestantism, the new faith had not been able to build on its initial successes. A letter written in 1596 by William Lyon, bishop of Cork and Ross, illustrates the dire state of the Reformed Church, sixty years after its introduction to Ireland:

> Hereby they are generally mightily drawn away from their loyalty to her Majesty's godly laws now within these two years so far, that where I had a thousand or more in a church at sermon, I now have not five; and whereas I have seen 500 communicants or more, now are there not three.…I have caused churches to be re-edified, and provided books for every church through[out] my diocese, as Bibles, New Testaments, Communion Books, both English and Latin…but none will come to the church at all, not so much as the country churls; they follow their seducers the priests and their superiors.…In Waterford, the Mayor and the Sheriff of the city come not to church, neither will they take the Oath of Supremacy, and in this city of Cork the bailiffs refuse the oath, neither come they to the church.[3]

Eight years later, the solicitor general Sir John Davies gave an equally pessimistic account of the state of the Church of Ireland:

> The churchmen for the most part throughout the Kingdom are mere idols and ciphers, and such as cannot read, if they should stand in need of the benefit of their clergy; and yet the most of those, whereof many be serving men and some horse-boys, are not without 2 or 3 benefices apiece.…And yet for all their pluralities they are most of them beggars, for…many gentlemen, and some women and some priests and Jesuits have the greatest benefit of our benefices though these poor unlettered clerks bear the name of incumbents.…But what is the effect of these abuses? The churches are ruined and fallen down to the ground in all parts of the Kingdom. There is no divine

service, no christening of children, no receiving of the sacrament, no Christian meeting or assembly, no, not once a year; in a word, no more demonstration of religion than amongst Tartars or cannibals.[4]

Why did the Tudor Reformation fail in Ireland? The most obvious reason is that its introduction lacked the spiritual foundation that existed in England. Since the fourteenth century, at least, a popular religious spirit had been evident in England, characterized by anticlericalism, attention to the Bible in the vernacular and doctrinal dissension on issues such as the Eucharist. These differences with Rome were buttressed by links to similar movements on the Continent and by the particular political situation of the sixteenth century in which England's main rivals were the Catholic powers of France and Spain. In Ireland the situation was, as ever, different. The church in Gaelic areas was to a great extent a church unto itself, with many practices—the acceptance of married clergy and the strong pagan elements in worship—antithetical to many fellow Catholics in England and on the Continent. Still, the papacy was unwilling to interfere as long as the Gaelic church continued to pay its dues. Nor was the church in the Pale or the towns in a significantly better condition. The feeble state of the Irish church acted not so much as an opportunity for Protestant reformers but as a hindrance. The ramshackle institutions were difficult to build upon, and the conformant clergy which the Church of Ireland inherited tended to be poorly educated and lacking in evangelical zeal. Such abuses as absenteeism and the holding of multiple offices were rife. An extreme, though telling, case is that of Miler McGrath, who secured five bishoprics and seventy-seven lesser offices. Nor did Ireland provide a climate attractive to suitable ministers. Although committed and suitable clergy did exist among Gaelic and Old English conformants and among newcomers from England and Scotland, the hostile, precarious conditions and the absence of training facilities hindered the establishment of an effective ministry.

COUNTER-REFORMATION
AND CONQUEST

The failure of the Tudor Reformation was not only due to its inadequacies, but also to the existence of a powerful reinforcement of Catholicism in the form of the Counter-Reformation. The Irish had taken little part in the Council of Trent, begun in 1545, that had sought to revitalize the Catholic Church from within, nor had an early mission to Ireland by a group of Jesuits—the driving-force behind the Counter-Reformation—met with any success. But by the end of the sixteenth century the principles of Tridentine reform, as they were called, had begun to make themselves felt. Education was central to this process. As Ireland did not have a university until 1592, the old noble families were likely to send their children to be educated in schools controlled by Catholics, whether at home or abroad. As Sir John Dowdall complained in 1595:

> Every town is established with sundry schools where the noblemen and gentlemen's sons of the country do repair; these schools have a superstitious or an idolatrous schoolmaster, and each school [is] overseen by a Jesuit, whereby the youth of the whole Kingdom are corrupted and poisoned with more gross superstition and disobedience than all the rest of the popish crew in all Europe. The townsmen do transport into Spain, Italy, Rheims and other places, young men both of the Irish and English nation, in the company of Jesuits, to be brought up in their colleges; and so when they have been thoroughly corrupted they return them again with letters of commendation, with instructions to seduce the people to disobedience and rebellion.[5]

These schools became centers in which Irish Catholics could be trained and a base from which Jesuits could be recruited. Henry Fitzsimon, the son of a Dublin merchant, was educated on the Continent and returned in 1596. He had great success in returning Protestant converts to Catholicism, but was arrested in 1599. From prison he wrote to the General Secretary of the Jesuits in 1604:

> Religion does not strike deep and firm roots here; people, by a kind of general propensity, follow more the name than the reality of the Catholic Faith, and thus are borne to and fro by the winds of edicts and threats. However the work of our Fathers, ever since their arrival, has been solid and brilliant. Those, who before were mere *tabulae rasae*, know the teaching of the faith, and piety flourishes where all had once been a waste, and where even the name of piety was not known.[6]

A report of 1613 from a papal envoy to the Vatican gave a positive view of the state of Catholicism in Ireland. The population was overwhelmingly Catholic, and they professed their religion openly. This, he believed, was because they were naturally inclined to the Catholic faith, having a long attachment to the papacy and hating the English, and always being tenacious of old customs and distrusting of novelty. The "heresy" of Protestantism was introduced against their wishes and with violence, so while Protestantism seemed externally to be in the ascendancy, the reality was very different. Though the rural population was quite ignorant in matters of faith, the Irish, he wrote, were well served by priests, especially those educated abroad. This, he believed, was due to the fact that the nobility and gentry remained mainly Catholic.[7]

His last point is particularly important. The great success of the Counter-Reformation was its ability to reinforce the majority of the descendants of Anglo-Norman settlers in their Catholic faith.

This group came to be known as the Old English, set apart from the New English, more recent arrivals who tended to be closer to the English administration in Ireland. In a choice between the latter group and the Gaelic Irish, the Old English found themselves allying with their coreligionists against the representatives of the Crown to which they professed loyalty.

At the start of the seventeenth century Protestantism in Ireland seemed in a weak position, but it was soon to dominate, if not as the religion of the majority, at least as that of the politically and socially powerful. This success was largely due to the political upheavals of the Tudor age. Between the 1540s and the 1600s, the constitutional relationship between Ireland and England, and the relationship of power not only between the two countries but within Ireland, underwent fundamental shifts. The wars of the Elizabethan period resulted in the effective conquest of Ireland and allowed for its full-fledged colonization; and colonization meant an increase in Protestant numbers, power and influence.

Since the twelfth century kings of England had ruled Ireland not as kings but as lords, a fact problematic to Henry VIII and the ruling power in the colony. The 1541 Act of Kingly Title, which declared Henry King of Ireland, stated:

> Lack of naming of the king's majesty and his noble progenitors kings of Ireland…hath been great occasion that the Irishmen and inhabitants within the realm of Ireland have not been so obedient to the king's highness and his most noble progenitors, and to their laws, as they of right and according to their allegiance and bounded duties ought to have been.[8]

The lordship of Ireland was, well before the sixteenth century, a failed colony. More direct control was desirable for a king who saw the danger of Ireland falling to one of his European enemies and to the insecure colonists of the Pale. Secondly, the Act of Kingly Title did something to remove the embarrassing suggestion that English authority was still based on the papal grant of the country to Henry II in 1155 (see p. 83–84). At the same time the policy known to historians as "surrender and regrant" was introduced. Native and "disobedient" colonial rulers were asked to surrender their territories and acknowledge Henry as king. In return, their lands were restored by feudal grant, they were accorded full legal rights and protection, and also given English titles of nobility. For example, the O'Neills became earls of Tyrone and the O'Donnells earls of Tyrconnell. Although these changes made little difference at first, with many lords only paying lip service to the agreements, this policy signaled a new interest in regarding English authority not just as a matter pertaining to a minority of loyal subjects, but to all the people of the island.

It was during Elizabeth's reign that this plan began to become reality. The policy of "surrender and regrant" produced a number of succession disputes amongst the Irish and the growing authority of the Crown prompted many to rebel. The Crown rose to these challenges, crushing some of the dominant Irish powers, and capitalized on the opportunities created by their destruction. The heart of the rebellion in the 1570s and 1580s was Munster. These rebellions were primarily reactions to the encroaching power of Elizabethan government, but a religious aspect was also present. The 1579 proclamation of the rebel leader James Fitzmaurice Fitzgerald declared that "this war is undertaken for the defence of the Christian religion against the heretics." Significantly, the rebels enlisted the support of the Catholic powers of Europe. Though the force of six hundred Spanish and Italian soldiers "sent by the pope for the Catholic faith" which landed at Smerwick on the Dingle peninsula had little military effect, its arrival marked the first impact of the religious wars of Europe on Ireland. The rebels were crushed and in 1585 vast areas of land held by the rebel leaders were confiscated.

The Crown used this land for a new "plantation" policy toward Ireland. Thousands of settlers were introduced from Britain, bringing with them English culture and the Protestant religion.

Most of Ireland had been subdued by the 1590s, but Ulster remained outside English rule. It was there that the most significant rebellion was launched. Hugh O'Neill, earl of Tyrone, had spent much of the previous decade consolidating his authority over the Gaelic rulers of Ulster, but it eventually became clear that the greatest threat to his position came from the encroachment of royal forces. In 1595 he and the other main ruler in Ulster, Rory O'Donnell, earl of Tyrconnell, appealed to the king of Spain. "Our only hope," they wrote, "of establishing the Catholic religion, rests on your assistance. Now or never our Church must be succoured." They also appealed to the Old English and to the pope. Despite some striking successes, the Ulster rebels were hard pressed to fight the forces of the Crown. Their chance for an offensive came in December 1601, when a Spanish army landed at Kinsale in County Cork. O'Neill and O'Donnell led their armies south, but they found it difficult to adapt to the military tactics of the Spaniards, and the combined forces were soundly defeated. The English followed this up with a large-scale campaign to subdue all rebels, and in 1603 O'Neill finally surrendered. The English conquest of Ireland was complete. Four years later O'Neill and O'Donnell, along with a hundred lesser chieftains and their families, went into voluntary exile on the Continent. "The Flight of the Earls" marked the defeat of Gaelic Ireland. As one poet put it: "Tonight Ireland is desolate, the banishment of her true race hath left wet-cheeked her men and her fair women; strange that such a dwelling place should be so desolate." It also marked the beginning of a new era for Protestant Ireland. The Reformation had been unsuccessful when English control over Ireland remained weak. Now, political success opened the way for a transformation of religious conditions in Ireland.

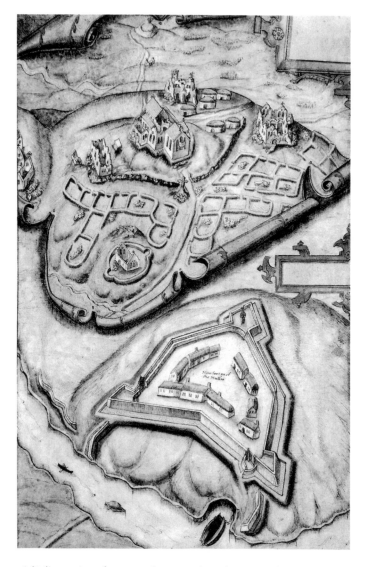

A bird's-eye view of a new settlement at Armagh, c. 1601, by Richard Bartlett

At this time, across the Atlantic, the American colonies were being established, but already English authorities had attempted planned settlements of a similar kind in Ireland. By taking the war to Munster in 1601 O'Neill and O'Donnell had all but destroyed the fledgling plantation there, but now the province of Ulster lay open to confiscation. The Ulster plantation was an ambitious project in which the six counties of Armagh, Cavan, Coleraine (now Londonderry), Donegal, Fermanagh and Tyrone were forfeited to the Crown. The major planters or "undertakers" were granted large areas of land, but were made responsible for the promotion of settlement and the fortification of their lands. Ex-soldiers and crown servants or "servitors" were granted smaller areas of land and were allowed to have Irish tenants. Companies also invested in the plantation, most notably the London businessmen who sponsored a settlement in Derry—hence the name Londonderry. Catholics were excluded from this settlement but were allowed to live outside the city walls in the Bogside area. "Deserving natives" got 20 percent of the land, but the former landowners tended to move west. Thousands of others remained behind in the wastelands and forests, menacing the settlers. The plantation was originally a government-planned enterprise, but it soon took on a momentum of its own. By 1630 thousands of Lowland Scots had moved into Ulster on their own initiative, mainly to Antrim and Down, originally outside the planned plantation area. The consequences of the plantation were great, establishing in Ireland a new ethnic and religious community. But the indigenous population, while often displaced from their lands, remained in Ulster in large numbers. The tensions and resentment between these two communities, originating in the seventeenth century, are still felt in the conflicts in Northern Ireland today.

Ulster, of all the Irish provinces, had been the most resistant to English rule and the most resilient in its old Gaelic ways. Now it had been conquered and successfully planted. The establishment of representative boroughs amongst the settlers meant that there now existed a Protestant majority in the Dublin parliament. Furthermore, the Lowland Scots had brought with them their Presbyterian faith, which differed in many ways from that of the Anglican New English (see p. 116–117). Still, the majority of the population of Ireland consisted of Catholic Gaels and Old English, bitter at defeat and dispossession and fearful for the future.

PROTESTANT IDENTITY

For the first six or seven decades of its existence the Church of Ireland was a pale reflection of its English counterpart. Small in numbers of adherents and largely irrelevant to the majority of the population, it did not possess any clearly defined identity. Nevertheless, despite the successes of the Counter-Reformation and the continued difficulties the Church of Ireland faced, the first decades of the seventeenth century saw this denomination develop a distinctive character and lay the foundations of "Protestant ascendancy." The Elizabethan wars had given the Protestant population a stronger grip on power, and the subsequent plantations increased their number. However, they remained a minority amongst the large number of Gaelic Irish and the stubbornly Catholic Old English, and this did much to shape their specific identity.

One of the central figures in the emergence of this identity was James Ussher, who was born in Dublin in 1581. His family had come to Ireland in the early days of the Norman colony, but they differed from most Old English families in their prominence in Dublin government and the fact that they were quick to conform to the Reformation. In 1594 Ussher began a career of scholarship when he entered the newly founded Trinity College Dublin. He went on to become a bachelor of divinity in 1607 and was made professor soon afterward. The idea of a university for Ireland had long been mooted but had not been accomplished until 1592. Queen Elizabeth's warrant for Trinity College stated that it was:

> …to serve for a college for learning, whereby knowledge and civility might be increased by the instruction of our people there, whereof many have usually heretofore used to travel into France, Italy and Spain, to get learning in such foreign universities, where they have been infected with popery and other ill qualities, and so become evil subjects.[9]

Trinity College had originally been intended as the first of a series of colleges that would make up the University of Dublin, but these were never built and Trinity expanded, so that to this day Trinity College and the University of Dublin are one and the same. The founders of Trinity intended it as an agent of Anglicization and Protestantism, a training ground for ministers and an intellectual center. Many of its earliest fellows came from Cambridge University and brought with them the puritan ethos current there. They laid a greater stress on the idea of the predestination of God's elect, taught a greater rejection of ritual than the mainstream Church of England and took a more aggressive stance toward the Catholic Church, identifying the pope as the Antichrist. Ussher shared this outlook, and he played a central role in the drawing up of the Church of Ireland's first confession of faith, the "Irish Articles" of 1615. This was based on the founding document of the Church of England, the "Thirty-Nine Articles" of 1562, but reflected the Calvinist leanings of its authors.

In 1621 Ussher became bishop of Meath and four years later was promoted to the see of Armagh. He was, however, above all a scholar. Described by Samuel Johnson as "the great luminary of the Irish Church," he devoted most of his life to the investigation of that church's origins. This involved, on the one hand, an exhaustive investigation of the writings of the early Christian church and, on the other, a thoroughgoing research into the antiquities of Ireland. He regularly consulted libraries in England and corresponded widely in Ireland and abroad, acquiring many almost forgotten documents of the early Irish church along the way, including the *Book of Kells*. His collection of books and documents is now held by Trinity College. The sum of his investigations was the assertion that the Irish church did not owe its Christian origins to Rome and that the Church of Ireland was the true heir to St. Patrick. In his great work on the subject, *The Religion of the Ancient Irish and Britons* (1631), he wrote:

> Onely this will I say, that as it is most likely, that S. Patrick had a speciall regard unto the Church of Rome, from whence he was sent for the conversion of this Iland....But that S. Patrick was of opinion, that the Church of Rome was sure ever afterward to continue in that good estate, and that there was a perpetual privildge annexed unto that See, that it should never erre in judgement, or that the Pope's sentences were alway to be held as infallible Oracles—that I will never beleeve: sure I am, that my countreymen after him were of a farre other beleefe, who were so farre from submitting themselves in this sort to whatsoever should proceed from the See of Rome, that they oftentimes stood out against it, when they had little cause so to do.[10]

Although Ussher had a good relationship with many Catholic clergymen, he was resolute in his opposition to the doctrines of their church. In his position as the first chair of theological controversies at Trinity, Ussher relentlessly refuted Catholic arguments. He not only believed that Catholic doctrines were wrong, but that their toleration was a grievous sin, and he played a prominent role in the emergence of a debate which was to be of central importance to

Irish Anglicans, that is, what ought to be the policy of the Protestant minority toward the Catholic majority? In the immediate aftermath of the rebellion of O'Neill and O'Donnell, the government policy was, for a time, one of coercion with fines imposed on those who did not attend reformed church services. However, in the 1620s the new king, Charles I (r.1625–49), entered upon a new policy. Faced with the spiraling costs of war, the king was prepared to render "matters of grace and bounty"—in other words, toleration of Catholics according to his prerogative—in return for increased taxation. These "Graces," as they became known, infuriated the New English and many amongst the hierarchy of the Church of Ireland. Ussher, along with other senior churchmen, drew up a document condemning the doctrines and practices of the Catholic Church and challenging those who condoned them. He wrote:

> The religion of the papists is superstitious and idolatrous, their faith and doctrine erroneous and heretical; the church in respect of both apostatical. To give them therefore a toleration, or to consent that they may freely organise their religion, and profess their faith and doctrine is a grievous sin.[11]

Ussher's approach to the problem of Catholicism—coercion and Anglicization—was not shared by all his colleagues within the Church of Ireland. Edmund Spencer, who spent nearly twenty years in Ireland as an official of Elizabethan administration and later as a planter in Munster, wrote in the 1590s:

> In planting of religion thus much is needful to be observed, that it be not sought forcibly to be impressed into them with terror and sharp penalties, as now is the manner, but rather delivered and intimated with mildness and gentleness, so as it may not be hated afore it be understood, and their professors despised and rejected.[12]

William Bedell was a friend and admirer of Ussher's; although he shared his Calvinist leanings and his love of scholarship, in other ways he could not have been more different. The son of an Essex farmer, he was educated at Cambridge and subsequently taught there. After a time as a clergyman in English parishes, he took up a position as a chaplain to the English embassy in Venice, an experience that did much to influence his policy in Ireland. In Venice, where it looked for a time that the Protestant faith would take root, he introduced Italian translations of the Bible, which had only been available in Latin previously, the Book of Common Prayer and other key texts. In the same way, when he came to Ireland in 1627 as provost of Trinity College, he sought to attract the Irish to the reformed faith on their own terms. As he wrote a few years later:

> The popish clergy is double to us in number, and having the advantage of the tongue, of the love of the people, of our exertions upon them, of the very inborn hatred of subdued people to their conquerors, they hold them still in blindness a superstition, ourselves being the chiefest impediments of the work that we pretend to set forth.[13]

Believing that the Church of Ireland could never win converts while its clergy could only speak English, Bedell learned the Irish language and put it on the curriculum at Trinity, with a native speaker to supervise pronunciation. In 1629 he was appointed bishop of Kilmore and Ardagh, and there he continued this policy. He arranged for daily services in Irish, a catechism in Irish and the translation of biblical texts. Though Bedell was often criticized by those amongst the Church of Ireland who favored an Anglicizing policy, and though his success in spreading the reformed faith was limited, he was well regarded by many, both within the Church of Ireland and without. On his death in 1642, a time when little love was lost between Catholics and Protestants, the oration at his graveside was given by a Gaelic chieftain.

The Anglican tradition is not the only Protestant tradition in Ireland. Since the seventeenth century Ireland has been the home of a large number of Presbyterians, most of them descendants of Lowlands Scots who settled in Ulster. The foundation of the Presbyterian Church in Ireland is officially dated to June 1642 when the first presbytery, a center for assembly and worship, was established at Carrickfergus, County Antrim. In reality, however, Presbyterianism began in Ireland three decades earlier when two Church of Ireland bishops of Scottish origin granted license to a number of Scottish ministers to preach in Ulster. These ministers were part of a branch of the reformed church that owed its origins to the ideas which had developed in Geneva under John Calvin the previous century and had been transmitted and developed by such Scotsmen as John Knox. At the core of their belief was the idea of the predestination of God's elect. Their church was also distinguished in organization and practice by its strict discipline, rejection of ritual, and government by groups rather than individuals. In the early decades of the seventeenth century, as its popularity spread through Lowland Scotland, this faith came into conflict with the established church, which made repeated attempts to impose bishops and Anglican ritual. These "nonconformists" or "dissenters," then, often found themselves in the position of rebels against establishment powers, stoutly defending their freedom of belief and practice.

In Ulster, however, these Scottish nonconformist ministers were allowed to act within the established church, and the success of their preaching was dramatic. A "revival movement" from 1625 to 1631, in which large crowds flocked to hear the gospel preached, helped to spread the doctrines of Calvin and Knox throughout eastern Ulster. This, coupled with continuing immigration from Lowland Scotland, helped to make nonconformists a majority amongst Ulster Protestants. The backlash began in 1633 when Thomas Wentworth was appointed lord deputy of Ireland. In an attempt to root out Calvinism from the Church of Ireland, he overturned Ussher's Articles of 1615 and brought the church into line with its English counterpart, prosecuting those who did not conform. In Ulster this meant the expulsion of the majority of Scottish ministers and the imposition, in 1639, of the "Black Oath," by which all property-owning Scots settlers were called upon to declare their loyalty to the established church. At the same time similar tensions between English authority and Scottish Presbyterians led to King Charles I's disastrous invasion of Scotland in 1640. The Scots had been supported by the puritan elements which dominated the English parliament and had for some time been in conflict with the king; this defeat for Charles was to pave the way for the English Civil War. Soon the affairs of Scotland and England came to be embroiled with those of Ireland as Ulster erupted in violence.

WARS OF RELIGION

In 1641 a royal report on the progress of the plantations stated optimistically that "the country is now full of persons of quality of British birth and of civilly educated Irish." It added that "plantations have certainly kept the peace and encouraged the Protestant religion."[14] That very year a rebellion broke out in Ulster which threatened to destroy not only the plantation, but the Protestant religion in Ireland. It is not difficult to find reasons for insurrection amongst the Catholic Gaelic population in Ulster. Dominant for centuries there, they had been dispossessed, moved to poorer land or forced into a subordinate position, and replaced by people with a different way of life and a different faith. They remained the majority in the province and they had little to lose. Now they had an added motive—fear of invasion from both Scottish Presbyterians and English puritans. Led by descendants of the Gaelic chieftains, the rebels claimed that they were loyal to King Charles, even producing a forged royal commission in which the king urged the Ulstermen to defend him against his enemies. Their immediate strategic aims were twofold: to capture Dublin Castle and its chief ministers, and to seize a number of strategic sites in Ulster. The first part of the plan failed when its details were revealed by a drunken conspirator, but the uprising in Ulster went ahead, albeit in a far more bloody and unruly manner than anticipated.

It is difficult to delve beneath the layers of interpretation and misrepresentation that have built upon the rebellion which began on October 23, 1641. One thing is clear: Thousands of Protestant settlers were massacred by their Catholic neighbors. A conservative estimate puts the numbers at two thousand and, in some places, such as Portadown, the majority of the settlers were wiped out. This was horrifying enough, not only for Irish Protestants but their English and Scottish neighbors, yet was made all the more so by lurid accounts that claimed casualties of up to fifty thousand and embellished the claims with tales of inhuman brutality. One such writer, Thomas Morley, reported:

> A man who had severell young children borne and alive, and his wife nere her time of delivery of another, was most cruelly murthered by the rebels, his wife, flying into the mountaines, the rebels hastily pursued her and her little children, and found her newly delivered of her child there; they pittying no such, nor any distresse, presently murthered her and her other children which runne with her thither, and in most inhumane and barbarous manner suffered their dogs to eat up and devoure the new borne child.[15]

Morley suggests that much of the brutality was inspired by contempt for the Protestant religion:

In the county of Cavan, James O'Rely, Hugh Brady and other rebels often tooke the Protestant Bibles and wetting them in puddle water, did five or six severell times dash the same in the faces of the Protestants, saying, come, I know you love a good lesson, here is a most excellent one for you, and come tomorrow and you shall have as good a Sermon.[16]

Through such accounts, the events of 1641 entered into the consciousness of many Irish Protestants as attempts at the concerted destruction of the Protestant people. In this way a true episode of brutality was turned into something even worse, and a genuine threat from the Catholics of Ulster became an overriding feature of their identity. In addition, 1641 and the events that followed caused the Anglicans and Presbyterians of Ireland to look to each other in unity against Catholics, if in dispute on other matters.

The year 1641 was also to begin the process of unifying the Catholics of Gaelic and Old English descent. They were different in many ways. The more numerous Gaelic Irish were generally poor and landless, and their leaders' declarations of loyalty to the Crown hid a general antipathy toward English authority. The Old English had retained much of their lands and wealth but had lost political dominance and, since they relied on royal prerogative, their loyalty to the crown was genuine. They were culturally different, with the Old English, proud of their roots and influenced by the Counter-Reformation, liable to scorn the simpler, more traditional customs and the unsophisticated religious practices of the Gaelic Irish. Still, there was much that united them, adversity in particular. Neither the status quo of Dublin Castle dominance and continued plantation nor the prospect of a puritan victory over King Charles afforded any cheer, though the Old English had more to lose than the Gaelic Irish by taking to arms. Above all, it was becoming evident, in Ireland as in most of Europe, that the clearest marker of political loyalty and advantage was now religious adherence.

Within two months the rebels had taken most of Ulster and were moving south. The Old English of the Pale, with civil war looming in England, threw in their lot with the Ulster rebels to form the "Confederate Catholics." Their stated aims are pithily expressed in their motto, *Pro Deo, pro rege, pro patria*—for God, king and country. They appealed for freedom of religious expression, proclaimed that they were acting in the king's defense against puritan attack (despite the fact that Charles had been quick to dissociate himself from the rebels), and they also rejected the authority of the English parliament to rule over Ireland. In October 1642, a year after the Ulster insurrection, the Confederates appeared in a strong position. They controlled most of the island, and they had begun to set up a parliament and administration in Kilkenny (hence "The Confederation of Kilkenny," the name often applied by historians to this alliance). However, they also faced new problems. Puritan armies from England and Scotland were beginning to check their advance, and serious splits had started to form within the alliance. The latter was due in part to the increasing influence of a clerical party, led by the papal nuncio, Archbishop Rinuccini. An Italian with little real grasp of the situation, Rinuccini pressed for a more extreme stance, urging not only the toleration of the Catholic Church but its elevation to the position of the established church. This alienated the Old English, who feared the confiscation of their lands and were prepared to settle for a de facto tolerance dependent on royal prerogative.

Over seven years the conflict in Ireland dragged on, as an important subplot of the English Civil War or, as it is sometimes more accurately called, the War of the Three Kingdoms (1641–53). Military confrontations, discussions between the Confederates and the Crown, and splits amongst the Catholic allies failed to break the deadlock. This only became possible with the execution of King

Hauing rauiſhed Virgens & Wifes they take there Children & daſe there braines againſt the Walls in ſight of there weepinge Parents & after deſtro; red them likewiſe,

From "The Teares of Ireland," an account of the 1641 rebellion (1642)

Charles in January 1649 and the succession of Oliver Cromwell (1600–58) as lord protector of the Commonwealth of England. One of his first acts was to prepare an army to settle the situation in Ireland.

The year 1649 occupies the same place in Catholic history as 1641 does for Protestants. Again, exaggeration, myth and propaganda have done much to obscure the reality, but a core of brutal truth remains. Cromwell landed in Dublin in August 1649 with a force of twenty thousand men and in September laid siege to Drogheda. When the siege was broken on the second attempt, that town, which had no association with the Confederate cause, became an example to all recalcitrant Catholics of Cromwell's determination to prevail and avenge as two thousand people were slaughtered by his soldiers. Cromwell's comment was:

> I am perswaded that this is a righteous Judgement of God
> upon these Barbarous wretches, who have imbrued their
> hands in so much innocent blood, and that it will tend to
> prevent the effusion of blood for the future.[17]

Cromwell went on to terrorize Wexford and other towns, but his
retribution did not only apply to these townspeople. All those
involved in the rebellion were liable under a radical new land settlement. While some were pardoned, many of those involved with
the Confederate side lost their lands in their entirety. Others were
allowed to keep holdings, but not their own. Instead they were
forced to transplant to the counties west of the Shannon, where
the land was poorest. This was not entirely an act of vengeance,
for Cromwell was indebted to creditors and to soldiers who had
fought for prospective lands in place of pay. This ambitious settlement did not turn out entirely as planned, for many Catholics
remained on their lands and many of the new owners quickly sold
up. However, there was a substantial shift in population from east
to west, with around three thousand Catholic landowners trans-
planted to Connacht, along with forty thousand tenants, and the
percentage of Catholics in Dublin dropped to little over a quarter. A dramatic shift in the ownership of the land east of the
Shannon had been effected. The great landlords were now
Protestant; where Catholics held land, it was almost always a small
holding. Yet, the Protestant landowners remained uneasy, subject
to everyday threat from dispossessed bandits and wary of changes
in the political situation in Britain and Europe.

During the Cromwellian years, nonconformist congregations multiplied. By 1660 Ulster had seventy-four Presbyterian
parishes, and Presbyterianism continued to flourish there, though
numbers remained relatively small outside that province. The
nature of that church, with its government by committee, meeting and session, and the severe discipline imposed by ministers

helped to make Presbyterian communities close-knit. Their industriousness and their experience in 1641 made them a resilient part of Ulster life.

The most radical of the nonconformist groups was the Society of Friends, or Quakers. Founded in England by George Fox (1624–91), the Quakers' challenging stance against secular powers and their spirit of enquiry into religious doctrine often left them open to persecution. In the 1650s an English-born merchant and Quaker convert, William Edmundson (1627–1712), traveled as a preacher around Ireland, setting up meetinghouses in Dublin and Ulster. He attracted converts from all walks of life, but especially from the military. The Quakers, despite persecution, developed a strong base, and by 1701 there were fifty-three meetinghouses and six thousand members. They were pioneers in trade and manufacture, particularly in the linen industry, and many became wealthy.

In 1660 the monarchy was restored under Charles II and the situation changed yet again. Catholics had reason to feel hopeful at the accession of this king, who was married to a Portuguese Catholic and whose father had received their loyalty. However, the new regime felt little inclination toward a full-scale restoration of land. Although some Catholics regained property they had lost under Cromwell, most did not, and Protestants continued to hold around 80 percent of the land. The twenty-five years of Charles's reign were a time of peace but also a time of instability, as Protestants feared for their newfound gains and Catholics stored up a sense of injustice and resentment. These tensions were to come to the fore in the last act of the wars of religion, which began with the accession of James II (1633–1701) in 1685. James was a Catholic—he converted in 1669—but also a pragmatist. He was quick to reassure his subjects that there would be no reversal of the existing position, and at first there was little fear amongst the Protestant community in

Britain or Ireland. However, tensions began to grow in Ireland with the appointment of Richard Talbot, earl of Tyrconnell (1630–91), as lord deputy in 1687. Tyrconnell soon began to show favoritism to Catholics in appointments to the army and local government. When a royal heir was born in 1688, there was a strong Protestant reaction. William, prince of Orange (1650–1702), ruler of the Dutch Republic, was invited to take the English throne and James fled to France. The conflict between these two men, both personally tolerant in religious matters, would mark the culmination of Ireland's religious wars.

James decided to make his stand in Ireland. In March 1669 he landed at Kinsale and made a triumphal march to Dublin. Now the people of Ireland were once again required to take sides. Most of the north went over to the Williamite side, which sent troops and equipment to Ulster. A decisive moment was the closing of the gates of Derry by the city's Apprentice Boys as the Jacobites—as James' forces were known—approached. The local commander, Robert Lundy, advocated surrender, but he was overruled and fled the city; his name became a synonym for a traitor to the Ulster Protestant cause. The people of the city held out for a hundred and five days in appalling conditions, until the Williamite forces broke through a boom which the Jacobites had placed across the river and came to the aid of the inhabitants. In June 1690 William landed at Carrickfergus with an army of fifteen thousand. He marched south and met the Jacobites at the River Boyne, where he won a famous victory, celebrated to this day by Protestants on July 12 as the "Glorious Twelfth." James fled to France and his forces fell back to Aughrim, County Galway, where they again suffered defeat. Finally, the following year James's army, under the command of Patrick Sarsfield (1655–93), surrendered at Limerick. Protestant victory was complete.

In 1655 a commentary on the state of the plantations had given the opinion that Catholic numbers were likely to decline, and with their decline would come the end of strife in Ireland: "They are likelyer to be swallowed up by the English, and incorporated into them; so that a few centuries will know no difference present, fear none to come, and scarce believe what were pas'd."[18] As it turned out, the differences of the seventeenth century lived on and gained sustenance from the memory of those years.

Jonathan Swift (1667–1745), by an unknown artist of the eighteenth-century Irish school

VI

CATHOLIC, PROTESTANT AND DISSENTER

Every year thousands of Protestants, not only in Ulster but throughout Ireland, celebrate King William's victory over James II. To those who march in orange sashes behind the Lambeg drums, the Battle of the Boyne marks a vindication of their way of life, and in particular their faith. The marking of the "Glorious Twelfth" is a statement that Protestant Ireland was and is here to stay. To many Irish Catholics, on the other hand, it symbolizes something different—not only defeat, but repression. That was the immediate consequence of 1690. The Protestant minority was unequivocally in the driving seat, their numbers larger and their power greater than at any other time in Irish history. Soon they would speak of "the Protestant Ascendancy" or "the Protestant Nation." Catholics were not only marginalized and dispossessed but disabled in various ways by punitive legislation. Yet victory and domination soon gave way to other forces: the development of a vibrant and distinctive culture amongst Irish Anglicans; the emergence of political radicalism amongst Ulster Presbyterians; and the return of the Catholics to the political mainstream.

THE PENAL ERA

Now may we turn aside and dry our tears,
And comfort us, and lay aside our fears,
For all is gone—all comely quality,
All gentleness and hospitality,
All courtesy and merriment is gone;
Our virtues all are withered every one,
Our music vanished and our skill to sing;
Now may we quiet us and quit our moan,
Nothing is whole to us that could be broke; nothing
Remains to us of all that was our own.[1]

The words of Aodhagán O'Rathaille (1670–1726), the foremost Gaelic poet of the era, sum up the mood of loss and despondency amongst the Catholics of Ireland after the defeat of King James. Now they had not only been comprehensively beaten, but the victors had begun to reinforce their position with measures which aimed at excluding the Catholic population from wealth and power. The transfer of land from Catholics to Protestants, which had begun in earnest with the plantations and had intensified with the Cromwellian confiscations, was now extended further. By 1700 Catholics amounted to three-quarters of the population but held only one-eighth of the land, mainly in Connacht. In 1692 parliament became a Protestant preserve when members were required to repudiate the Catholic Mass, transubstantiation and the authority of the pope. No Catholic would sit in parliament until 1828. The will and the opportunity existed to shore up the Williamite settlement.

King William himself had been gracious in victory. The Treaty of Limerick, which followed Sarsfield's defeat, pardoned the Jacobite soldiers and allowed thousands of them to join regiments in France (they became known as "the Wild Geese"). It also permitted a generous degree of religious toleration:

> The Roman Catholics of this kingdom shall enjoy such privileges in their exercise of their religion as are consistent with the laws of Ireland, or as they did enjoy in the reign of King Charles the Second: and their Majesties, as soon as their affairs will permit them to summon a parliament in this kingdom, will endeavor to procure the said Roman Catholics such farther security in that particular as may preserve them from any disturbance upon the account of their said religion.[2]

But after half a century of religious wars, not all of the victors were prepared to be so magnanimous. In 1641, and again in 1689, Protestants had perceived the power of the Catholics' numerical might to threaten and destroy them. Now, when Protestants were more secure than they had ever been, they sought to reinforce their position.

The penal laws, or the "popery laws" as they were known to contemporaries, began with the exclusion of Catholics from the 1692 parliament. Over the following decades, intensifying during the reign of Queen Anne (1702–14), a body of restrictions was established on Catholic civil rights and property holding. Catholics could not bear arms and were effectively barred not only from parliament, but from Crown offices, the legal profession and the army, and even from the right to vote. Catholic bishops, monks and friars were expelled, priests were to be registered and no children were to be educated in Catholic schools, whether at home or abroad. Catholics were not allowed to buy land, and they could not take out a lease longer than thirty-one years. A Catholic could not inherit from a Protestant; when a Catholic landowner died, his land was to be subdivided amongst his sons. Most notoriously, if a

Catholic owned a horse, he was required to sell it to a Protestant on presentation of five pounds.

Catholics were not the only group to be penalized. Despite the sufferings and efforts of dissenters in the religious wars, the Presbyterians in particular, they were not allowed a full share in the victory. Wary of the continued immigration from Scotland, parliament excluded dissenters from that body and from senior civil and military office by means of a sacramental test. The validity of Presbyterian marriage was questioned, and members of dissenting churches were required to pay tithes to the Church of Ireland. Though less punitive than the anti-Catholic legislation, these laws helped to foster a sense of suspicion and resentment against the government, especially amongst Ulster Presbyterians, and it contributed to their large-scale emigration from Ulster to America, which began in the eighteenth century.

There remains a popular image of the Catholic Church under the penal laws of a hidden faith clinging on despite repression, of "Mass rocks," where fugitive priests would lead their flock in secret, and "hedge-schools," where Catholics were instructed furtively. Glimpses from contemporary writings suggest that this is not an entirely mythical image. For example, we can sense the danger in this letter, written in 1711 by a certain Father Dominic Lynch under a pseudonym to another priest. Father Lynch had taken over the administration of the province of Tuam in place of his uncle, the archbishop, who had fled to the Continent and feared to return:

> The times are bad and we have reason to [observe] caution. You take great care of yourselves lest you be surprised as we are informed is intended. You must keep no sort of a station or meeting, but from village to village serve your people at unseasonable hours. I dare not goe further your side. I believe you may better serve or distribute the sacred

liquor [the holy oils] in some house there at the Neale than where we thought to meet this day.[3]

A similar caution is evident in this letter written from the Irish College in Salamanca, Spain, in 1751:

Last post I was agreeably surprised by some lines from you in Mr. Rourke's letter, a favour I had so long before expected. If you have written before to our college it was certainly an error I had forgot to apprise you of as it is probable maney letters to me were intercepted. You will for the future be more cautious and follow the directions in Mr. Rourke's letter.[4]

The writer's caution was justified. This letter appeared as part of a dossier for prosecution under the penal laws.

However, in general the stark picture presented by the legislation was not matched by the reality. Despite sporadic persecution of Catholic clergy, most people were able to practice their religion openly. By the middle of the eighteenth century it is estimated that there were around eight hundred monks and friars in Ireland and that there were at least three times as many Catholic priests in the country as their Church of Ireland counterparts. By this time some churches of good quality were being built in cities and towns. A 1731 *Report on the State of Popery* revealed the existence of five hundred and forty-nine Catholic schools, certainly an underestimate. Priests also continued to be trained in seminaries overseas, in contravention of the penal laws. The resilience of Catholics in the face of penalization is striking. The 1731 report named seven hundred and four leading families of the gentry who had conformed, but this statistic seemed to have little impact on the religious picture. Catholics remained 38 percent of the households in Ulster, 77 percent in Leinster, 89 percent in Munster and 91 percent in Connacht.[5]

This resilience may be explained by the steadfastness of the mass of the people and the preference for faith over prosperity. But it also must be said that there was never a large-scale drive toward the conversion of Catholics. A push toward missionary enterprise in the first decade of the eighteenth century, with the provision of some Irish-speaking ministers and translations of key texts, soon fizzled out. One is forced to the conclusion that there was no real interest amongst the Church of Ireland elite in converting the whole of the people. This was conceded by the Church of Ireland archbishop William King in 1724 when he said, "It's plain true…there never was nor is any design that all should be Protestants." This was also suggested by the Act of 1728 that curbed the numbers of converts practicing at the bar. The penal laws, then, were not aimed at preventing Catholicism, but at limiting the rights, power and wealth of the large numbers who were Catholics.

Central to the motivation behind the penal laws was fear. As Archbishop King succinctly put it: "…there is no medium but either we or they must be undone." The horrors of the seventeenth century remained strong in people's minds, and the "Catholic menace" never seemed far away. Accounts of the Catholic massacres of Protestants in 1641 proved so popular that they were reprinted throughout the first half of the eighteenth century. If we examine the wording of the legislation, the legacy of war and its continued threat seem predominant. "An Act For Banishing All *Papists* Exercising Any Ecclesiastical Jurisdiction, And All Regulars Of The *Popish Clergy* Out Of This Kingdom" of 1697 does not attack them for their role in promoting their church, but for their alleged part in sedition:

> Whereas, it is Notoriously known, that the late Rebellions in this Kingdom have been Contrived, Promoted and Carried on by Popish Arch-Bishops, Bishops, Jesuits and other Ecclesiastical Persons of the Romish Clergy. And forasmuch as the Peace and Publick Safety of this Kingdom is in Danger,

by the great number of the said Arch-Bishops, Bishops, Jesuits, Friars and other Regular Romish Clergy, now residing here, and settling in Fraternities and Societies, contrary to Law, and to the great Impoverishing of many of His Majesty's subjects in this Kingdom, Who are forc'd to maintain and support them; which said Romish clergy do, not only endeavour to Withdraw His Majesty's Subjects from their Obedience, but do daily stir up, and move Sedition, and Rebellion, to the great hazard of the Ruine and desolation of this Kingdom.[6]

Similarly, "An Act to Prevent the Further Growth of Popery" of 1704 explains how:

…many persons so professing the popish religion have it in their power to raise division among protestants, by voting in elections for members of parliament, and also have it in their power to use other ways and means tending to the destruction of the Protestant interest in this kingdom.[7]

Such a mentality was sharpened by the fact that England was at war with France in 1689–97 and 1702–13. The close links between Irish Catholics and the French, and also Ireland's strategic position, were matters of great concern. At times like this, religious tolerance was hard to find anywhere in Europe. Both Spain and France had introduced anti-Protestant measures of equal or greater severity. Thousands of Huguenots, Calvinistically inclined Protestants, were expelled from France by Louis XIV, and around one hundred thousand of them settled in England and Ireland, where they took a leading role in such industries as linen manufacture. The peculiarity of Ireland's situation, however, was that it was the majority rather than the minority who were penalized.

Some have argued that the penal laws were motivated not only by fear but by vengeance, greed and malice. The Dublin-born writer and parliamentarian Edmund Burke (1729–97) described the penal code as "a machine as well fitted for the oppression, impoverishment and degradation of a people, and the debasement in them of human nature itself as ever proceeded from the perverted ingenuity of man." He saw the code as "manifestly the effects of national hatred and scorn towards a conquered people whom the victors delighted to trample upon and were not afraid to provoke....They were not the effect of their fears but their security."[8] Even if the impoverishment of the Catholic people was not the original intention behind the legislation, it became the consequence. While the laws which limited religious expression were soon ignored, those relating to the holding of land and power were more stringently enforced. The subdivision of land between sons, coupled with a population boom in the eighteenth century, meant that the mass of the Irish peasantry was greatly impoverished, relying on potato cultivation. The exclusion of Catholics from parliament meant that, for the first half of the century at least, its interests were exclusively those of the Protestant elite. The fact that the majority of the population were Catholic gave the Protestants the opportunity to penalize them. In this sense, full-scale conversion was unwanted, as it would have undermined the monopoly on wealth and power which the Protestants hoped to maintain.

But if the majority of the Catholic population were amongst the poorest people in Europe at the time, not everyone was reduced to the same position. A land-owning gentry remained, particularly in Connacht and in parts of Munster and Leinster. There were many ways for Catholic landholders to circumvent the laws. Most obviously one could convert to the Church of Ireland in name, if not in conscience, for the sake of holding larger lands or, as often happened, a Protestant could hold lands for Catholic relatives. The exclusion of Catholics from certain professions sometimes allowed their success in others. In particular, the eighteenth century saw the emergence of a Catholic merchant class. Catholics dominated commerce in Galway,

Limerick, Cork and Waterford, and they also featured prominently in Dublin. These middle-class townspeople were able to help in the support of religion by contributing to the maintenance of chapels and Mass-houses. They were also to play a leading role in the reemergence of Catholics into the political mainstream in the second half of the century.

If the reaction of many Catholics to their position in the Penal Age reflected that of Aodhagán O'Rathaille, others, such as the eighteenth-century poet Eileen O'Leary, could foresee a time when the wheel would turn again:

> The world hath conquered, the wind hath scattered
>   like dust
> Alexander, Caesar, and all that share their sway:
> Tara is grass, and behold how Troy lieth low—
> And even the English, perchance their hour will come.[9]

THE ASCENDANCY

The eighteenth century was the century of the Anglo-Irish—the landed aristocracy and middle-class townspeople of Anglican faith. Their culture may have been founded on domination, but it flourished by virtue of their own creativity and inventiveness. Irish Protestants had never seen such a time of peace and prosperity as the century which followed the Battle of the Boyne; never before did they have the opportunity to make such a commitment to Ireland. No longer an embattled few in a hostile environment, they now began to set down roots. The permanence of their commitment may be seen in the building of large, stately homes throughout the country—the "Big House," as locals would call it. There landlords, formerly absentees for the most part, now took a greater interest in the running of their estates. Many also had a townhouse in Dublin, which in the eighteenth century became one of the great cities of Europe.

A walk south from Fitzwilliam Square through the center of Dublin and out to Ballsbridge and Donnybrook is both an architectural tour and an encounter with Anglo-Irish identity. In the early decades of the eighteenth century, Luke Gardiner laid out a number of streets and squares on the then-fashionable north side of the city. Fitzwilliam Square, Henry Street and Henrietta Street were built according to the practical but elegant style which has since become known as Georgian (after the reigning monarchs of that name). Sackville Street, now O'Connell Street, remains the widest main thoroughfare in any European capital. To the end of that street and across the river we come to the central focus of Anglo-Irish life, namely College Green. There stands Trinity College, since the late sixteenth century the symbol of Protestantism and Anglicization, opposite the parliament building begun in 1729 by the Irish architect Sir Edward Lovett Pearce. Its magnificence and expense were a deliberate shot at competition with Westminster. The establishment of the Wide Streets Commission in 1757 promoted the extension of this style to Leinster House, Merrion Square and out to the southeastern suburbs. The picture was completed with the introduction

J. Tudor, "A prospect of the Parliament House in College Green, Dublin" (1753)

The Custom House, Dublin

of French neoclassicism in the Custom House, Four Courts and Rotunda Hospital by the English Huguenot James Gandon. Along with the reshaping of Dublin's architectural landscape came the opening of public libraries, the foundation of the Royal Dublin Society in 1731 to promote agriculture and crafts, and the Royal Irish Academy to promote the study of Irish antiquity. More than a building programme, this was a statement of permanence and a claim to a primary position in the emerging British Empire. William Dunkin's poem, "On the New Bridge Built on the Eastern Side of Dublin," written in 1755 to commemorate the opening of what is now called Grattan's Bridge, seems to sum up the new confidence:

> Swift rushes Liffey to the main, afloat
> Against the stream slow tugs the lab'ring boat
> The waving multitude promiscuous flow
> Through streets in air, and spurn the tide below
> Hence learn what labour's persevering part
> Performs, attended with her hand-maid, art:

The wit of man, superior to the might
Of nature, bade the distant banks unite.[10]

It seemed nothing less than its due when in 1742 Handel chose
Dublin for the premiere of his "Messiah." But along with confidence came the will to question:

Remove me from this land of slaves,
Where all are fools, and all are knaves;
Where every knave and fool is bought,
Yet kindly sells himself for nought;
Where Whig and Tory fiercely fight
Who's in the wrong, who's in the right;
And when their country lyse at stake
They only fight for fighting's sake
While English sharpers take the pay,
And then stand by to seek fair play.[11]

These are the opening lines of the poem "Ireland" by the defining
figure of Ireland's eighteenth century, Jonathan Swift. He was born
(or, as he put it, "I happened to be dropped") in 1667 in "wretched
Dublin, in miserable Ireland." Of an Anglo-Irish family, he fled to
England in 1688 and there became an Anglican priest. He returned
to Ireland in 1699 and held various positions in rural parishes
before being appointed dean of St. Patrick's Cathedral, Dublin, in
1713. Though best known for *Gulliver's Travels*, Swift's writings deal
with many of the central themes in Irish life of the time. Not least
because of his caustic pen, it is often easy to forget that Swift was a
churchman and that one of his greatest concerns was the defense
of the privileges of the Church of Ireland. One of his earliest
works, *A Tale of a Tub* (1704), is an allegory concerned with the different Christian churches. A father bequeaths a new coat to each of
his sons, Peter (representing the pope), Jack (Calvin) and Martin
(Luther). Each son begins to embellish the coat, with Peter taking

to wearing three hats at once and otherwise behaving eccentrically. While Martin succeeds in carefully removing the embellishments on his coat, Jack—and the satire appears more bitter toward dissenters than Catholics—rips them off with such vigor that the coat is torn to shreds.

But if Swift had contempt for the Catholic religion, he nevertheless retained a concern for the poverty of the Catholics whom he saw around him every day in his walks through Dublin. He wrote his most savage satire, which still retains the ability to shock, in response to the famine of 1729, a comment on the state to which the poor of Ireland had been brought. Entitled *A Modest Proposal for Preventing the Children of Poor People from Being a Burthen to their Parents or the Country; and for Making Them Beneficial to the Publick*, it suggested slaughtering one-year-old children to make flesh, "a most delicious, nourishing and wholesome food." He added: "It would greatly lessen the *Number of Papists,* with whom we are yearly overrun; being the principal Breeders of the Nation, as well as our most dangerous Enemies; and who stay at home on Purpose, with a Design to *deliver the Kingdom to the Pretender.*"[12]

Swift identified Ireland's ills primarily with the nature of its relationship with England. Instead of being treated by England as a sister kingdom, he saw Westminster stifling Ireland's political independence and crippling the country's economy. The Declaratory Act of 1720 had given the British parliament power to legislate for Ireland "in all causes whatsoever." Jobs in the church, the army and the legal profession tended to be given to members of the English establishment. Since 1690 the English parliament had attempted to ban the export of wool and other products from Ireland. In 1720 Swift anonymously published *A proposal for the universal use of Irish manufacture*, in which he suggested that "the Irish should burn everything English but the peoples and the coals." Then, under the pseudonym M. B. Drapier, he attacked English policy in Ireland, asking: "Were not the people of Ireland born as free as those of England?"

Here Swift was tapping into a more general sense among the Anglo-Irish, which grew as the century progressed. In manners, culture and religion they looked to England; they were completely committed to the constitutional connection to the Crown. Even so, they inevitably developed responses to their environment which moved them further away from the English. One feature of this was the growth of interest in Ireland's past and even in the Irish language amongst Protestants. This was not quite "going native," as many of the Anglo-Norman settlers had done. Rather, it was the emergence of an identity distinct from both Catholic Ireland and Protestant England. On another level it manifested itself in political demands for free trade and constitutional reform. *The Patriot Party,* led by the parliamentarians Henry Flood and Henry Grattan, campaigned to remove English protectionism and allow greater independence to the Dublin parliament.

The Patriots' position was a classic colonial one and was echoed at the same time in America, where a growing sense of distinctiveness from England amongst the colonists was combined with resentment toward the government over constitutional and free-trade issues. When the American War of Independence broke out in 1775 its impact in Ireland was great. The war meant a diversion of large numbers of troops to the American colony and a resulting vulnerability to attack from France. The solution found in Ireland was the formation of a volunteer corps. Drawn primarily from the Protestant gentry and middle class, the *Volunteers* expanded in numbers, reaching a membership of some ten thousand, and soon took on a social and political life of their own. When the French threat receded, the Volunteers did not disband, but instead used their numbers and influence to support the Patriots' demands for free trade and legislative independence for Ireland. Free trade was granted in 1779, and a huge assembly of Volunteers at Dungannon in February 1782 forced concessions on constitutional and civil issues. Most importantly, the Dublin parliament (known during the period 1782–1800 as "Grattan's parliament" after its main agitator) gained considerable legislative independence.

Many of those who pressed for these measures believed that an essential part of the movement toward greater rights for Ireland was the relaxation of penalties on Catholics. As Grattan put it, "…the Irish Protestant could never be free, till the Irish Catholic had ceased to be a slave." From 1782 onward, the "Catholic Question" was to dominate Irish politics. By the second half of the nineteenth century the penal laws were an anachronism and an embarrassment. While most Protestants still retained the belief and desire that the Catholic masses should be kept in check, the sort of repression that prevailed in the decades after the Treaty of Limerick no longer retained the same appeal. The memory of religious wars had receded and the danger from Catholics seemed less pressing. Part of this had to do with the peace and prosperity of the previous seventy years, the collapse of the Jacobite cause and the defeat of France in the Seven Years War (1756–63). In the era of the Enlightenment, persecution on religious grounds appeared increasingly unacceptable and jarred with the Patriots' demands for universal rights. When Catholics in the West Indies and Canada were guaranteed religious liberties, the Irish situation appeared anachronistic even in a colonial context. Furthermore, a Catholic voice began to emerge.

In 1760 the *Catholic Committee* was formed to represent their interests. It was mainly made up of middle-class Catholic merchants and was led by the antiquarian Charles O'Conor (1710–91). O'Conor's writings, in particular his *Dissertations on the Ancient History of Ireland,* sought to reject the prevailing notion of the Gaelic Irish as a barbarous people, undeserving of full rights. The other prong in their approach was an emphasis on loyalty. The Committee was at pains to present the Catholic population as loyal and unthreatening to the British connection and reliable as defenders of Ireland against foreign invasion, and they presented a number of petitions of this kind to the parliament and the king. In the 1770s the Catholics had some moderate but important successes. By 1778 the worst aspects of the penal legislation had been watered down and that same year the prime minister, Lord North, promised "justice for Ireland" as a reward for its loyalty during war. In 1782, with the aid of the more radical Volunteers, a Catholic Relief Act was passed to accompany constitutional reform. Catholics could now purchase lands and teach—on license—and their clergy had greater freedom.

The Patriot Party, the Volunteers and the Catholic Committee had achieved successes, but they were moderate ones. Their constituency was the respectable, moderate, well-to-do Catholic and Anglican classes. Soon others became prominent who had more radical aims regarding both Ireland's position in relation to England and the position of Catholics in Ireland.

RADICAL POLITICS

The driving force behind this movement was Belfast Presbyterianism. At the end of the eighteenth century Belfast was a prosperous city of twenty thousand people, its wealth founded primarily on the export of linen. The population of Belfast was overwhelmingly Presbyterian, and the city had developed a reputation for radicalism and religious tolerance. This was in part due to the relatively monolithic nature of the population (which would soon change with the influx of rural Catholics and Protestants during the next century), but it was also due to the history of dissenters over the previous century. The penal laws had affected dissenters as well as Catholics. The sacramental test on office holders was not repealed until 1780, and they still had to pay tithes to the Church of England. This had bred a distrust of the Anglican-dominated Irish polity and of the British government. Such ideas had been bolstered by the influence of the eighteenth-century "Scottish Enlightenment," which challenged notions of absolute monarchy. A further factor was the emigration of around a quarter of a million people from Ulster to America between 1716 and 1776 (see p. 174–75). This had forged strong links between Ulster and the rebellious colonists, where the Scots-Irish role had been particularly strong in the War of Independence. Six of the signatories to the Declaration of Independence were of Scots-Irish roots, as were six of the early presidents. Amongst the secure, prosperous and outward-looking Belfast middle classes, protective of their commercial interests and suspicious of both London and Dublin rule, the Catholics appeared more as potential allies than as enemies.

The French Revolution of 1789 had an inspirational effect in Belfast, where the anniversary of the fall of the Bastille was celebrated for many years, and Tom Paine's pamphlet *The Rights of Man* was widely disseminated. In this environment it was not surprising that such views were taken up and applied to Ireland. The organization which channeled these energies was the *United Irishmen,* founded in Belfast in October 1791. Largely made up of middle-class Presbyterians, they were avowedly nonsectarian and nonviolent. Its founding resolutions were:

> *First, Resolved,* That the weight of English influence in the Government of this country is so great, as to require a cordial union among ALL THE PEOPLE OF IRELAND, to maintain that balance which is essential to the preservation of our liberties, and the extension of our commerce.
> *Second,* That the sole constitutional mode by which this influence can be opposed, is by a complete and radical reform of the representation of the people in Parliament.
> *Third,* That no reform is practicable, efficacious, or just, which shall not include Irishmen of every religious persuasion.[13]

The author of these words and the name synonymous with the United Irishmen is that of Theobald Wolfe Tone (1763–98), a young Anglican barrister from Dublin. Tone had already attracted the attention of the Belfast radicals with his tract *An Argument on Behalf of the Catholics of Ireland,* in which he argued that "the proximate cause of our disgrace is our evil government, the remote one is our own intestine division, which, if once removed, the former will be instantaneously reformed."[14] Through Tone's influence, a second branch of the United Irishmen was founded in Dublin in the same year.

Tone's significance was not only in his eloquent articulation of the ideals of the United Irishmen, but in the manner in which he drew together a range of forces for change. One of these was the revitalized and newly radical Catholic Committee, which engaged Tone as assistant secretary. Pressure on parliament resulted in the Catholic Relief Act of 1792, which removed restrictions on education and allowed Catholics to practice at the Bar and occupy some lower positions in government. In December of that year, as a show of strength, a great representative assembly of Catholics met in Dublin. The Catholic Committee drew up a petition that they presented directly to King George III, pointedly bypassing the Dublin parliament. Significantly, the petitioners made their way to London via Belfast, where they were cheered on by the United Irishmen. The result was the Catholic Relief Act of 1793, which Dublin grudgingly accepted under pressure from Westminster. Now Catholics could vote, serve on juries and carry arms. Within two years a seminary was founded at Maynooth for the education of Catholic clergy. Catholics had come a long way, thanks in no small measure to their alliance with radical Anglicans and Dissenters, and their achievements had been gained by nonviolent, constitutional means.

But by 1795 a real crisis was looming. The measures of 1793 had raised hopes but had not delivered them; Catholics remained excluded from parliament and from senior government positions.

Theobald Wolfe Tone (1763–1798), by an unknown artist of the eighteenth-century Irish School

Deeper forces were now at work, beyond parliament and the debating clubs.

THE 1798 REBELLION

For most people in Ireland, Catholic and Protestant, the loftier questions of constitutional reform and admission to senior positions held little relevance. In 1700 the population of Ireland was around two million; at the end of the century it was five million. This, along with land enclosure and the transfer of land to pasture, created land hunger, higher rents and accompanying problems. One response to this situation was the emergence of secret societies in rural areas. Groups such as the Whiteboys and the Rightboys, which emerged in Catholic areas of the south, were bound together by oath and engaged in acts of destruction and intimidation: leveling ditches and stone walls, burning houses and threatening landlords. They were not originally sectarian organizations— though they resisted the payment of tithes they also opposed the level of dues to the Catholic Church—but they were swiftly branded as such by the landlord class. In the most extreme case of anti-Catholic reaction, Whiteboy disturbances in Tipperary in 1766 resulted in a Catholic priest, Father Nicholas Sheehy, being sentenced on trumped-up charges and then hanged, drawn and quartered. In the 1780s and 1790s similar organizations emerged which had the added feature of sectarianism.

In much of Ulster, beyond Belfast, the resentments of the plantation era remained, and became sharpened by economic factors. The focus was the "weaving triangle," which covered much of Armagh and parts of East Tyrone. Setbacks to the linen industry and the growing number of Catholics being employed contributed to Protestant resentment in the region. At the same time, the competition over land which prevailed throughout Ireland had taken on a sectarian character in Ulster. As a petition to the lord lieutenant of Ireland put it, "...some of us by refusing to pay the extravagant rent demanded by our land lords have been turned out, and our lands given to papists, who will pay any rent."[15] Organized groups emerged: the Oakboys, Steelboys and Peep-o-Day-Boys on the Protestant side; the Defenders and Ribbonmen on the Catholic side. A contemporary local who called himself J. Byrne, a "dyer and publican" of Armagh, described this growing polarization:

> The Defending parties, combine among themselves, not to purchase any goods from any Protestant that they knew to be any way active in aiding or abetting the Peep-o-day boys; and that was the worst sort of revenge, that any set of men in their senses could think of; for it turned many well-disposed Protestants against them, that hitherto espoused their cause: for who else in the county of Armagh, could be of any service to them, in a time of distress? And by turning their best friends against them, they have got both the rich and poor for their enemies. The Peep-o-Day boys have pursued much the same career against such of the Papists as they usually used to deal with, and both parties have got a kind of cant word, "that we'll deal with none but our own sort."[16]

He goes on to describe a typical clash between the groups:

> It is a common saying with old women in the North, that the Scotch and Irish fairies, have had desperate quarrels, on Holy-eve, but as the Scotch and Irish fairies have either killed or banished each other to some distant climes, the Peep-o-day-boys and Defenders have taken up the cudgels in their place: for on Holy-eve, this year, they appointed to fight at midnight, in the neighbourhood of Cocklehill, near Laughall; the Defenders assembled in Willis-Grange, with handkerchiefs round their bodies, as a mark to know

each other in the dark; they repaired to the appointed spot, and took a refreshment of native whiskey, with a tenant of Mr. A–r, in that quarter. The Peep-o-day-boys assembled at a Mr St.. C–s, at Cocklehill; several shots were fired by both parties, as signals to give notice of their respective rivals; but captain whiskey, by his great activity, cast some of them into the ditches, and others fell to fighting amongst themselves, so that their respective generals, had enough to do, to keep their troops from mutiny, and it was accounted good manoeuvring to get each party to his respective home before day light.[17]

The actions of the secret societies could sometimes be farcical, but they could also be very serious. By 1790 they were present all over Ulster, and thereafter they spread to the south. The *Defenders,* in particular, began to mobilize in North Leinster and Connacht, concentrating on issues of tithes, taxation, employment and land, but retaining their sectarian character.

In the 1790s Ireland drifted toward crisis. The Catholic Relief Act of 1793 had been accompanied by repressive measures, partly prompted by the outbreak of war with the French Republic. Political assemblies were outlawed, the importation of arms was limited and special powers of arrest were granted. The government set up a militia, prosecuted opponents for sedition and used terror tactics against the local population. If government policies were especially draconian, they were responding to a real threat, in particular the spread of the Defender movement and its alliance with the United Irishmen. As the Defenders gained strength and became increasingly politicized, Tone sought to take advantage of their grass-roots base. The United Irishmen, originally a nonsectarian, nonviolent organization, became a revolutionary movement with many of the anti-English and anti-Protestant sentiments of the Defenders. In 1795 a formal alliance was made between the two organizations. In the same year the *Orange Order* came into being.

On December 21, 1795, Protestant attempts to prevent Defenders from holding armed demonstrations led to the "Battle of the Diamond" at Loughgall, County Armagh, in which the Defenders were routed. In its aftermath the Orange Order was founded, its name recalling the victory of King William in 1690. Initially made up mostly of Anglicans, it stood for the Protestant faith and loyalty to the Crown. But the provisional nature of that loyalty is expressed in their oath: "I...do solemnly swear, that I will, to the utmost of my power, support and defend the King and his heirs as long as he or they support the Protestant ascendancy." The Order spread rapidly in Ulster and was blamed for pogroms against Catholics. While there was undoubtedly much truth in this, the exaggerated Orange menace also helped the Defenders to recruit more members in the south. As the United Irishmen allied themselves with the Defenders and appeared set for war, the landed classes and the government, albeit reluctantly, looked to the Orange Order as their first line of defense.

In 1795 Wolfe Tone was implicated in a seditious plot and sent into exile. He went first to America and then to France, where he engaged in a successful diplomatic mission aimed at persuading the Republican army to aid an Irish rebellion. In December 1796 almost fifteen thousand troops set sail from France for Bantry Bay, County Cork, but fell foul of stormy conditions. The fleet was scattered and lost thousands of men; those remaining were forced to return without landing. "We were near enough to throw a biscuit ashore," wrote Tone in his diary. "England has not had such an escape since the Spanish Armada." Despite its failure, this mission was deeply shocking to the government. More draconian laws were introduced and the government militia expanded, with troops given license to flog, torture or hang anyone suspected of treason.

When the United Irishmen rebellion finally took off in 1798, it was crippled by the arrest and execution of its leaders and the reluctance of the French to commit large numbers. That summer, localized rebellions broke out throughout the country. While Ulster also witnessed insurrection, the main focus was Wexford, where sectarianism immediately came to the fore. Wexford had the largest Protestant population outside Ulster, and when the rebels, overwhelmingly Catholic, seized control of the main towns, they adopted brutal measures toward their Protestant inhabitants. In Scullabogue near New Ross, men, women and children were herded into a barn and burned to death. Government forces quickly regained the initiative, and reprisals were taken against Catholics. With the rebellion all but defeated throughout the country, the French eventually landed at Killala Bay in County Mayo. They declared the "Republic of Connacht" and managed to rout government forces but, as elsewhere, early successes gave way to swift defeat. Tone was captured and committed suicide in custody.

By now the idea of a union of Irish people of all faiths was long dead. But even before 1798, the original ideals of the United Irishmen had been soured by sectarianism. In the aftermath of the rebellion, positions became even more polarized. The Act of Union of 1801 scrapped the Irish parliament for which Grattan and other "Patriots" had fought so hard. Dublin, once the showpiece of the Empire, fell into decline as a provincial backwater. Ulster Presbyterians, formerly the champions of Catholic emancipation, turned in increasing numbers to the Orange Order. The national movement took on a distinctly Catholic color.

On June 20, 1798, a month before his death, Tone wrote in his diary:

> To-day is my birth-day. I am thirty-five years of age; more than half the career of my life is finished, and how little have I yet been able to do....I had hopes, two years ago,

that, at the period I write this, my debt to my country would have been discharged, and the fate of Ireland settled for good or evil. To-day it is more uncertain than ever. I think, however, I may safely say, I have neglected no step to which my duty called me, and, in that conduct, I will persist to the last.[18]

Wolfe Tone was a complex figure in life and in death. He advocated unity among Catholic, Protestant and Dissenter, but the rebellion which he led degenerated into sectarian slaughter. He has been hailed as a hero by liberal democrats and by republican advocates of physical force alike. And although his efforts ended in failure, his legacy remains as strong as ever, more than two centuries later.

The Cathedral of the Holy Cross, Boston, Massachusetts

VII

THE MAKING OF
MODERN CHRISTIANITY

Much of what is considered traditionally Irish is in fact a creation of the nineteenth century. This is especially true of the modern character of Irish Christianity. The familiar image of Catholic Ireland, which lasted until recent decades—of a devout and somewhat puritanical people, strongly under the influence of their priests and bishops—originates in this century, a consequence of great social upheavals and the vigorous efforts of their clergy. The popular concept of the dissenting Protestant churches—of preaching, an emphasis on the Bible, and political conservatism—also derives from this time, influenced by the evangelical movement. At the same time, the established church declined in influence and in numbers, at least in the south, though its imprint on the country remained strong. These developments were closely tied up with political trends: the emergence of the Catholic Irish nation as a powerful political force, the union of northern Protestants in response to what they perceived as the nationalist threat, and the retreat of the Anglo-Irish.

The funeral of the Fenian Jeremiah O'Donovan Rossa, 1915

POPULAR RELIGION

The people who loom largest in the history of Irish Christianity are those at the top. The archbishops, bishops and abbots, the intellectuals and politicians who had greatest influence tended to leave the most enduring marks on posterity, whether by their own writings or by virtue of their presence in the writings of others. But the story of Christianity in Ireland was not only shaped by public figures, but by the masses of people who constituted the reality of Christian life but left few traces. In particular, the Catholic rural peasantry, who made up the majority of the population before the Great Famine of the 1840s, had a rich and influential religious culture, but did not have as loud a voice as the wealthier and more influential scions of the churches. The practices of popular religion were distinctive to Ireland, but they reflected older pagan traditions found in many societies. For rural Catholics at the lowest level of society, religion was just as much about wakes, holy wells and celebrations of the agricultural calendar as it was about Sunday Mass and the sacraments. These traditions date back hundreds of years, and elements of them remain today, but they fell away sharply in the nineteenth century. Even before the Famine, they had begun to decline under pressure from the church hierarchy. The physical and psychological effects of these years dealt such traditions a fatal blow by wiping out vast numbers of the rural peasantry and changing the life and attitudes of those who remained.

Visitors to Ireland often remarked upon the piety of the people, their chastity, and the low rate of illegitimacy. But behind this apparently healthy picture, the religious lives of the mass of the people was still a matter of concern to the church authorities. Though people were inclined to attend Mass and receive the sacraments, their approach to such matters appeared lax. Before the time of the Famine many areas did not boast a church; private homes were often the focus for the religious life of the parish. More worrying for the hierarchy was the range of practices and beliefs which betrayed pre-Christian origins. In many rural areas the preoccupation with natural forces, and the attribution of magical powers to those forces, had not died out with the coming of St. Patrick. People would speak of fairy people living in mounds, or of the banshee (a wailing spirit) and the pooka (a hobgoblin).

The peasant population also remained attached to the celebration of key days in the agricultural year. On St. Brigid's Day, which coincided with the pagan feast of Imbolc in which spring was welcomed (see p.17), crosses were woven from rushes and placed in houses and farm buildings as protection against harm. May Eve and St. John's Eve, in the harvest season, were marked by bonfires and great celebrations. The most characteristic feature of popular religion in Ireland at this time was the celebration of the feast of a saint at a holy place associated with that figure. Robert Bell, a visitor to Ireland in 1804, wrote:

> Of all the amusements of the native Irish, there was none so remarkable for variety, for the multitudes that partook of them, and for the interest they excited, as those which were called *Patrons*....It was a large assemblage of people from all parts within a distance of ten or twenty miles, collected together round a sacred fountain dedicated to, and called after the name of the Saint, in honour of whom this festival was celebrated.[1]

These celebrations, usually known as "patterns," a corruption of the word *patron*, were usually held at wells, mountains or trees. The novelist William Makepeace Thackeray described the proceedings at a pattern held at Croaghpatrick in County Mayo:

> The first station consists of one heap of stones, round which they must walk seven times, casting a stone on the heap each time, and before and after every stone's throw saying a prayer.
>
> The second station is on the top of the mountain. Here there is a great altar—a shapeless heap of stones. The poor wretches crawl on *their knees* into this place, say fifteen prayers, and after going round the entire top of the mountain fifteen times, say fifteen prayers again.
>
> The third station is near the bottom of the mountain at the further side from Westport. It consists of three heaps. The penitents must go seven times round these collectively, and seven times afterward round each individually, saying a prayer before and after each progress.[2]

The pagan elements seem pronounced at all patterns. In some places even cattle were brought on May Eve to drink the water from a holy well at which stations were performed. However, it was not just the pagan nature of the ritual that attracted the attention of observers, but also its social side. Thackeray continued:

> The pleasures of the poor people—for after the business on the mountain came the dancing and love-making at its floor—were wofully spoiled by the rain, which rendered dancing on the grass impossible; nor were the tents big enough for that exercise. Indeed the whole sight was as dismal and half-savage a one as I have seen.[3]

Robert Bell offered a similar description:

> In the morning or forenoon the priest of the parish performed Mass on a large stone, which was called an altar. Several old men and women at the same time performed penance round the well. Here were all sorts of hawkers, mountebanks, conjurers and itinerant musicians: and tents and booths were erected chiefly for the sale of liquor. The day was not uncommonly concluded by a general battle.[4]

This boisterous aspect to the proceedings attracted a great degree of criticism from the clergy. In 1782 the Catholic Bishop Troy of Ossory complained:

> Our deluded people assemble on these days for wicked purposes. Instead of praying they wish damnation to themselves and acquaintances with most horrid and deliberate imprecations. They profane the name of God and everything else that is sacred by most execrable oaths and finish the day by the perpetration of the grossest impurities, by shedding their neighbour's blood, by murder, and the transgression of every law.[5]

What many outsiders found most puzzling was that both the pious and the rowdy element went hand-in-hand, and that each aspect was approached with great enthusiasm: The ceremonials were not simply a pretext for merrymaking. In 1854 it was observed that:

> It is quite usual to see young men and women devoutly circumambulating the well or lake on their bare knees, with all the marks of penitence and contrition strongly impressed upon their faces; whilst again, after an hour or two, the same individuals may be found in a tent dancing with ecstatic vehemence to the music of the bagpipe or fiddle.[6]

By this time, however, the pattern was a dying practice. The attempts by the clergy to suppress it, which intensified just before the Famine years, bore fruit in the aftermath of the devastation of the 1840s.

There were other occasions when the sacred entered into a strange alliance with the profane. Christenings and weddings, for example, were times of indecorous celebration. Most of all, the wake that marked a death was an occasion when the solemnity which it might be expected to demand was overcome by enthusiastic game-playing and dancing. An account from 1778 described the wakes as:

> ...meetings of merriment and festivity, to which they resort from far and near. The old people amuse themselves in smoking tobacco, drinking whiskey and telling stories in the room with the corpse; whilst the young men, in the barn or some separate apartment, exhibit feats of activity; or, inspired by their sweethearts, dance away the night to the melodious *pleasing* of a bagpipe.[7]

Amongst the outlets for merriment and festivity were dancing, singing, storytelling and feats of strength and intellect. There was also a strong sexual element in the activities reported. A contemporary visitor to Ireland described a game called "Frimsy Framsy":

> A chair or a stool is placed in the middle of the flure, and the man who manages the play sits down upon it, and calls his sweetheart, or the prettiest girl in the house. She, accordingly, comes forward and must kiss him. He then rises up and she sits down. "Come now," he says, "fair maid—*frimsy framsy*, who's your fancy?" She then calls them she likes best, and when the young man she calls comes over and kisses her, he then takes her place, and calls another girl—and so on, smacking away for a couple of hours. Well throth, its no wonder that Ireland's full of people; for I believe they do nothing but coort from the time they're the hoith of my leg.[8]

An appropriately named Dr. Prim recorded some of these games, prefaced with the warning: "So marked are they in every part by the all-pervading licentiousness of Paganism, that to spare the feelings of the modest reader, if written at all, they should be confided to the guardianship of a dead language. In this place I can but refer to their nature in the most general terms." He continued:

> The "game" usually first performed was termed "Bout" and was joined in by men and by women, who all acted a very obscene part which cannot be described. The next scene generally was termed "Making the Ship," with its several parts of "laying the keel," forming the "stem and stern," and erecting "the mast," the latter of which was done by a female using a gesture and expression, proving beyond doubt that it was a relic of Pagan rites. The "Bull and Cow" was another game strongly indicative of a Pagan origin, from circumstances too delicate to be particularised…in

that called "Drawing the Ship out of the Mud," the men engaged actually presented themselves before the assembly, females as well as males, in a state of nudity, whilst in another game the female performers attired themselves in men's clothes and conducted themselves in a very strange manner.[9]

This aspect of Irish peasant life may seem odd to those accustomed to the image of a people locked in sexual puritanism, but there are many recorded examples of open sexuality in dance and celebration. An observer described a May Day celebration in County Louth around 1838:

> The figure of the female is made up, fixed upon a short pole and dressed in a fantastic manner, with flowers, ribbons etc. This figure they call "The May Baby."…Around this figure a man and woman (generally his wife) of the humble class, dressed also fantastically with straw etc. dance to the sound of a fiddle, and entertain the people with indecent shows and postures, the figure at the same time being kept moving by the rustic maiden that supports it. These exhibitions cause great merriment among the assembled populace; women who have had no children to their husbands also attend (some of them from a considerable distance) to see this figure and exhibition, which they imagine will promote fruitfulness in them and cause them to have children.[10]

But if such lack of prudery was socially accepted, at least amongst the lay in the poor peasant communities, sexual incontinence was not. Illegitimacy and sexual relations outside marriage were thoroughly frowned upon in rural society. Why this aspect of life should be so prominent in Irish Catholic morality is not entirely clear, but the landholding situation seems to have been a contributing factor. Because there was so much concern about securing a good inheritance, marriage was expected to be late and judiciously thought out, and sexual continence outside marriage was insisted upon. The close family and local structure also meant that it was easier to monitor the potentially wayward young. The clergy, then, often accused of instilling sexual puritanism in their congregations, were in fact reflecting the ethos of laypeople. It should be added that the illegitimacy rate amongst Irish Protestants was significantly lower than amongst Protestants in the rest of the United Kingdom. Still, priests did take a role in the enforcement of this strict moral code. In the pre-Famine years, it seems that the clergy were becoming louder and more successful in their attempts to limit the opportunities for sin.

Apart from the growing clampdown on patterns and unruly wakes, dances were targeted. John Casey, parish priest of Ballyferriter, County Kerry, is remembered as "a deadly enemy of pipers and card-players." The diary of a fellow priest records how he happened to visit a house where a dance was being held in secret:

> His anger knew no bounds, he rushed over, laid hold of the innocent but unfortunate piper, kicked, cuffed and beat him unmercifully, broke his pipes and completely dispersed the whole assembly.[11]

The impact of the Famine and the growing authority of the clergy over its flock meant that the exuberant practices that had been a part of rural Irish life since pre-Christian times, and that had already been declining, were soon almost wiped out.

EMANCIPATION AND "THE LIBERATOR"

If the late eighteenth century was a time of optimism for the Catholic cause, the new century brought with it a major obstacle to their interests: the Act of Union of 1801. This created the United Kingdom of Great Britain and Ireland, dissolved Ireland's parliament and allowed for an Irish representation of thirty-two peers in the House of Lords and one hundred members in the House of Commons. The Catholic hierarchy and many leading Catholic politicians initially supported the union with Britain. They did not lament the passing of the Dublin parliament, which had stood as the bastion of Protestant privilege for more than a century. In fact, it took extensive bribery, including the creation of twenty-eight peerages, to persuade the Dublin MPs to surrender their parliament. The Catholic clergy believed that, in return for their support, the London government would speedily remove the remaining restrictions on Catholics, in particular the prohibition on their entering parliament. The clergy were mistaken in this, as the Westminster parliament, influenced by the vehemently anti-Catholic King George III (1738–1820) and his son the Regent (1762–1830), refused to grant Catholic emancipation. Most Catholics also failed to take the longer view of the consequences of union. Even if Catholics had immediately been granted the right to sit in the London parliament and won every Irish seat, they would still have been outnumbered by English, Scottish and Welsh MPs. Therefore, Catholics were locked into a position of permanent minority.

These issues, Catholic emancipation and repeal of the Union, came to dominate Irish politics in the pre-Famine years. The name synonymous with both of these causes is Daniel O'Connell. A popular song of the time hailed him as the Irish Moses, leading the Catholics out of captivity:

> The bondage of the Israelites
> Our Saviour he did see,
> He then commanded Moses
> To go and set them free,

And in the same we did remain
Suffering for our own
Till God has sent O'Connell,
To free the Church of Rome.[12]

O'Connell won the epithet "The Liberator" for his success in winning Catholic emancipation, but his achievement went beyond legislative change. O'Connell was the first to mobilize the Catholic masses into a disciplined and peaceful political movement. Greater than the removal of the remaining penal laws was the gift that O'Connell gave his people: a loud and influential political voice.

Daniel O'Connell was born in 1775 in County Kerry to a modestly landed family. He was part of the first wave of middle-class Catholics to benefit from the loosening of the penal laws on professions, becoming a highly successful barrister. His early education in France, where he witnessed the violence of the postrevolutionary terror, gave him a lifelong hatred of violence, and so he was highly critical of the 1798 rebellion. He was also a vocal opponent of the Act of Union, and his first major political speech in January 1800 was at a protest meeting against it. Strongly influenced by his Christian faith, he worked against slavery and colonialism and supported the emancipation of Jews. More a conservative than a radical, he became the model for future Catholic constitutional politicians.

The first two decades of the nineteenth century had been frustrating ones for the Catholic Committee. There seemed little prospect of getting the Westminster parliament interested in emancipation, especially as long as the Committee members were engaged in endless squabbles amongst themselves. It had traditionally been run by the Catholic middle classes, the landlords, merchants and professionals who had benefited most from the relaxation of the penal laws. To the majority of the Catholic populace, the Catholic

Committee and its aims seemed distant and irrelevant. Indeed, most people would never have heard of it. O'Connell changed all this by founding the *Catholic Association of Ireland* in 1823. While the leaders of this organization remained middle class—lawyers, in particular—O'Connell managed for the first time to attract mass membership to a constitutional movement for the rights of Catholics. This was achieved through an ingenious innovation, namely "the Catholic Rent," a membership fee of one shilling a year. Now every Irish Catholic could afford a stake in the movement. As a ballad of the time put it:

> A penny each month is your just due,
> collected by some faithful brother
> Then why should Patrick's friends refuse
> In this grand plan to assist each other.[13]

Revenues from mass subscription could be put toward propaganda, court cases and agitation. Another important part of this movement was the prominent role played by the clergy, especially parish priests, who were responsible for the collection of subscriptions and for organization at a local level.

The Association was an immediate success, reaching a membership of perhaps half a million. In 1824 the Church of Ireland bishop of Limerick commented:

> Throughout all parts of Ireland the Catholic Association is omnipotent; its mandates are respected as much as the Acts of Parliament are condemned. In any district or parish the Catholic Rent needs only to be proposed, and it is hailed with acclamation....There is what we of this generation have never before witnessed, a complete union of the Roman Catholic body....In truth, an Irish Revolution has, in great measure, been effected.[14]

The *Dublin Evening Post* reported on an emancipation meeting in Longford in 1825:

A space near the altar was appropriated for the accommodation of the Gentlemen who took an active part in the proceedings. The aisles and galleries of the Chapel, which is, we understand capable of accommodating two thousand persons, were completely occupied by the crowds of peasantry who thronged in as if to show that they felt deeply their degrading condition.[15]

When the government suppressed the Association in the same year, frightened by the rapid growth of this popular movement, O'Connell immediately founded the *New Catholic Association*. It was officially dedicated to "public and private charity," but was indistinguishable from the organization it had replaced.

When a general election was held in 1826 the Association mobilized its membership to support sympathetic candidates. All adult males who held land worth than forty shillings were entitled to vote, but that did not mean that they could vote as they pleased. Ballots were not secret until 1832 and tenants, fearful for their lands, would obediently vote as their landlords instructed them. Now, the pressure of the landlords was matched by that of the other figure of local authority, the parish priest. The novelist Harriet Martin recalled a conversation between a tenant and a priest at the election in Galway for which her father stood as a pro-Catholic candidate:

"My blessing to ye! Phanick O'Dea!" said Father John, "how long is it since you turned Protestant?"

"Me turn Protestant, is it Father John! The Lord save us!" And Phanick crossed himself reverentially. "Sure I'm no Protestant, nor one belongin' to me; the heavens betwixt us an' harum!"

"If you aren't Protestant, and a bitter black one, too, how do you come to vote for the Orange candidate, my man?"

"Avoch, Father John, sure it isn't of our own will we're voting! didn't Pat Sullivan threaten to burn the houses over our heads and banish us the place, if we didn't vote the way we were ordhered. An' how would we stand in country, Father John, if we didn't? always in arrares of rint, you know."[16]

The Association's great success was in Waterford, where the notoriously anti-Catholic Beresford family had held the seat for seventy years. An energetic and well-organized campaign resulted in the election of Henry Villiers Stuart on the Catholic emancipation ticket. When Beresford responded with eviction, the Association stepped in to support the dispossessed tenants.

Stuart was a Protestant; as yet, no Catholic had stood for parliament. The 1678 Test Act required that each MP take oaths of allegiance and supremacy, testify on oath his disbelief in

Joseph Haverty, "O'Connell and his contemporaries; the Clare Election, 1828"

transubstantiation and his firm conviction that "the invocation or adoration of the Virgin Mary or any other saint and the sacrifice of the mass, as they are now used in the Church of Rome, are superstitious and idolatrous." But there was nothing to prevent a Catholic from standing in an election. In 1828 a by-election was held in Clare, and O'Connell was put forward as a candidate. A highly disciplined campaign, in which voters pledged to abstain from whiskey, resulted in O'Connell's election with an overwhelming majority. Fearing violence, the government (under the Duke of Wellington) agreed to remove the restrictive oaths, and in 1829 King George IV tearfully signed the Bill for Catholic Emancipation. It did have a sting in its tail, however. The voting qualification was raised from forty shillings to ten pounds, thereby disenfranchising large numbers of people, mainly poor Catholics.

The achievement of emancipation made O'Connell a hero to millions and a famous international figure. He was described as "the King of the beggars," "the counselor" or "the Liberator." He now turned his attention to other issues. Catholics were still required to render a tithe, a tenth of their tillage crop, to the Church of Ireland. Spurred on by O'Connell's call to a campaign of nonpayment, localities throughout Leinster and Munster became flashpoints for conflict between Catholic farmers and the authorities. At Graiguenamanagh, County Kilkenny, in 1831 farmers successfully resisted the attempts of a force of six hundred police and soldiers to collect tithes. But in 1834, near Rathcormac in County Cork, the authorities killed nine unarmed protesters who were trying to defend a certain widow Ryan from seizure of property. O'Connell received much of the blame in the English press for the disturbances of the "tithe war." The *Times* wrote:

Scum condensed of Irish bog!
Ruffian, coward, demagogue!
Boundless liar, base detractor!

Nurse of murders, treason's factor!
Of Pope and priest the crouching slave,
While they lips of freedom rave,
Of England's fame the viprous hater,
Yet wanting courage for a traitor.[17]

However, the campaign eventually proved successful. In 1838 the payment of tithes by Catholics was effectively abolished. O'Connell also supported the churches in their demands for denominational education, condemning the establishment of the nondenominational National School system in 1831. Yet, although these schools were nominally nondenominational, the realities of Irish life meant that a school in a Catholic area became effectively a Catholic school, and a school in a Protestant area became a Protestant one.

In 1840 O'Connell shifted his attention to the issue of the Union and set up the National Repeal Association. Modeled on the Catholic Association, it used the same tactics of mass mobilization and the spreading of the message through huge assemblies, or "Monster Meetings." Priests again played a prominent role, and the movement was backed by a newspaper, the *Freeman's Journal*. However, this time O'Connell faced the determined efforts of prime minister Robert Peel. When a proposed monster meeting at Clontarf in 1843 was banned, O'Connell, wary of violence, backed down. The following year he was imprisoned for six months on a charge of sedition. When O'Connell died in Genoa on his way to Rome in 1847, repeal of the Union remained a distant hope.

O'Connell introduced certain elements to the Irish political scene which were to remain prominent for the rest of the century and beyond. One was the mobilization of the masses, which was deployed in agitation over land and Home Rule and eventually in the events which led to the formation of the independent Irish state. There was now a growing sense of the Irish nation as distinct from its government. Always present was the implicit threat of violence, contained for much of O'Connell's era, but erupting periodically thereafter. Another feature was the newly prominent role of the Catholic priesthood in politics. They had taken a lead in the emancipation and repeal movements, and they continued to influence political affairs, although their relationship with the newly emergent nationalism became more troublesome. O'Connell was a great liberal democrat, but his campaigns helped to reaffirm the divisions between Catholics and Protestants in Ireland. He was guilty of sectarian triumphalism, referring back to Cromwell and pointing to the Catholics' superiority in numbers. When he attempted to spread his message to Belfast, he was run out of the town. Though emancipation and repeal had Protestant supporters, they were overwhelmingly Catholic demands and served to cement the common cause among Protestants of all denominations. These feelings were reflected in the words of a contemporary song:

> For we are true blue, and Orange too,
> and will never consent to see,
> O'Connell Dan, return the man,
> who'd blindly vote for Popery.[18]

THE FAMINE

By the mid-1840s such political issues were overshadowed by an unprecedented disaster. Between 1800 and 1841 the population of Ireland rose from around just under five million to over eight million. This population was supported by the potato crop, which formed the nutritious staple diet of the vast majority. The potato prospered in the wet climate of Ireland and was ideally suited to cultivation by small landholders. However, the dependence of millions on a single crop had begun to worry some in authority. In 1844 a commission reported:

The potato enabled a large family to live on food produced in great quantities at a trifling cost, and as a result the increase of the people has been gigantic. There had, however, been no corresponding improvement in their material and social condition, but the opposite....Their sufferings were, in the opinion of the Commission, greater than the people of any other country in Europe had to sustain.[19]

A year after the commission reported, calamity struck. A fungal disease called potato blight, which had already been reported in the United States and England, destroyed almost half of the nation's crop. It recurred over the next four years, resulting in extreme loss of life, not only from starvation, but also from such diseases as typhus and cholera which accompanied it. The *Cork Examiner* described the horrifying scene in 1846:

> Disease and death in every quarter—the once hardy population worn away to emaciated skeletons—fever, dropsy, diarrhoea, and famine rioting in every filthy hovel, and sweeping away whole families....seventy-five tenants ejected here, and a whole village in the last stage of destitution there....dead bodies of children flung into holes hastily scratched in the earth without shroud or coffin....every field becoming a grave, and the land a wilderness.[20]

The response of British prime minister Robert Peel was immediate. He purchased £100,000 worth of Indian corn from the United States and sold it at a penny a pound, and introduced public works, soup kitchens and workhouses. However, in 1846 Lord John Russell's Liberal Party took office. Although they continued with soup kitchens and workhouses, they refused, as enthusiastic supporters of free trade, to interfere with market forces by importing grain or blocking exports. How much such policies exacerbated the agony is still hotly debated, but they certainly roused the anger of many. Addressing Lord Russell, the Catholic Archbishop MacHale of Tuam thundered:

> If you are ambitious of a monument, the bones of a people, slain with the sword of famine, piled into cairns more numerous than the ancient Pyramids, shall tell posterity the triumphs of your brief but disastrous administration.[21]

Though it was the poor who suffered most from the effects of the Famine, landlords also found themselves in a difficult financial situation. They were required by the government to finance relief measures, but at the same time their income was endangered by the inability of their tenants to pay rent. While some landlords sacrificed their personal fortunes to save their starving tenants, others responded by evicting those who could not pay. The *Illustrated London* News described how:

> Not a roof-tree is to be seen where the happy cottage of the labourer or the snug homestead of the farmer at no distant day cheered the landscape. The ditch side, the dripping rain, and the cold sleet are the covering of the wretched outcast the moment the cabin is tumbled over him; for who dare give him shelter from "the pelting of the pitiless storm"? Who has the temerity to afford him the ordinary rites of hospitality, when the warrant has been signed for his extinction?[22]

"How I wish," wrote Father William Flannelly of Clifden, County Galway, "the real sufferings of the people could reach the ears of the rich of this life!" Nor were the Protestant landlords solely to blame. James Browne, parish priest, declared:

> Ballintubber is *gone*, alas! My fine virtuous, holy people have been starved to death. The landlords of all sects have

conspired for their destruction—the Catholic Landlords the most cruelly disposed.[23]

In addition to the relief works introduced by the government, private charity played a role in lessening the suffering. Contributions came from all over the world. In 1847 Pope Pius IX issued an encyclical appealing for three days of public prayers and almsgiving. The response was great, particularly from Catholics in Britain, Australia and the United States; Anglo-Irish officers in India also sent a large contribution. Most effective of all was the Central Relief Committee of the Society of Friends, which brought shiploads of food from the United States. The *Freeman's Journal* reported:

> The Catholic and Protestant clergymen vie with one another in acts of benevolence. They are the most active members of relief committees—they confer together, remonstrate together, evoke together the aid of a dilatory government, and condemn together its vicious and dilatory refusals.[24]

The famine affected Protestant and Catholic alike, but its effects were felt hardest by the Catholic peasantry. The overwhelmingly Catholic west of Ireland was particularly vulnerable; Ulster, which had an industrial base, more mixed farming and more flexible landholding practices, was least affected. The Catholic clergy was criticized by some for not coming to the aid of their people. The radical paper *The Nation* commented in 1847:

> Independent of their local duties, which they have discharged with a devotion unsurpassed in the annals of martyrdom, have they in their political capacity, as...citizens, raised their voices against the murder of their people...? Or have they...backed the abettors of that infamous pol-

icy which gave to the butcher two million of their flock? Have they whispered when they should have denounced, or been silent when they should have thundered?[25]

A committee of Meath priests voiced similar opinions in writing to the hierarchy, stating that had their lordships "taken the position between the starving people and their rulers, the poor would not have been neglected as they were." Such criticisms were somewhat unfair. The hierarchy had not openly criticized the government at first because they believed a more temperate approach would bring a greater commitment to relief. However, when the scale of the Famine and the inadequacy of the state's response became clear, they took concerted action, approaching the viceroy and putting forward criticisms of government policy. At the Synod of Thurles in 1850 they released a strongly worded statement which interpreted the Famine as a combination of natural disaster and human negligence:

> We behold our poor not only crushed and overwhelmed by the awful visitation of heaven, but frequently the victims of the most ruthless oppression that ever disgraced the annals of humanity....One of the worst fruits of the false teaching of the age, has been to generate a spirit of contempt, hard-heartedness, and hostility to the poor. The mammon of iniquity, not the Spirit of Christianity.[26]

The Famine had effects which went well beyond the mere statistics of death. It was a trauma from which, in a sense, Ireland has never recovered. Still, some positive consequences came of it. For those who remained behind, conditions remained difficult, but in certain ways improved. Though evictions continued, land hunger was less of an issue, and many farmers found themselves in a more prosperous condition. Another was the spread of Irish people and culture abroad. For those who left Ireland for Britain, America and

Australia, this was a decision born of necessity and entered into reluctantly. As it turned out, many of them found a better life abroad and Irish communities emerged all over the world.

THE IRISH IN AMERICA

The Irish have long been an itinerant people. In the early Middle Ages, Irish monks made their mark on broader Christian consciousness through their monastic foundations in Britain and Europe. After the religious wars of the sixteenth and seventeenth centuries, many Irish Catholics settled in continental Europe, where they played an important role in the armies, universities and churches of the Catholic powers. And throughout history, Irish people have settled in Britain, drawn by greater economic opportunities. But their greatest impact has been on the New World, and religion played an important part in that impact.

The earliest substantial Irish presence in the Americas was in the West Indies. In the seventeenth century some twelve thousand Irish men and women traveled to the Caribbean, most of them as servants. Despite these large numbers, they did not form a distinctive community. The first time that happened was in the eighteenth century, when more than a quarter of a million Irish people settled in North America. They were overwhelmingly Ulster Presbyterians of Scottish origin driven to leave Ireland by famines and crises in the linen industry, and drawn by the promise of economic opportunities and religious tolerance. The main centers of settlement were Pennsylvania and the backcountry South, where Scots-Irish influence may still be heard in the music of the Appalachian Mountain region. One settler wrote home to his minister in County Tyrone of this "bonny country" where "aw that a man works for is his ane, there are ne Ravenus Hunds to rive it from us here....there is ne yen to take awa yer Corn, yer Potatoes."[27] Supporters of colonial grievance, they played a prominent role in the Revolutionary War. George Washington declared, "If I am defeated everywhere else I will make my stand among the Scotch-Irish of my native Virginia."[28] The seventh president of the United States, Andrew Jackson (1767–1845), was the son of a farmer who had led emigrants from Ulster to settle in South Carolina.

In 1760 there were three hundred Presbyterian congregations in the United States, but due to schisms and the enthusiastic Americanism of the Scots-Irish, many became members of the expanding Methodist and Baptist churches. And although integration with other groups resulted in some loss of distinctive identity, they continued to call themselves Scots-Irish so as to set themselves apart from the growing number of Catholic Irish immigrants. This is especially evident in Canada, where Irish immigration—some Catholic but more Protestant—grew to a peak in the 1840s. There the Orange Order (see p.149) grew rapidly, with 154 lodges founded by 1834. By 1900 one-third of English-speaking Canadians were members of a lodge, and the "Glorious Twelfth" was an important celebration.

In the 1820s Catholics were a minority among Irish immigrants, numbering around 100,000. Most were servants, and did not form a distinct group. But from then onward mass migration made Catholics the dominant group among Irish Americans. The Great Famine gave massive impetus to a movement which had already begun. Between 1845 and 1900 almost four million Irish Catholics settled in the United States, the most popular places of settlement being Massachusetts, Connecticut, New York, New Jersey and Pennsylvania. Though in the immediate aftermath of the Famine, most Irish immigrants arrived as families, thereafter young single people, particularly women, came to predominate. The majority came from rural backgrounds, but they tended to settle in urban areas. Just as the Scots-Irish were early pioneers, Irish Catholics were pioneers of the American cities, the first large group there aside from Anglo-Saxon Protestants. They frequently faced hostility from "nativist" groups and learned to form themselves into communities. They banded together in labor unions and in local government, and became an important force in social and political life. The Catholic Church was also very important as a focus for Irish identity.

Some of the Catholic clergy in Ireland were concerned about the impact of the New World on the morals of their emigrant flock. A Patrick Murphy wrote home to his mother in 1885, reassuring her that in his new home, New York, "there are plenty of good Catholic people, and no fear of losing our way, as Father Dwyer said."[29] There was also concern among non-Irish Catholics in the United States that the Irish would have a detrimental effect on their church. In 1840 it was said that "nobody can deny that in external decorum and the ordinary moral and social virtues the Irish Catholics are the most deficient class of our community," and warnings were made of the danger to the church if it became associated with "Irish hoodlumism, drunkenness and poverty."[30] But over time the Irish contributed greatly to the transformation of the Catholic Church in the United States from a poorly organized minority church to one which played an important role in American life. They helped to move the church closer to good relations with the Protestant culture. The Irish also played an important part in creating a Catholic higher education system in the United States. Symbolic landmarks in the history of Irish Catholicism in America were the openings of St. Patrick's Cathedral in New York and the Cathedral of the Holy Cross in Boston. Although the proportion of Irish Americans within the Catholic Church has declined since 1900, they are still great in numbers and continue to dominate the hierarchy.

At home, too, at the same time all the major churches were going through a period of renewal.

RELIGIOUS REVOLUTIONS

Although the eighteenth century had been the age when the Anglican population dominated political and social affairs, they found their church at the close of the century a weak and ineffective organization. In part this was due to the peculiar situation in which the Church of Ireland found itself, as the privileged, established church of the country, but only commanding the adherence of a minority. The church was closely linked to secular authority, with bishops and abbots being nominated by government, and patronage playing a large role. Although in the heartland of Anglicanism churches might be generously endowed and ecclesiastical discipline strict, particularly in Dublin, in other parts of the country priests and bishops governed areas too large for effective administration. Many of the clergy held more than one benefice, causing widespread absenteeism, and the quality of the clergy was often criticized. In 1801 William Stuart, archbishop of Armagh, complained that of the six bishops serving in his province, three were men of tolerable moral character but "inactive and useless," while two were men "of acknowledged bad character." The nineteenth century saw a revitalization in the Church of Ireland which has been termed the "Second Reformation." In the first three decades the authorities made concerted attempts to curb abuses amongst the clergy and engaged in an extensive church-building project. This was followed by a period of sustained, and often controversial, missionary activity.

The pioneers behind the evangelical movement in Ireland were the Methodists. This movement had originated in England in the 1750s with the itinerant preaching of John and Charles Wesley. John Wesley made numerous trips to Ireland, where he traveled throughout the country preaching the Gospel and urging confession of sins, and placing particular emphasis on the importance of personal conversion and salvation by faith. By 1800 there were twenty thousand Methodists in Ireland, mainly concentrated in the Anglican heartland of south and west Ulster. Though the Methodists wished to remain within the established church, Anglican concern over their activities and their ordination of ministers led to a split in 1818. Nevertheless, they continued to grow in number, reaching more than forty thousand in the 1840s. Another influential evangelical group was the Baptists, whose name derives from their conviction that baptism should be undertaken by adults. They originated in England in the 1650s, but had little presence in Ireland until a group of English missionaries established the Baptist Irish Society in 1814. Growth was mainly in Ulster, particularly amongst small farmers and industrial workers, though substantial numbers were also attracted to the church in Dublin. Though neither denomination is as prominent in Ireland as in England, Wales or the United States, both retain substantial numbers to this day.

The nineteenth-century success of the Methodists and Baptists had an impact on the Church of Ireland. Soon popular religious enthusiasm, gospel halls and revivalist meetings became part of the established church. They also had the effect of instilling a new missionary zeal into the Church of Ireland. Many of those converted to the Methodist or Baptist churches were members of other Protestant denominations, but these groups also reached out to the Catholic population. In 1799 Methodists dispatched Irish-speaking missionaries to work amongst the Catholic population. Their efforts acted as a catalyst to a similar mission within the established church, and the 1820s saw a sustained attempt to convert Catholics. The Hibernian Bible Society, the Scripture Readers' Society and similar groups trained and supported itinerant preachers, some of whom were fluent Irish speakers. Their work in preaching and in distributing Bibles in Irish was often accompanied by what appeared to some as inducements, for example the provision of free elementary education. Most controversial were their efforts during the Famine. In 1849 Alexander Dallas founded the Society for Irish

Church Missions to Roman Catholics; by 1854 he had set up 125 mission stations across the country. Numerous complaints from the Catholic bishops, amongst others, were raised that evangelists were luring Catholics toward conversion with food, clothing and other material benefits. Catholics accused converts of "taking the soup." The Quaker Alfred Webb noted in his diary:

> A network of well-intentioned Protestant associations spread over the poorer parts of the country, which in return for soup and other help endeavoured to father the people into their churches and schools, really believing that masses of our people wished to abandon Catholicism.... The movement left seeds of bitterness.[31]

The Presbyterian Church did not face the same problems. The self-governing nature of the congregations meant that neglect or abuse of authority was firmly dealt with. The Presbyterian Church did, however, suffer from theological schism. Already in 1726 some ministers had seceded from the church and in the second decade of the nineteenth century there were serious divisions between the "Old Light" orthodox group and the "New Light" advocates of a looser doctrine. The growth of evangelicism helped to boost the orthodox faction, while the New Light group was becoming more open in its challenges. Henry Cooke (1788–1868), a minister in County Down, launched an attack on unorthodox teaching in the Belfast Academical Institute, the main body for training ministers, and in 1828 succeeded in getting the synod to introduce regulations providing for formal scrutiny of the beliefs of all prospective ministers. The New Light group withdrew to form the Non-subscribing Presbyterian Association. Cooke's victory left much bitterness and contributed to Presbyterians moving ever further away from the liberal political stance which some had taken in the previous century. Nevertheless, despite the schism, there was also growth within the church. A temperance movement had great success, and by the end of the century a large proportion of the ministry were total abstainers. In the middle decades of the century Presbyterians were central to missionary activity to Britain's African colonies. In 1859 a great religious revival spread from America to Ulster, stimulating huge public meetings and mass conversions.

Protestant evangelicalism had the effect of forcing a revitalization of the Catholic Church. The central figure in the "devotional revolution" of the nineteenth century was Cardinal Paul Cullen. Born in 1803 to a prosperous farming family, Cullen spent his formative years in Rome, first as a student and then as rector of the Irish College there. He was fascinated by the ecclesiastical triumphalism he found in Rome, and by the intellectual excitement of the times, when ideas of papal absolutism were developing. This movement, ultramontanism ("beyond the mountains," referring to Italy's position beyond the Alps) which culminated in the declaration of papal infallibility in 1870, found in Cullen one of its greatest advocates. He vigorously opposed gallicanism—the French nationalist movement which argued that churches should be free to manage their own affairs with little interference from Rome—and also liberalism and revolutionary movements, which he saw as a threat to the papacy. In 1849 Cullen was appointed archbishop of Armagh and the following year returned to Ireland after twenty-one years at the papal see. In 1852 he became archbishop of Dublin and later, in 1866, Ireland's first cardinal. His immediate move as archbishop of Armagh was to hold a full canonical synod at Thurles in 1850, the first of its kind in Ireland since the sixteenth century. All the Catholic bishops of Ireland attended, and their resolutions were submitted to Rome for ratification. The synod introduced a comprehensive code of church law and initiated reforms in baptism, confession and marriage. Greater uniformity of observance was imposed and links with Rome were bolstered. Cullen also began to make new appointments to the church by which he shaped it in his own image.

At the start of the nineteenth century, the majority of the people were Catholics; by the second half of the century they were truly practicing Catholics. This transformation has been termed a "devotional revolution."[32] Attendance at Mass became almost universal, the sacraments became a more regular feature of religious practice, and such devotional practices as benedictions, stations of the cross and processions became more common. The shifting focus of religious practice from the home to the church was facilitated by a programme of church building. The clergy became better educated and more disciplined, increasingly set apart from the laity by their dress and manners.

This was also a time when the religious orders, in particular nuns and the Christian Brothers, increased in number and played an ever more important role in their communities, especially in relation to education. A state system of education had been established in 1831, and although it was meant to be nondenominational, the churches soon took on a crucial role as teachers and patrons. The government attempted to provide third-level education for Catholics—excluded from Trinity College—in the form of the nondenominational Queen's Colleges of Belfast, Galway and Cork, but they were condemned by Cullen and others as "godless," and vigorously resisted. In 1854 the English theologian John Henry Newman (1801–90) established a Catholic university in Dublin, two years after the publication of his plea on behalf of liberal education, *The Idea of a University*. Although it foundered due to lack of state funds, it was later revived in the form of the National University of Ireland.

THE CHURCHES AND POLITICS

Since the sixteenth century politics and religion in Ireland had been closely bound up together. While Catholics and Protestants tended to side with "their own kind," there had always been attempts by some to go against this way of thinking, most notably by the United Irishmen. Nor did everyone fit neatly into this pattern of matching political and confessional identities. The threatened French landing in 1796 (see p. 149) had prompted the formation of a local Catholic militia in Cork to resist any invasion; the most hated figures in Famine times were not the landlords but the gombeens, Catholic middlemen who collected the rent. Although many Protestants were involved in the emancipation and Home Rule movements, many Catholics were happy to acquiesce in the status quo; and, in addition, there had generally been friendly relations between the church authorities and much cooperation between Catholics and Protestants at a local level on a day-to-day basis.

But in the decades after the Famine, polarization became starker. The rise of ultramontanism in the Catholic Church and evangelicalism in the Protestant Churches led to a more militant stance by each. Furthermore, the expectations of Catholics had risen over the decades, and their numbers had been successfully mobilized to the concern of the Protestant population. Additionally, the psychological trauma of the Famine had caused many to be more resentful and mistrustful of others and to stick to their own.

Many Catholic advocates had argued that emancipation and repeal were ambitions which would benefit all. O'Connell had said that he did not wish to create a Catholic ascendancy. Such protestations notwithstanding, the movements seemed to be clerically dominated, exclusive of Protestants and damaging to their interests. Nor was this situation helped by the increasingly combative stance taken by the Catholic hierarchy, illustrated by Cullen's boast that he had never dined with a Protestant. The 1850 Synod of Thurles expressed disapproval of interdenominational marriages, and the church authorities remained adamant in their opposition to the establishment of a nondenominational university. Papal militancy also played a part, with the proclamation of papal infallibility proving especially objectionable to members of other churches.

In Catholic eyes, the Church of Ireland was a symbol of privilege, unrepresentative of the people of Ireland. James Doyle, the Catholic bishop of Kildare and Leighlin, claimed it would not survive a day without state support. Members of the Church of Ireland, however, as the threat of disestablishment loomed, came to the defense of their church and its position in Irish life. Archbishop Beresford of Armagh declared that:

> ...a church that embraces so large a proportion of the educated classes, which numbers among its members the inheritors of the great historic names of the country, a majority of the learned professions, and the mercantile classes, and which has implanted the principles of industry, order and loyalty for which the Protestant population is so remarkable, cannot be said to have failed in its mission.[33]

Similarly, the dean of Cork claimed that the Church of Ireland could truly be considered a national Church because "it asserts the idea of a free national life against the anti-national despotism of the papacy." The problem, as they saw it, was that they were "hemmed in, by two opposite descriptions of professing Christians—the one, possessing a church, without what we can call a religion; and the other, a religion, without what we can call a church."[34] Not only did Anglicans see their church as being increasingly under siege, but also their way of life came under threat as the post-Famine years saw the progressive dismantling of their economic, social and political privileges.

If many southern Anglicans remained dismissive of Presbyterians, the Protestants of Ulster were increasingly making common cause. The political radicalism which had featured so prominently in the United Irishmen movement did not disappear entirely from Ulster Presbyterianism, but the success of Henry Cooke and the changing political scene caused more Presbyterians to see themselves as part of an embattled minority throughout the whole island. In 1834 Cooke was the principal speaker at a rally at Hillsborough aimed at uniting Protestants against nationalism. He also led a rally to celebrate the "repulse" of O'Connell from Belfast in 1841. An important factor in the change of attitude was the emergence of Belfast as a prosperous industrial city. In the words of Henry Cooke: "Look at Belfast and be a repealer, if you can."

The attitude of the Catholic hierarchy toward political involvement changed after the Famine, partly because of changes within the church and partly due to changes in the nature of politics. Cardinal Cullen was a nationalist who had no qualms about the clergy taking a political role in such controversies as education. Even so, in most cases he was keen to withdraw the clergy from the role of political agitators. Cullen's views were rooted in his ultramontanism. Ultramontanists had for some time criticized gallican-minded clergy for being too close to state authorities, rather than taking their line from Rome, but now in Ireland there appeared another rival for the Vatican's attentions in the form of the nationalist movement.

Cullen's greatest opponent was John MacHale, Archbishop of Tuam. Born in County Mayo in 1791, a native Irish speaker, educated at a "hedge school," MacHale was a relentless critic of the political establishment and a fervent nationalist. To Cullen, MacHale was attempting to subordinate religion to the cause of nationalism. The growing reluctance of the Catholic hierarchy to become involved in politics may also have been connected to their rising status in society. As one nationalist put it, quoting the seventeenth-century scholar Father Luke Wadding: "Time was when we had wooden chalices and golden priests but now we have golden chalices and wooden priests."[35] The ties that had bound them to local communities had weakened and it was the priests on a local level who tended to take a greater part in politics.

The state of politics at the time also put the Catholic Church hierarchy in a difficult position. Whereas the pre-Famine era was a time of constitutionalism and peaceful protest, the 1840s saw an upsurge in violence which developed over the following two decades. The *Young Ireland* movement emerged from the ruins of the repeal campaign. Its followers were interested in fostering a sense of Irish identity and history through their journal *The Nation*; they looked not to the aims and methods of O'Connell but to Tone and Emmet. This meant approval of physical force, but their planned insurrection in 1848 failed miserably, ending as a scuffle in a cabbage patch belonging to a certain Widow McCormack of Tipperary.

After the failure of this rising, many of its leaders fled overseas to join others who had emigrated due to the Famine. In the United States in 1858 the *Irish Republican Brotherhood* (IRB), better known as the *Fenians*, was founded. It was a secret oath-bound military society which sought the complete separation of Ireland from England by force, and it quickly gained a large membership in the United States as well as in Ireland. By 1864 it is estimated that 54,000 people had taken the oath, ranging across all social classes. Of course, its expansion compromised its secrecy, and an insurrection in 1867 was foiled by informers. In the same year three Fenians were executed for the murder of a constable in Manchester, England, and their names were added to the growing roll call of martyrs to the republican cause.

The Catholic Church had always opposed secret societies, considering them occultist, unholy and subversive. In the mid-nineteenth century there was added a fear of liberalism, socialism and revolutionary movements. The Fenians were condemned on all of these grounds, but also because the church saw their aims as hopeless and destructive both to individual life and to the country. Bishop

Moriarty of Kerry's denunciation of them has become famous: "God's heaviest curse, his withering, blasting, blighting curse upon them…eternity is not long enough, nor hell hot enough for them."[36]

Fenians were refused absolution in the confessional and priests who spoke out in favor of them were disciplined. When the Fenian Terence Bellew McManus died in the United States in 1861, Cullen refused to allow his burial in Dublin's Pro-cathedral. Nevertheless, eight thousand mourners marched at McManus's funeral and, despite the bishops' condemnation of commemorative Masses for Fenians, clergy were found to conduct them. Some Catholics clearly believed that duty to the nation took precedence over obedience to the strictures of the bishops; others simply believed that priests should keep out of politics. Charles Kickham, a senior Fenian but also a devout Catholic, wrote: "We never uttered a word against the priests as ministers of religion. But we challenged and do challenge their right to dictate to the people in politics."

The Young Ireland and Fenian movements were in part a response to the failure of constitutional politics. The Conservative government had faced down O'Connell over repeal and his successors had not had any success in attracting the support of British governments. This changed with the election of a Liberal government under William Gladstone. As early as 1845 Gladstone had said that Ireland's unhappy condition was the result of "cruel, inveterate, and half-atoned injustice" and, on his appointment as prime minister in 1868, he declared that his mission was to "pacify Ireland." Though a devout Anglican, one of the first steps he took was to disestablish the Church of England in 1869—that is, to remove its position in law as the official Church of the land, financed by taxation. This was, understandably, much resented by Anglicans and was opposed by the Conservative leader Disraeli. However, although some of its endowments were removed, the Church of Ireland remained in possession of extensive estates, had the continued support of the wealthy land-holding classes and was not supplanted by any other church. To an extent, the disestablishment of the Church of Ireland could be seen as a revitalizing factor: its constitution was revised, the evangelical spirit was fostered, and the role of the lay within it increased. However, this was one step on the way to the dismantling of Protestant privileges. Others were the Ballot Act of 1872, which provided for secret ballots, and the Representation of the People Act of 1884, which gave the vote to all adult males, irrespective of property. Half of the landowners in the country were Anglicans, and they tended to have the largest and richest holdings. They also retained a great degree of influence in government, but that was increasingly under threat. The two main issues which proved a battle of strength were repeal of the union, or "Home Rule," and land reform.

In 1870 the *Home Rule Association* was founded by Isaac Butt, the son of a Church of Ireland clergyman, who had been deeply affected by the Famine and politicized by his work representing Fenian prisoners. His party gained sixty seats in the general election of 1874, but found that it was insufficient to influence parliament to put Home Rule on the agenda. The Irish MPs responded by obstructionism; blocking the business of parliament by using the rules of the house, for example, by speaking all night to keep a bill from being dealt with.

One of the principal obstructionists, Charles Stewart Parnell, succeeded Butt as leader of the party in 1879. A Protestant from County Wicklow, Parnell's great achievement was in bringing together the disparate forces of nationalism: constitutionalism in the form of the Home Rule party, physical force in the form of the Fenians and rural agitation in the form of the Land League. In 1873 the Fenians had amended their constitution to say that the movement would "confine itself in time of peace to the exercise of moral force" and that "the IRB [the Fenians] shall await the decision of the Irish people, as expressed by a majority of the Irish people, as to the fit hour of inaugurating a war against England," in the meantime lending "support to every movement calculated to advance the cause of Irish independence."[37] Knowing that without the United States on his side he would never succeed, Parnell sailed there in 1879 and persuaded the Fenians to give his party financial support. His next step was to form an alliance with the land movement. In the aftermath of the Famine, tenants continued to live in miserable conditions, and landlords, themselves facing bankruptcy, continued to evict. The late 1870s saw the beginning of a great agricultural depression, accompanied by agrarian violence. The Land League, under the leadership of Michael Davitt (1846–1905), who had himself experienced eviction as a child, organized rent strikes and other forms of direct action. One such tactic was "boycotting," named after Captain Boycott of County Mayo, a particularly notorious target. In 1879 the *Irish National Land League* was founded, and Davitt asked Parnell to become its leader. This union of different nationalist forces was dubbed "The New Departure."

In 1881 Gladstone's Land Act strengthened tenants' rights and set up land courts to fix rents. However, the Home Rule Bill of 1886 was defeated by Conservatives in the House of Lords. Parnell and the Liberals were determined to try again, but in December 1889 a bombshell landed. Captain William O'Shea, a former supporter of Parnell, filed a petition for divorce from his wife Katherine, citing her adulterous relationship with Parnell. They had been living together for some time, but this was not known to the majority of Parnell's supporters. The initial push to remove Parnell came not from the Catholic Church, as is often believed, but from English Nonconformist Protestants within Gladstone's party. But when support began to slip away from Parnell, the church hierarchy joined in his condemnation, calling on the people of Ireland to repudiate him. Parnell refused to step down and traveled the country to whip up support, but the party split, with only one-third of

MPs siding with Parnell. He died in 1891 at the age of forty-five, a broken man politically, but at last married to his beloved Katherine.

The fall of Parnell shocked Ireland and split the nationalist population. It was also an event which endured in the memory of all those who witnessed it. James Joyce, in his *Portrait of the Artist as a Young Man,* describes Stephen Dedalus's memory of his aunt's two hairbrushes, one featuring a picture of Michael Davitt, the other Parnell, and how one day she returned home and smashed the image of Parnell. The other great Irish modernist, W. B. Yeats, wrote his poem "Come Gather Round Me, Parnellites" in 1936, a time when church authority was again flexing its muscles in the political arena:

> The Bishops and the Party
> That tragic story made,
> A husband that had sold his wife
> And after that betrayed;
> But stories that live longest
> Are sung above the glass,
> And Parnell loved his country,
> And Parnell loved his lass.[38]

Huguenot Cemetery, St. Stephen's Green, Dublin

THE UNION AND
THE NATION

The formal division of the island of Ireland came about in the 1920s, but its integrity had been crumbling for some time. In the latter decades of the nineteenth century, the union with the United Kingdom came under unbearable strain. Catholic ambitions grew from devolved government to outright separation, while the Protestants of Ulster stood firm to resist change. The rise of Irish nationalism on the one hand and Ulster unionism on the other culminated in the revolution of 1916–21, which ushered in two new political entities: one overwhelmingly Catholic in its orientation, the other dominated by Protestant interests. But as the century progressed, both states began to come under strain from within and without, leading to a crisis of identity in the south and war in the north.

ULSTER UNIONISM

Parnell's *Irish Parliamentary Party* claimed to speak for the Irish people, but in reality they spoke mainly for the Catholics of Ireland.

191

It was the Catholic population who were likely to benefit from reform of the landlord system, and Catholics who would form the majority within any Home Rule parliament. Although some Protestants were prominent in the nationalist movement, it was dominated by the interests of Catholic tenant classes and the urban middle class. The Anglicans of Munster, Leinster and Connacht watched their political influence wane in the latter decades of the nineteenth century with something akin to resignation. They tended to support Conservative candidates sympathetic to their land interests and the integrity of the Union, but their response was not a militant or radical one.

It was a different story in Ulster. There Protestants were not an embattled minority but a majority, at least in the four northeasterly counties of Antrim, Armagh, Down and Londonderry, and there the Protestant political tradition encompassed not only Anglican constitutional politics, but also Presbyterian radicalism. They had shown themselves prepared to fight for their livelihoods and identity over the years, and the nineteenth century brought economic, political and religious developments which reinforced Ulster Protestants in their identity. Ulster, alone of the four Irish provinces, had reaped the benefits of the industrial revolution. This was particularly marked in Belfast, where linen and ship-building industries had produced a boom in the economy and in the population. In 1841 Belfast's population had been one-third of that of Dublin; fifty years later it had edged ahead at over a quarter of a million. This economic success depended to a great extent on trade with Britain; therefore, fear of the severance of that link and of the introduction of protectionist policies by a Dublin government sharpened opposition to Home Rule.

Sectarianism had long been a part of the Ulster landscape, and in the nineteenth century it continued to prosper. Rural clashes persisted, notably at Dolly's Brae (County Down) in 1849, where at least thirty Catholics were killed when they attacked an Orange parade. But during this period such clashes also spread to urban areas, as Catholics and Protestants flocked from the countryside to the factories and shipyards of Belfast. The first recorded sectarian affray in Belfast was on July 12, 1813, and others followed in 1832, 1835, 1843 and 1852. In 1857 a sectarian riot in Belfast, sparked by street preaching, lasted for ten days, with serious loss of life; and in 1864 a nationalist demonstration provoked two weeks of rioting and left eleven people dead. Sectarian clashes were also noted in other urban centers during the summer's "marching season." Although these violent encounters tended to take place within the poorer social groups, sectarianism was also rife amongst the better-off. The growth of ultramontane Catholicism and the increasing political militancy of the Catholic population throughout Ireland intensified the fear, common amongst Protestants, that Home Rule meant "Rome Rule."

As nationalism became more militant, so too did unionism, particularly in Ulster. Again and again speakers called on their representatives to defend the Protestant religion and way of life against the perceived threat from Catholics. On July 12, 1867, the unionist politician William Johnston addressed ten thousand Orangemen at an open-air meeting at Bangor. Speaking in their name to their MPs, he said: "Gentlemen, we have put you into Parliament by Orange votes, and by Orange votes we will keep you there; but you must support Orange and Protestant principles."[1] If these principles were abandoned, it was argued, their bonds of loyalty could legitimately be thrown off. In the wake of the disestablishment of the Church of England, the Reverend John Flanagan, rector of Killeevan in the diocese of Clogher, addressed an Orange meeting in these terms:

> Protestant loyalty must make itself understood. People will say, "Oh, your loyalty is conditional." I say it is conditional, and must be explained as such....It appears wonderful that

there is one thing upon which we can confidently throw ourselves which has been overlooked by all the speakers— I mean the Queen's coronation oath. She should be reminded that one of her ancestors who swore to maintain the Protestant religion forgot his oath, and his crown was kicked into the Boyne. We must speak out boldly, and tell our gracious Queen that, if she breaks her oath, she has no longer any claim to the crown.[2]

The general election of November 1885 is rightly seen as a triumph for Parnell's party, but it was also a triumph for unionism in Ulster, with many Orangemen winning seats. In its aftermath the Orange Order set up a separate political party, the *Unionist Party*. This was not initially an Ulster party; their objective was the maintenance of all Ireland within the Union. But the introduction of the Home Rule Bill of 1886 began to make the issue of Ulster more pressing.

Ulster's resistance to Home Rule was galvanized by the decision of many in the Conservative Party to "play the Orange card." The phrase "Ulster will fight, and Ulster will be right" was coined by Randolph Churchill, a Conservative MP who organized large-scale demonstrations all over the province in 1886 and also addressed audiences in Britain. At a meeting in London he stated his case for the defense of Protestant rights:

England cannot leave the Protestants of Ireland in the lurch. England is bound to the Protestants of Ireland; you, as Englishmen, are bound to the Protestants of Ireland by every conceivable tie. The Protestants of Ireland on an occasion such as this, and in a national crisis such as this, are the only nation which is known to the English people in Ireland. On four successive occasions they have conquered Ireland practically at the request of England.

During 680 years [sic] the Protestants of Ireland have held Ireland mainly for the benefit of England. They have developed the resources of Ireland by their capital and their industry under the protection and guarantee of England. They are one with England, one with the English people, one with you in race and religion. They are essentially like the English people, a dominant and imperial caste.[3]

There was a strong religious element to the opposition to Home Rule. The Ulster Loyalist Anti-Repeal Union, founded in 1886, made all Protestant clergymen honorary members, just as O'Connell's associations had done with Catholic priests. The same year the Presbyterian General Assembly carried the resolution that Home Rule would:

> …in our judgment, lead to the ascendancy of one class and creed in matters pertaining to religion, education and civil administration. We do not believe that any guarantees, moral or material, could be devised which would safeguard the rights and privileges of minorities scattered throughout Ireland against encroachment of a majority vested with legislative and executive functions.[4]

Sometimes political and religious identity was explicitly linked to history. A pamphlet for a successful parliamentary candidate in the 1886 election carried the question:

> Q. Have the Irish ever had Home Rule and how did they behave?
> A. They murdered every Englishman and Protestant they could lay their hands on in 1641.
>
> They were set on by the priests, who said that the killing of them was a meretricious act. Altogether they

killed in that year 150,000 Protestants—men, women and children.[5]

At other times it was linked to economics. The Reverend R. M. Edgar of Dublin wrote in 1886: "Ulster, least favoured of the provinces by nature, has become the leading province, mainly through Presbyterian industry and energy."[6]

The introduction of the first Home Rule Bill in 1886 was met by serious rioting in Belfast from June to December, leaving at least thirty-two people dead. Orangemen began to drill with wooden guns. William Johnston declared: "We are prepared to take the Bible in one hand and the sword in the other....We will defend the Protestant religion and our liberties won at the Boyne with rifles in our hands."[7] The year 1886 had marked a turning point in the history of Ulster. Now it was clear that the Protestants of Ulster could, and would, fight. The introduction of a second Home Rule Bill in 1893 was not taken quite as seriously, even though the Anglican Archbishop Knox of Armagh called it "a Bill to suppress the Protestant faith." Its defeat was followed by a period of Conservative rule with which the Protestants of Ulster felt more comfortable.

Although during the two decades after the fall of Parnell the immediate threat of Home Rule receded, it was not removed. During this period Ulster unionism came to be reinforced by the decline in influence of Protestants in the southern provinces. The Conservative policy of "Constructive Unionism"—sometimes derisively called "Killing Home Rule by Kindness"—involved a large-scale transfer of land mainly from Protestant landlords to predominantly Catholic tenants. This was achieved by advancing millions of pounds in government loans to tenant farmers and compensation to landlords. Through this policy, Ireland was turned into a land of owner-occupiers. This transfer of land also marked the death knell for the Anglican land-holding classes and a consequent decline in Church of Ireland numbers, at least outside Ulster. The increasingly isolated minority that remained became, if not entirely reconciled to a loosening of ties with Britain, at least more resigned to it than their coreligionists in the North. They sought to influence a possible settlement and were not prepared to stake all in an attempt to block change.

In 1905 the Liberals were back in government in London. Five years later they were again returned, but with a reduced majority. The Irish Parliamentary Party, now led by John Redmond, held the balance of power, and in turn for their support the Liberal leader, Herbert Asquith, introduced a third Home Rule Bill. Twice, in 1886 and again in 1893, Home Rule had been voted down by the House of Lords, but now, under the Parliament Act of 1911, the Lords only had the power to delay legislation. By this point, the differences amongst Ulster Protestants appeared less important than what united them. Two-thirds of their adult males were members of the Orange Order and they had made it clear that they would not stand idly by. The Unionist party elected a Dublin-born barrister, Edward Carson, as leader. He was joined by James Craig, a Belfast-born grandee who organized mass meetings throughout Ulster. In September 1911 Carson told the crowds: "We must be prepared the morning Home Rule passes, ourselves to become responsible for the government of the Protestant Province of Ulster." A year later the vast majority of Protestant adults signed up to a Solemn League and Covenant, first submitted for approval to Protestant clergymen. It read:

> Being convinced in our consciences that Home Rule would be disastrous to the material well-being of Ulster as well as of the whole of Ireland, subversive of our civil and religious freedom, destructive of our citizenship and perilous to the unity of the Empire, we, whose names are underwritten, men of Ulster, loyal subjects of His Gracious

Majesty King George V, humbly relying on the God whom our fathers in days of stress and trial confidently trusted, do hereby pledge ourselves in solemn Covenant throughout this our time of threatened calamity to stand by one another in defending for ourselves and our children our cherished position of equal citizenship in the United Kingdom and in using all means which may be found necessary to defeat the present conspiracy to set up a Home Rule Parliament in Ireland.[8]

Already Orange Lodges had begun to drill in preparation for war, and early in 1913 Carson united these units into the *Ulster Volunteer Force*. They rapidly grew in numbers and successfully imported arms from Germany and Austria. Early in 1914 British troops based at the Curragh in Kildare declared that they would disobey any order to subdue the Protestants of Ulster. In response to such pressure, the Home Rule Bill was amended to allow for the exclusion of some, or all, of the counties of Ulster from Dublin rule. But that summer, while debates and negotiations were continuing as to whether such a partition of the island was to be permanent or temporary and what area it would encompass, war with Germany broke out. The implementation of Home Rule was suspended until the end of the war, and both unionists and nationalists set off for the fields of Flanders. Soon war was also in the air at home.

IRISH NATIONALISM

Unionism in Ulster emerged, if not as a religious movement, at least as one deeply imbedded in Protestant faith, history and culture. Irish nationalism and Irish Catholicism had a somewhat more troubled relationship. While they often went hand-in-hand, sometimes a stark choice had to be made between church and nation.

But the movement which culminated in the 1916 rising and the subsequent war of independence, though not coordinated by the Catholic Church and often at variance with its ideology, was suffused with Catholic history and imagery. When the nation emerged triumphant, the door was open for the Catholic Church to take on a leading role.

The Irish Parliamentary Party was the official face of nationalism, but Irish nationalism had by this time taken on many forms. Cultural movements, labor activism, economic protectionism and physical force all played their role in bringing about Irish independence. In the second decade of the twentieth century these movements came together to give birth to revolution—what W. B. Yeats called "a terrible beauty." The nationalist movement was also fostered by the mobilization of the Ulster unionists and the crisis of war in Europe. Personalities such as Douglas Hyde, James Connolly, Arthur Griffith and Patrick Pearse, to name but a few, gave it shape.

From the late nineteenth century onward, many Irish people began to take a greater interest in their past and, in particular, their Gaelic heritage. The *Gaelic League* was founded for the promotion of the Irish language and the *Gaelic Athletic Association* for the "preservation and cultivation of national pastimes." At the same time poets and dramatists such as W. B. Yeats, Lady Gregory and J. M. Synge took an interest in the literature of Ireland's Celtic past. Another movement which developed during this period was *Sinn Féin,* founded in 1907 by the Dubliner Arthur Griffith. Meaning "ourselves," this organization advocated self-sufficiency, protectionism and the setting up of Irish alternatives to such British institutions as parliament and the civil service. These were nonsectarian organizations. Douglas Hyde, the founder of the Gaelic League, was the son of a Church of Ireland rector, and the Irish literary revival had a distinctly Anglo-Irish character. Still, their existence helped to identify the Irish experience increasingly with the Celtic and, by extension, Catholic experiences. They also provided a fertile environment for the development of political movements, including physical-force nationalism.

For many, however, questions of nation were less pressing than those of survival. Since the eighteenth century Dublin had declined as a political and economic center, and many of the great Georgian buildings had fallen into slums. Families lived in cramped conditions and in poverty, their breadwinners being unemployed or living on meager wages. In response to these appalling conditions, Ireland's first labor movement emerged. Church authorities had always been quick to condemn socialist movements abroad and they were alarmed to see them appear at home. The socialist leader James Connolly hit back:

> Is not this attitude symbolic of the attitude of the Church for hundreds of years? Ever counselling humility, but sitting in the seats of the mighty; ever patching up the diseased and broken wrecks of an unjust social system, but blessing the system which made the wrecks and spread the disease; ever running divine discontent and pity into the ground as the lightning rod runs and dissipates lightning, instead of gathering it and directing it for social righteousness as the electric battery generates and directs electricity for social use.[9]

However, Connolly did not see socialism and religion as incompatible:

> It is not Socialism but capitalism that is opposed to religion; capitalism is social cannibalism, the devouring of man by man, and under capitalism those who have the most of the pious attributes which are required for a truly deeply religious nature are the greatest failures and the heaviest sufferers.
>
> Religion, I hope, is not bound up with a system founded on buying human labour in the cheapest market,

and selling its product in the dearest; when the organised Socialist working-class tramples upon the capitalist class it will not be trampling upon a pillar of God's Church but upon a blasphemous defiler of the Sanctuary, it will be rescuing the Faith from the impious vermin who have made it noisome to the really religious men and women.[10]

Connolly also saw labor and nationalism as intertwined: "The cause of labour is the cause of Ireland: the cause of Ireland is the cause of labour. They cannot be dissevered." Though its significance later came to be played down, it was this labor movement which proved one of the foundations of insurrection. A massive lockout and strike in Dublin in 1913 led to the formation of the *Irish Citizen Army*, a militia intended to defend workers from attack by the police. At the same time, in response to the formation of the *Ulster Volunteer Force*, southern nationalists set up the Irish Volunteers, which, despite its motto "Defense, not defiance," contained a strong Fenian element. The catalyst for insurrection was the outbreak of war in Europe. In an effort to express loyalty to Crown and country, thousands of Protestant Ulstermen volunteered for the war effort, but so did thousands of Catholic nationalists. Some, however, saw this as an ideal time to launch an offensive against British authority. The IRB made plans for the Easter weekend of 1916 and the Citizen Army gave its support.

The leader of the rising was Patrick Pearse (1879–1916), a schoolteacher who had made his way toward nationalism via the cultural revival. As a young man he had become involved in the Gaelic League, and in 1908 he set up Ireland's first bilingual (Gaelic-English) school, St. Enda's. Though he initially favored constitutional nationalism, he was prompted by the mobilization of unionism to help set up the Irish Volunteers and to join the IRB. A prolific poet and essayist, Pearse's writings provide the best example of the union of Catholic imagery and Irish patriotism. This

Patrick Pearse

union was not something new. Although the stance of Tone and others against sectarianism and the standoff between the Fenians and the Catholic Church might have suggested that these forces were opposed, Irish nationalism, perhaps more than most other forms of nationalism, tended to link the two. The Fenian movement continually used Christian imagery of rebirth. The Fenian Peter O'Neill Crowley's deathbed words were: "Father, I have two loves in my heart—one for my religion, the other for my country. I am dying today for fatherland. I could die as cheerfully for the faith."[11] And a priest said of the Fenian Jeremiah O'Donovan Rossa that, while he was a criminal in the eyes of the British government, "his crimes were the title deeds of sainthood in Ireland's patriotic litany."[12] Pearse explicitly linked religion and nation. He wrote:

> Like a divine religion, national freedom bears all the marks of unity, of sanctity, of catholicity, of apostolic succession. Of unity, for it contemplates the nation as one; of sanctity, for it is holy in itself and in those who serve it; of catholicity, for it embraces all the men and women of the nation; of apostolic succession, for it, or the aspiration after it, passes down from generation to generation from the nation's fathers.[13]

That God spoke to Ireland through Tone and through those who, after Tone, have taken up his testimony, that Tone's teaching and theirs is true and great and that no other teaching as to Ireland has any truth or worthiness at

all, is a thing upon which I stake all my mortal and immortal hopes. And I ask the men and women of my generation
to stake their mortal and all my immortal hopes with me.[14]

In particular, Pearse developed the idea of a Republican martyrol-
ogy, most explicitly in his poem "Oath":

In the name of God
By Christ His only Son,
By Mary His gentle Mother,
By Patrick the Apostle of the Irish,
By the loyalty of Colm Cille,
By the glory of our race,
By the blood of our ancestors,
By the murder of Red Hugh,
By the sad death of Owen Roe,
By the dying wish of Sarsfield,
By the anguished sigh of Fitzgerald,
By the bloody wounds of Tone,
By the noble blood of Emmet,
By the Famine corpses,
By the tears of Irish exiles,
We swear the oaths our ancestors swore,
That we will free our race from bondage,
Or that we will fall fighting hand to hand
Amen[15]

In his most famous speech, at the funeral of O'Donovan Rossa in
August 1915, he declared: "The fools, the fools, the fools—they
have left us our Fenian dead, and while Ireland holds these graves,
Ireland unfree shall never be at peace."

In Pearse's view, the national goal could only be achieved by
sacrifice in blood. He wrote of bloodshed as a positive, redemptive

force. While others were alarmed at the militarization of the Orangemen, he wrote:

> We must accustom ourselves to the thought of arms, to the sight of arms, to the use of arms. We may make mistakes in the beginning and shoot the wrong people; but bloodshed is a cleansing and a sanctifying thing, and the nation which regards it as the final horror has lost its manhood. There are many things more horrible than bloodshed; and slavery is one of them.[16]

Referring to "a new regeneration and cleansing," he wrote: "…with what joyousness and strength should we set our faces towards the path that lies before us, bringing with us fresh life from the place of death, a new resurrection of patriotic grace in our souls!"[17] It was no coincidence, then, that the sacrifice and resurrection were set for Easter weekend.

From the beginning, the Rising looked set to fail. Arms shipments from Germany were intercepted and plans to mobilize the Irish Volunteers were cancelled, but the IRB went ahead nonetheless. On Easter Monday they struck, capturing strategic buildings throughout Dublin, and made their headquarters the general Post Office on Sackville (now O'Connell) Street. There, before bemused passersby, Pearse read out the Proclamation of the Republic, beginning with the words: "Irishmen and Irishwomen: In the name of God and of the dead generations from which she receives her old tradition of nationhood, Ireland, through us, summons her children to her flag and strikes for her freedom." Though the government was taken by surprise, the rebellion in Dublin was not matched throughout the country. The British army soon mustered and, although fighting continued for almost a week, the rebels' surrender was inevitable. Comprehensively defeated, lacking public support and treated with widespread derision, the Rising had proved a disaster.

Within weeks, however, this situation had been turned around, largely thanks to inept management by the government. The leaders of the Rising were hastily tried in secret and executed in Kilmainham Prison, thereby immediately joining the ranks of republican martyrs and arousing public sympathy. The internment of hundreds of suspects encouraged this sense of injustice. Though the reaction of the Catholic Church to the Rising was initially muted, in the following years church leaders began to voice greater sympathy for the rebels' cause. When the government attempted to introduce conscription to the Great War in 1918, the Catholic hierarchy took an active part in its resistance.

The great political beneficiaries of the Rising were Sinn Féin. Though they had played only a minor role in the insurrection, and few had heard of them beforehand, newspapers and politicians identified them as the prime movers and on the back of this attribution they came to replace the Irish Parliamentary Party as the main nationalist voice. In the general election of December 1918, Sinn Féin won seventy-three seats to the unionists' twenty-six and the Irish Parliamentary Party's mere six. On January 21, 1919, rejecting the legitimacy of the Union, Sinn Féin met at the Mansion House in Dublin as Dáil Éireann ("the Parliament of Ireland") and declared the establishment of a sovereign Irish Republic. On the same day the Irish Volunteers shot two policemen dead at Soloheadbeg, County Tipperary, marking the outbreak of a war which was to last for over two years.

The War of Independence, or the Anglo-Irish War (1919–21), was a dirty, low-level conflict, involving a series of guerrilla attacks and reprisals, with atrocities committed on both sides. The *Irish Republican Army* (IRA), the new military wing of Dáil Éireann, led by the capable general Michael Collins (1890–1922), set about attacking members of the Crown forces and making the country ungovernable. They were matched by newly demobbed soldiers from the Western Front, the "Black and Tans" and the Auxiliaries, who took retribution ruthlessly. The most notorious episode was "Bloody Sunday," November 21, 1920, when the shooting of eleven British intelligence officers was answered by the killing of three prisoners in Dublin Castle, and the shooting dead by the Black and Tans of fourteen players and supporters at a Gaelic football match.

The events of these years met with panic amongst unionists. Not only Home Rule, but total separation from Britain now seemed a possibility and, with it, the threat of Catholic domination. Constitutional means had been exchanged for violence, and the frequent IRA attacks on the landlord classes in the south made northern Protestants particularly uneasy. In these circumstances, they willingly accepted the new settlement established by the Government of Ireland Act of December 1920: Home Rule for Dublin over twenty-six counties, and for Belfast over the six counties of Antrim, Armagh, Down, Fermanagh, Londonderry and Tyrone. This was rejected outright by the Dáil, however, and the war continued. By the summer of 1921 the IRA could see defeat looming and it was forced into negotiations.

Although it may seem strange today, the main point of discussion was not the position of Northern Ireland, but the relationship of any Irish government to the British Empire. Lloyd George, the Prime Minister, managed to sideline the issue of partition by suggesting that the present arrangement was of a temporary nature and proposing a boundary commission to investigate. The Irish delegation, led by Arthur Griffith and Michael Collins, hoped that such a commission would reduce the territory of Northern Ireland to an unworkable area which would inevitably wither away. On the matter of sovereignty, the Irish negotiators did not fare much better, with Lloyd George insisting that Ireland should remain within the empire and that an oath of allegiance to the Crown should remain. Facing a British ultimatum and fearing that this was the best that could be achieved, the Irish delegation agreed to sign a treaty with the British government on December 6, 1921.

There were no celebrations. Collins accurately foresaw the divisions which the treaty would cause, saying: "I have signed my own death warrant." In January 1922 the Dáil approved the treaty by a margin of sixty-four to fifty-seven, and the Irish Free State came into being. It subsequently won the support of a clear majority of the southern electorate, but faced opposition from influential figures, in particular from Éamonn de Valera (1882–1975). De Valera, who was to dominate Irish politics for much of the century, had been a commander in the 1916 Rising and only escaped execution thanks to his United States passport. He had stayed in Dublin during the peace negotiations, and when the treaty was approved he led a large faction out of the Dáil in protest. By June 1922 the pro- and anti-treaty factions were at war. The Civil War lasted less than a year, but it was particularly bitter, with high casualties on both sides, including the new leader of the Dáil, Michael Collins. The eventual victory of the pro-treaty side brought peace, but it did not end bitterness, and to this day civil war allegiances continue to influence domestic politics. It was perhaps inevitable that, following the trauma in which both political entities, north and south, had been born, the new establishments would see majorities dominate minorities.

CATHOLIC IRELAND

> For the virtues of his ancestors the Irishman has a country, not only fair and green but one of saints and scholars....Irish nationality is so bound up with the foundation of all true nobleness, the Catholic Church, that the words "Irish" and "Catholic" are linked constantly.[18]

So wrote the Catholic paper, the *Father Mathew Record*, ten years after the foundation of the State. Every new state requires an identity, and the identity of the Free State was founded on Catholicism.

Not only were 90 percent of the population Catholic, but, thanks to the "devotional revolution" of the previous century (see p. 180–81), they were particularly committed Catholics. Furthermore, the emergence of Irish nationalism had been closely bound up with their religious faith. That the Free State, and the Republic of Ireland which followed in 1949, developed as a Catholic state was not inevitable, however. In its early days, the Catholic Church hierarchy showed great concern for the future. A decade of violent instability had given way to a precarious settlement, and the anti-treaty camp continued to oppose the new State, occasionally by force. The world outside seemed to hold dangers for the people of Ireland. The most pressing concern of the church hierarchy at the time was the perceived threat of sexual immorality. The bishops' pastoral letter of 1927 declared that:

> The evil one is ever setting his snares for unwary feet. At the moment his traps for the innocent are chiefly the dance hall, the bad book, the indecent paper, the motion picture, the immodest fashion in female dress—all of which tend to destroy the virtues characteristic of our race.[19]

Immodest female dress was a recurring concern. In 1924, for example, Cardinal Logue of Armagh complained that:

> ...the dress, or rather the want of dress, of women at the present day is a crying scandal. There seems to be a rivalry among them as to how little dress they can wear without incurring universal reprobation.[20]

However, if the Church ever feared that the new state would allow such influences to prosper, they did not appreciate the conservative nature of its first governors, who turned from revolutionaries to conservatives of the deepest hue. The first government, led by the *Cumann na nGael* party (which later became *Fine Gael*), made little attempt to break with the British legal and administrative institutions which they had inherited, and their economic policies were cautious in the extreme. They also began to court the most powerful and conservative sectors of Irish society, namely the wealthy farming and business interests, and the Catholic Church.

The State began life as a liberal secular democracy in which religious equality was guaranteed. The Constitution of the Free State stated:

> Freedom of conscience and the free profession and practice of religion are, subject to public order and morality, guaranteed to every citizen, and no law shall be made either directly or indirectly to endow any religion, or prohibit or restrict the free exercise thereof or give any preference, or impose any disability on account of religious belief or religious status.[21]

However, while the Constitution made no mention of the Catholic Church, that institution quickly began to hold a highly influential position in the State and its power continued to grow when the Free State became a republic. It is too simplistic to say that the State became a theocracy, for the clergy played no overt role in government and political leaders did not always bow to clerical pressure. But, within a few years, the government had implemented a number of measures which put Catholic morality at the center of legislation.

In 1925 divorce was outlawed. The Prime Minister, William T. Cosgrave, stated:

> I have no doubt but that I am right in saying that the majority of the people of this country regard the bond of marriage as a sacramental bond which is incapable of being dissolved. I personally hold this view. I consider that the whole fabric of our social organisation is based upon the

sanctity of the marriage bond and that anything that tends to weaken the binding efficacy of that bond to that extent strikes at the root of our social life.[22]

The Censorship of Publications Act 1929 established a Censorship Board, headed by a Catholic priest. The import and sale of books considered "indecent or obscene" were banned. This definition was used to exclude the writings of James Joyce and Seán O'Casey, amongst others, just as they were gaining worldwide acclaim. Furthermore, the act prohibited the publication, sale and distribution of literature advocating contraception.

The strongly Catholic character of the state was in part a creation of the exertions of the church hierarchy and the willingness of successive governments to please them, but was also founded on the conservative Catholic character of the overwhelming majority of the population. The early years of independence from Britain saw the Irish people more committed to Catholicism than ever before or since. The advances of the previous century flourished in the form of very high attendance at Mass, participation in novenas, missions and retreats, membership of confraternities devoted to the Sacred Heart and the Virgin, and temperance and charitable movements. It was in these years that certain features of Irish life became commonplace: roadside grottos with statues of the Virgin, pictures of the Sacred Heart in the home, rosary beads and "miraculous medals." This was not just a people who had become more pious, but who had, it believed, found its identity. With British rule removed, Ireland now looked to Catholic nations abroad, and to Rome.

This was given its fullest expression in Dublin's hosting of the Eucharistic Congress of 1932. Coinciding with the legendary 1500th anniversary of St. Patrick's arrival in Ireland, this international celebration of the Eucharist was marked by an extraordinary level of religious enthusiasm. The papal legate was greeted at Dun

Laoghaire port by fifty thousand people. Huge, well-drilled processions followed and Masses were celebrated all night in Dublin. The climax of the congress was a Mass in the Phoenix Park, attended by one million people. The Dutch newspaper, *De Tijd*, referred to "Dublin the kneeling city, the city of millions of candles, the worshipping town, Dublin the heart of the Catholic world," while France's *Figaro* wrote: "One felt that one heart was beating in a whole nation."[23] But were all full members of that nation?

At the formation of the State, Protestants numbered around 7 percent of the population, most of them members of the Church of Ireland. For at least half a century, the number of Protestants outside Ulster had been falling, and they continued to decline throughout the twentieth century to the present level of around 3 percent. Emigration was partly to blame, but more significant was the Pope's *Ne Temere* decree of 1907 (since modified), which bound Catholic partners in a "mixed marriage" to rear their children as Catholics. From its foundation, most Protestants and their church leaders gave full allegiance to the state and played an active part in it. While alienated by the enshrining of Catholic moral teaching in legislation, there was no outcry against it from Protestants; after all, they were not necessarily enthusiastic about divorce, birth control or "indecent or obscene" publications. But, on occasions, cases of outright discrimination came to the fore. Most notorious was the blocking in 1930 by the Mayo Library Committee of the appointment as county librarian of Mayo of Mrs. Letitia Dunbar-Harrison, a Protestant, and worse, a graduate of Trinity College. The dean of Tuam explained: "We are not appointing a washerwoman or a mechanic, but an educated girl who ought to know what books to put into the hands of the Catholic boys and girls of this county." Councilor J. T. Moraghan put it in more extreme terms. He was:

> ...opposed to the appointment of a product of Trinity to the position of Librarian in this County. Trinity culture is

not the culture of the Gael; rather it is poison gas to the kindly Celtic people....At the command of the bigoted and Freemason press, Catholic rights are ignored....We are the connecting link between the past generations of our great Catholic dead and the generations yet unborn. We are the spearhead of the far-flung empire of Erin's exiled sons and daughters....Tolerance is synonymous with slavishness.[24]

The government capitulated to pressure, transferring Dunbar-Harrison.

The few voices critical of the direction the state was taking tended to be those of literary figures. During the divorce debate of 1925 W. B. Yeats, now a senator, put the case for pluralism:

I think it is tragic that within three years of this country gaining its independence we should be discussing a measure which a minority of this nation considers to be grossly oppressive. I am proud to consider myself to be a typical man of that minority. We, against whom you have done this thing, are no petty people. We are one of the great stocks of Europe. We are the people of Burke; we are the people of Grattan; we are the people of Swift, the people of Emmet, the people of Parnell.[25]

The domination of Catholic morality was not only contrary to the vision of Ireland put forward by those Protestant "Patriots"; it was also a departure from the republican tradition—the inclusiveness of Tone and Davis and the egalitarianism of Davitt and Connolly. One might have expected the republican movement to present a challenge to the State's ideology. After all, anti-treaty republicans had been excommunicated by the Catholic hierarchy during the Civil War, and they refused to enter the Dáil until 1927. But five years later they were in government, in the form of the

Fianna Fáil party, led by Éamonn de Valera. If some within the church were suspicious of Fianna Fáil, representing as they did the more revolutionary side of Irish nationalism, they need not have worried. As de Valera said in 1931: "If all comes to all, I am a Catholic first." Fianna Fáil had already outdone Cumann na nGael in their opposition to the appointment of Letitia Dunbar-Harrison as county librarian, and the 1932 general election became a contest between the holier-than-thou. It was reported that when the Angelus bell rang out during a local Fianna Fáil rally "Mr. de Valera immediately ceased speaking, blessed himself and silently said the Angelus prayer, [and] the crowd reverently followed his example."[26]

Part of the reason that de Valera left such a mark on the Ireland of the twentieth century is that he had an all-encompassing vision. It was given its most famous expression in his St. Patrick's Day speech of 1943:

> The Ireland which we dreamed of would be the home of a people who valued material wealth only as the basis of right living, of a people who were satisfied with frugal comfort and devoted their leisure to the things of the spirit—a land whose countryside would be bright with cosy homesteads, whose fields and villages would be joyous with the sounds of industry, with the romping of sturdy children, the contests of athletic youths and the laughter of comely maidens, whose firesides would be forums for the wisdom of serene old age. It would, in a word, be the home of a people living the life that God desires that man should live.[27]

There were two main elements to this vision, namely the "de-Anglicization" of Ireland and the fostering of its Catholic character, and throughout his political life de Valera took steps to make them a reality. Early in his premiership he launched an economic war with Britain and attempted to make Ireland economically self-sufficient. In 1935 his government introduced statutory restrictions on the sale and importation of contraceptives. Two years later he made his boldest step in introducing a new Constitution, drafted with the aid of John Charles McQuaid, soon to be Archbishop of Dublin.

The Constitution of 1937 established an Irish Republic in all but name (a republic was not declared until 1949). The name of the State was changed from the Irish Free State to "Ireland," or "Éire," and the head of government was called the "Taoiseach." No mention was made of the State's relationship with the United Kingdom, and an elected head of state was established in place of the British monarch. Most provocatively, the Constitution made a claim to Northern Ireland, stating that "[t]he national territory consists of the whole island of Ireland, its islands and the territorial seas."

Apart from these, the clauses which have attracted most comment concern the family and religion. Article 41 states:

> 1.1 The State recognises the Family as the natural primary and fundamental unit group of Society, and as a moral institution possessing inalienable and imprescriptible rights, antecedent and superior to all positive law.
> 1.2 The State, therefore, guarantees to protect the Family in its constitution and authority, as the necessary basis of social order and as indispensable to the welfare of the Nation and the State.

It went on to prohibit divorce, and to emphasize the woman's place within the home. Article 44, which was expunged in 1972, addressed religion:

1.1 The State acknowledges that the homage of public worship is due to Almighty God. It shall hold His Name in reverence, and shall respect and honour religion.

1.2 The State recognises the special position of the Holy Catholic Apostolic and Roman Church as the guardian of the Faith professed by the great majority of the citizens.

1.3 The State also recognises the Church of Ireland, the Presbyterian Church in Ireland, the Methodist Church in Ireland, the Religious Society of Friends in Ireland, as well as the Jewish Congregations and the other religious denominations existing in Ireland at the date of the coming into operation of this Constitution.

There is no doubt that de Valera's vision was of a state which would embody Catholic morality. In his St. Patrick's Day broadcast of 1935 he stated:

Since the coming of St. Patrick, fifteen hundred years ago, Ireland has been a Christian and a Catholic nation. All the ruthless attempts made down the centuries to force her from this allegiance have not shaken her faith. She remains a Catholic nation.[28]

But the 1937 Constitution did not single-handedly create such a state. It was created by the special position of the Catholic Church in the hearts and minds of the vast majority of the population, and was only strengthened by the church authorities and the complicity of politicians.

In 1949 the first president under the 1937 Constitution, Douglas Hyde, an Anglican, died, and his funeral was held in the Church of Ireland cathedral, St. Patrick's. The cabinet of the State's government, under instructions from their bishops, remained outside in their cars, rather than enter a Protestant church. One could be head of state, it seemed, and still not be accorded full respect as a member of that state.

THE DIVIDED PROVINCE

With the partition of Ireland, it must have seemed to some—outside Ireland at least—that the "Irish problem" had been solved. Three quarters of the island, overwhelmingly Catholic and resistant to British rule, had their own state, while the Protestants of the northeast retained their link with Britain. But there was an inherent imbalance in this settlement. While those who did not share in the ethos of the southern state suffered real discrimination, their numbers were small, and they presented little resistance. In Northern Ireland, one-third of the population found itself excluded. And while the issues of contention in the southern state related to personal morality, those in Northern Ireland concerned the more concrete matters of representation, housing, policing and employment. The southern state suffered alienation and stagnation, but stability was preserved; in Northern Ireland, the eventual consequence was war.

The partition of Ireland was not something immediately favored by either Catholics or Protestants: the former favored rule from Dublin, the latter rule from London, but both envisaged a united Ireland. Partition was embraced as a reluctant compromise. For the unionists of Ulster, it was a safeguard against Catholic domination; for those nationalists who approved the treaty, it was a price worth paying for an independent Irish state, and one which they believed would not last for ever. Partition did not separate Protestants from Catholic, nor was it meant to. Northern Ireland at its foundation had a Catholic minority of around 34 percent, which has since increased to around 43 percent. Of the six northern counties which remained within the U.K., Tyrone and Fermanagh had a Catholic majority. Moreover, whereas the rural northeast was very largely Protestant, mid-Ulster and the cities of Belfast and Derry were mixed (though they would become increasingly segregated with the coming of the Troubles in 1969). Northern Ireland constituted the largest possible area that Protestants would be able to control.

Many nationalists have seen the partition of Ireland as the core of the problem, but the division of Ireland did not of itself make Protestant domination inevitable. This was facilitated, more particularly, by the way in which the province was allowed to rule itself, with a permanent Protestant majority untroubled by interference from London.

Northern Ireland, like the Free State, was founded on a non-sectarian basis. The Government of Ireland Act 1921 stated that the Northern Ireland parliament should not:

> ...make a law so as to either directly or indirectly to establish or endow any religion, or prohibit or restrict the free exercise thereof, or give a preference, privilege, or advantage, or impose any disability or disadvantage, on account of religious belief or religious or ecclesiastical status.[29]

In 1921 the leading figure in the formation of Ulster unionism, Edward Carson, stated:

> From the outset let us see that the Catholic minority have nothing to fear from the Protestant majority. Let us take care to win all that is best amongst those who have been opposed to us in the past. While maintaining intact our religion let us give the same rights to the religion of our neighbours.[30]

But it was not easy to paper over the centuries of distrust and hatred. Northern Protestants remained insecure, with pogroms in the south, IRA attacks on the border, and the proposed review by the boundary commission hanging over them. Immediate measures were taken to limit any threat from northern Catholics. The Special Powers Act (1922) effectively created a state of emergency. Catholics complained of harassment by the exclusively Protestant "B-Special" reserve police force and were subject to internment without trial. Meanwhile, thousands of Belfast Catholics were expelled from their homes and jobs. When the report of the Boundary Commission in 1925 resulted in no changes to the border, four hundred thousand Catholics found themselves in a state which had the means and the will to ensure Protestant dominance.

The initial response of the Catholic community was nonparticipation, with Nationalist MPs declining to sit in the Belfast parliament. Many Catholics withdrew into their own communities, based around their own churches, schools, workplaces and social clubs. This was, perhaps, an understandable reaction to the shock of permanent partition, but in retrospect it seems a misstep. The minority voice was lost at a crucial time and the political development of the Catholic community was held back. Furthermore, it reinforced the view amongst Protestants that Catholics posed a threat to their position. A future prime minister of Northern Ireland, Basil Brooke, stated in 1933: "Ninety-seven, if not one hundred, per cent of the Roman Catholics in Northern Ireland were disloyal and disruptive."[31]

The following year the Prime Minister William Craig spoke of a "Protestant parliament for a Protestant people." As a statement of fact, it could not be faulted. Basic arithmetic dictated that one party, the *Ulster Unionist Party (UUP)*, held power from the formation of the Northern Ireland parliament in 1920 to its suspension in 1972. The majority was further boosted by the suspension of proportional representation for local elections in 1921 and for parliamentary elections in 1929. Restrictions on non-property-holders and extra votes for businesses served to shore up the Protestant vote. If this were not enough, local electoral boundaries were blatantly gerrymandered. The liberal unionist, Hugh Montgomery, observed the anomalies in 1941:

> How is the fact to be explained that in Fermanagh some 25,000 Unionist[s] have 17 seats in the County Council, while some 35,000 Nationalists get only 7; and that in Tyrone, some 60,000 Unionist[s] get 16 seats while some 75,000 Nationalists have only 11?[32]

Discrimination was also felt in the allocation of council houses and in the Protestant domination of the police force. At the most basic level, Catholics tended to be less wealthy, unhealthier and with fewer skills than their Protestant neighbors.

Northern Ireland remained subject to Westminster, but until 1969 the British governments of all parties remained very reluctant to interfere in the affairs of the province. The position of the Irish government also contributed to the situation in the North; while politicians were ever ready to employ republican rhetoric, they did little to help northern Catholics. Indeed, in creating a state so unattractive to Protestants and by laying claim to the six northern counties, they helped to shore up more conservative unionist attitudes. The loyalty of Northern Ireland during World War II (the Republic stayed neutral) served to reinforce its position within the Union, as did the declaration of an Irish Republic in 1949. The British government, in the Ireland Act of the same year, established that there would be no change in the constitutional position of Northern Ireland without the consent of the Belfast parliament. Northern Ireland seemed more secure as a political entity than ever before.

It was undoubtedly a Protestant-dominated state, but it was also a relatively peaceful and prosperous one. Nor did it seem as if Catholic dissatisfaction was rife. Northern Catholics found themselves, thanks to the economic fillip of the war and the fruits of the

Welfare State, better off in material ways than their southern counterparts. Their increasing reconciliation to the state was most clearly illustrated by the failure of the IRA's campaign of attacks on the border between 1956 and 1962, a failure that the republicans placed at the door of the Catholic community:

> Foremost among the factors motivating this course of action has been the attitude of the general public whose minds have been deliberately distracted from the supreme issue facing the Irish people—the unity and freedom of Ireland.[33]

Even in 1968, on the eve of nearly three decades of violence euphemistically known as "the Troubles," opinion polls were showing only a minority of Catholics in support of a united Ireland.

In fact, the Troubles emerged at the end of a decade when Catholics and Protestants seemed to be coming together as never before. There was still mistrust and resentment, but these sentiments seemed in decline. For the first time, the Protestant churches were engaging in contacts with the Catholic Church, as the ecumenical movement began to flourish. The growth of the Catholic middle class saw them play a greater, if still marginalized, role in the state. On the political level, too, there were signs of a thaw, with the leadership of Seán Lemass in the Republic and Captain Terence O'Neill in Northern Ireland. Lemass, a modernizer who turned his back on de Valera's isolationism, signaled a willingness to recognize the legitimacy of Northern Ireland and encouraged northern Catholics to play a greater role in its affairs. O'Neill, for his part, launched a programme of rapprochement with the Republic, and a reconciliation of Catholics to Northern Ireland through an improvement of their material conditions. The strongest symbol of this new approach came in 1965 with the invitation of Lemass to Belfast and O'Neill's reciprocal visit to Dublin. This may have been the way forward to peace and reconciliation in Northern Ireland, but O'Neill was undermined by more conservative Unionists on one side and Catholic activists on the other. O'Neill had been appointed rather than elected leader of the Unionist Party and he never had wide-ranging support amongst its membership. Senior figures made frequent challenges to his position, leading to his gradual isolation.

Outside the Ulster Unionist Party, challenges were also emerging. The most immediately recognizable face of diehard unionism, then and since, is the Reverend Ian Paisley. The son of a Baptist preacher, Paisley came to prominence as a staunch evangelical and an opponent of papalism, founding the Free Presbyterian Church of Ulster in 1951. In the 1960s he opposed the nascent ecumenical movement, calling it "the sickly growth of ecclesiastical expediency," and led protests to Lemass's visit with the slogan, "no Mass; no Lemass." In 1966, in response to O'Neill's policy, he founded the Protestant Unionist Party, which later developed into the *Democratic Unionist Party (DUP)*. A powerful orator and a master of dramatic public gestures, Paisley succeeded in giving a high profile to opposition to Catholicism, the Republic and Protestant compromise. At the same time, violent opposition emerged in the form of the Ulster Volunteer Force, responsible for the sectarian murder of a young Catholic in Belfast in 1966.

While some felt threatened by the pace of change, others believed it was progressing too slowly. O'Neill's approach was to raise Catholics' standard of living and thereby reconcile them to the state. But he failed to appreciate that northern Catholics saw the problem in terms of rights. While he made many gestures toward the Catholic community, visiting Catholic schools and nationalist areas, real change was slow in coming. A downturn in the economy made conditions for many Catholics particularly difficult. O'Neill's premiership coincided with the emergence of a popular movement for reform, the backbone of which was formed by a new wave of young educated Catholics. Inspired by the black civil rights movement in the United States, and later by the student protests of 1968, they began to take direct action.

The civil rights movement has been characterized by its opponents, then and since, as a front for nationalism, or even republicanism. Undoubtedly there were many nationalists and republicans within it, and many others later joined nationalist and republican groups, but it was a broad-ranging movement, composed of many different parties, that addressed the issue of the position of Catholics within the state. The launch of the *Campaign for Social Justice* in 1964 was followed by the formation of the *Northern Ireland Civil Rights Association (NICRA)* in 1967. The central objective of the civil rights movement was the establishment of the same standards in Northern Ireland as pertained in the rest of the United Kingdom in relation to elections, housing, the security forces and local government accountability. Although it was a peaceful movement which did not directly address the national question, it was seen by many Protestants as provocative, and its policy of direct action soon led to confrontation. In October 1968 a banned civil rights march was attacked by police and images were shown around the world. As sectarian tension rose, O'Neill announced a sweeping package of reforms, addressing housing, local election and police powers. NICRA, hoping to reduce tensions, suspended its protests. In a television broadcast O'Neill declared this a crucial turning point in Ulster's history:

> Ulster stands at the crossroads.... What kind of Ulster do you want? A happy and respected province in good standing with the rest of the United Kingdom? Or a place con-

tinually torn apart by riots and demonstrations and regarded by the rest of Britain as a political outcast?[34]

But by now the genie was already out of the bottle and Northern Ireland was set for an increasingly bitter downward spiral of tension and violence.

The Carmelite Priory, Aungier Street, Dublin

INTO THE
NEW MILLENNIUM

R eligion has played a marginal part in the recent history of most western societies, but in Ireland it has been central. From the 1960s the position of the Catholic Church in Irish life came under question, with consequences for the Republic's sense of identity. In Northern Ireland, long-standing sectarian divisions burst into violent conflict which dragged on until the closing years of the century. At the start of the new millennium, Ireland, north and south, seemed radically different compared to just a few decades before. In particular, Christianity as a force for shaping the history of its people, for good or ill, seemed less relevant than ever before. But did this mean the end of Christian Ireland?

THE TROUBLES

For the first forty years of its existence, Northern Ireland made little impact on international consciousness. Winston Churchill referred to the "dreary steeples of Fermanagh and Tyrone" harboring an

A republican mural from Belfast commemorating the IRA hunger strikers of 1981

interminable and incomprehensible quarrel, but while it remained at the level of animosity and resentment, few took the time to notice it. But when Northern Ireland erupted into flames in 1969, the terraced streets of Belfast and the green landscape of rural Ulster provided the incongruous setting for a war which would become known to television viewers the world over. Riots, explosions, armored cars and paramilitaries became familiar images of the province as the roll call of Protestant and Catholic dead became a regular part of nightly news bulletins.

The temperature had been rising for some time, but January 1969 marked the point of no return. That month the radical, non-sectarian, student-based civil rights group *Peoples' Democracy* decided to go ahead with a march from Belfast to Derry, passing through areas traditionally considered Protestant. On Burntollet Bridge, outside Derry City, they were attacked by a combination of police and loyalists, and that night there were further attacks on the Catholic Bogside area of Derry. The provocation of Protestant opinion had met with an uncompromising response. Within months Terence O'Neill had resigned, after elections had shown little unionist support for his reform project, and he was succeeded by his cousin, Major James Chichester-Clark. That summer's marching season saw rioting and sectarian clashes in Belfast and Derry, and at the same time mobs began to drive large numbers of Catholics from their homes. The Taoiseach, Jack Lynch, warned that "the Irish government can no longer stand by and see innocent people injured and perhaps worse."[1] While ambiguous, this statement conjured up the possibility of military intervention by the South and all-out war.

In August the British government finally stepped in. Their approach was twofold: to press the Northern Ireland government to continue the reforms which O'Neill had initiated and to contain the security situation. Within a year virtually the entire civil rights case had been conceded, with widespread reforms of local government, housing and security. At the same time, British troops made their appearance in Northern Ireland, a sight that would soon become very familiar. The troops were initially welcomed by Catholics, who saw them as their only protection against sectarian attack. Whereas in the early years after partition Catholics had looked to the IRA to defend them, they were now nowhere to be seen: "IRA—I Ran Away" read the graffiti on the walls of Catholic ghettos. The IRA's decision not to intervene reflected its leadership's recent shift to a strictly nonsectarian and nonviolent Marxist approach to the Northern Ireland problem.

The new climate of crisis brought a challenge to the leadership and led to the formation of the *Provisional IRA* (the term deriving from the establishment of the "provisional government" in 1916). The split within the IRA coincided with growing Catholic resentment toward the British Army, largely caused by heavy-handed security measures. Many young Catholics were driven toward the IRA, which was developing as an effective military force. February 1971 saw the killing of the first British soldier in Northern Ireland. Soon after, internment without trial was introduced, a disastrous policy which served to further alienate Catholics by arresting many innocent, while making no real impact on the strength of the para-militaries. On "Bloody Sunday," January 30, 1972, soldiers fired on unarmed protestors at a banned anti-internment rally, killing four-teen. That night nationalist areas of Northern Ireland exploded in anger, and the British embassy in Dublin was burned to the ground. As paramilitary violence reached a peak, not only from the IRA but also from the newly founded loyalist terrorist groups, the British government took the decision to suspend the Northern Ireland par-liament and to introduce direct rule.

The 1970s were a time of terror and disillusion for Northern Ireland. Old fears intensified, new ones emerged and hopes were repeatedly shattered. After decades of peace and security, Protestants saw their way of life again under threat. The British government, supposedly the guarantors of their interests, had been instrumental in removing Protestant privilege and even their parliament. In addition, Protestants faced the terror of republican violence, and a new hostility from some of their Catholic neigh-bors. Minorities in rural mid-Ulster felt particularly vulnerable and the 1970s saw a large movement of population to the northeast. Moderate unionist opinion fell into confusion as extremists prospered, with new support for Ian Paisley and for loyalist paramilitaries. The decade opened more hopefully in some ways for Catholics. Despite continued sectarian attacks, they now found themselves accorded fuller civil rights, and for a time it seemed that radical constitutional change was in the offing for Northern Ireland. However, hopes of such change soon faded when Catholics found themselves subject to new civil rights abuses, in the form of harassment and brutality by the

A loyalist mural from Belfast representing the pope celebrating the victory of King William of Orange in 1690. William did indeed have papal support.

security forces, seen more and more as an army of occupation. Meanwhile, most Catholics came to be outraged by the IRA's violent campaign and also found themselves vulnerable to attack from loyalist paramilitaries.

The Troubles had an impact beyond Northern Ireland. The British, so long indifferent to the province, were woken up to their responsibilities by its constant presence on their television screens. In 1974 the IRA took the war to the mainland, with devastating results, the Guildford and Birmingham pub bombings of that year leaving a total of twenty-six dead. That same year the Republic suffered violence, with a total of thirty-three people killed by loyalist car bombs in Dublin and Monaghan. Those atrocities apart, the southern population managed, in general, to escape the ravages of war, but the Troubles had a deep effect on the Republic in other ways. The new realities forced a painful reassessment of southerners' attitudes toward Northern Ireland, which could no longer be shrouded safely in republican rhetoric. The Troubles also served to drive a further wedge between the people of the South and their northern neighbors, both Protestant and Catholic. For most southern Irish, London remains more familiar than Belfast.

The 1970s were most dispiriting for those who actively sought peace. It soon became clear that this was to be a long war, apparently impossible to win, but also impossible to end. The first serious attempt at a peace settlement came in the form of the Sunningdale Agreement of December 1973, which proposed an executive with power shared amongst the province's parties, accompanied by an "Irish dimension." Although the executive was set up early in 1974, the proposed Council of Ireland, a cross-border body, proved unacceptable to many Protestants. Within months a general strike by the Ulster Workers' Council led to the collapse of the initiative and with it any hope of a speedy settlement. Thereafter the British government moved toward a policy of containment. While the security forces met with some success against the paramilitaries, violence continued in the form of attacks on government targets in Northern Ireland and Britain, and a seemingly endless cycle of sectarian "tit for tat" murders.

The litany of everyday violence was sporadically punctuated by crises which threatened to tip the province over into something even worse. One such crisis occurred in 1981 when ten Republican prisoners starved themselves to death in the Maze prison in protest at the removal of their status as political prisoners. The intransigence of Prime Minister Margaret Thatcher and the addition of ten men to the list of republican martyrs did much to boost support for Sinn Féin, the political wing of the IRA. Bobby Sands, the first to die, was elected MP in a by-election; two other hunger strikers were elected to the Dáil. Though the hunger strikes raised tensions to a level not seen since the early 1970s, in the long term it is possible to see in this crisis the roots of the peace process. The republican movement, noting its electoral gains, began to take a more positive approach to constitutional politics, a move which culminated in the cease-fires of the 1990s. Similarly, the British and Irish governments, alarmed at growing republican support, began, for the first time in a decade, to take concerted steps toward a settlement.

By the 1980s constitutional nationalist thinking had begun to move beyond the stark demand for a united Ireland to consider other constitutional arrangements. The driving force behind this development was John Hume, leader of the *Social Democratic and Labor Party (SDLP)* which had, since its formation in 1970, been the main voice of the Nationalists in Northern Ireland. The SDLP, along with the Republic's main political parties and representatives of the main churches—Catholic and Protestant—met between 1983 and 1984 at the New Ireland Forum, which aimed to examine new paths toward peace and justice. The forum's report acknowledged that Nationalists had tended to underestimate the importance of the Unionist identity and it proposed, in addition to a unitary state, two other options: a federal or confederal arrangement, or joint authority between Britain and Ireland. Thatcher immediately rejected all three proposals but, ironically, it was this most hard-line of politicians who was responsible for making the greatest concessions to date to nationalist opinion in the form of the Anglo-Irish Agreement of November 1985.

Since 1981, British and Irish leaders had met regularly at an Intergovernmental Conference, and the agreement entrenched the role of the Republic in the affairs of Northern Ireland, establishing a permanent secretariat near Belfast. While stressing the principle that a majority of the people of Northern Ireland must consent to any change in the constitutional position of the province, the agreement also signaled a readiness for reform. The agreement was sprung on unionists without consultation, and it provoked an angry reaction, but mass protests and campaigns of civil disobedience brought no concessions from Downing Street. If the Anglo-Irish Agreement was meant to isolate extremists, it seemed to have little effect, judging by the outrages of the following years: the bombing of Protestant civilians on a Remembrance Day march in

Enniskillen in 1987 and the loyalist grenade attack on mourners at a republican funeral in Belfast the following year, to name but two. But it did succeed in initiating a process which was to bring to Northern Ireland the best chance yet of peace.

NORTHERN IRELAND: A RELIGIOUS CONFLICT?

The protagonists in the Northern Ireland conflict may be described as nationalists and unionists, republicans and loyalists, but more often than not they are called Catholics and Protestants. Historically, political divisions in the region have tended to go according to religion, with parties winning the vote of one community or the other, but seldom gaining cross-community support. Northern Ireland is also a place where religion has meant much to the people, with church attendance levels much higher than in most other places in Europe. But to what extent is the conflict in Northern Ireland a religious one? While few scholars of the conflict would see it as primarily religious, pointing instead to national or ethnic issues, most would accept that the religious element is nonetheless an important one.

To be a member of one church or another is, in Northern Ireland, more than a matter of where one attends Sunday services. Most people are born in a hospital run by their church and educated in a Catholic or Protestant school, and integrated education represents only 1 percent of the school population. Their church might be the focus of social activities—religious ones, such as the Legion of Mary or Sunday school, or nonreligious, such as Gaelic games or the Scouts. Religious affiliation has played a role in segregating the two communities and in shaping the identity of each. The segregation of the communities has intensified since the beginning of the Troubles. From 1969 to 1972 between eight and fifteen thousand families, the majority Catholic, were forced to evacuate their homes in Belfast. The center of Derry City has been all but abandoned by the minority Protestant population, who moved east of the Foyle to the Waterside district. Nowadays half of the population of Northern Ireland lives in an area which is more than 90 percent Protestant or Catholic, whereas only 7 percent live in areas with a roughly equal mix. Typical is the comment of a middle-class Protestant who recalled playing soccer with Catholic children when he was a boy: "We knew what religion we were all right, but we played anyway. Now my kids don't really meet Catholics at all. In Belfast there's the odd pub where the two sides would drink together, but that's becoming more and more rare."[2]

The Catholic and Protestant communities are not mirror images. While the vast majority of the population is affiliated to a Christian church, active membership is higher among Catholics, around 60 percent of whom attend weekly Mass. Protestants in Northern Ireland, while much more active than their coreligionists in Britain, have a lower level of commitment than Catholics, particularly among the urban working class. Also, while all Catholics are members of the same church, Protestants are divided among many denominations. The largest reformed church in Northern Ireland is the Presbyterian Church of Ireland, with over three hundred thousand members, followed by the Church of Ireland. But there are more than forty other Christian churches in the province, notably the Methodist and the Baptist congregations. Within the main churches there are also divisions between "evangelical" and "liberal" wings, with a small majority of Presbyterians tending toward the former, and a larger majority of Anglicans tending toward the latter.

Catholics and Protestants also differ in their attitude toward the conflict. It is accepted by most commentators that Protestants are more likely to see the conflict in religious terms. This is in part related to their historical position as a besieged minority in Ireland and their perception of the Catholic Church. The way the Free

State and the Republic developed and the continued affront caused by the church's legislation on mixed marriages have contributed to the image amongst some Protestants of a church which is politically aggressive, intolerant, and with too strong a hold over its people. Hostility to Catholicism is stronger amongst the evangelical wing of Protestants; Ian Paisley is the most notable example of the combination of evangelical religion, anti-Catholicism and staunch loyalism. In a typical statement he declared:

> The struggle to destroy Ulster Protestantism cannot be viewed in isolation. Ulster is the last bastion of Bible Protestantism in Europe, and as such Ulster stands as the sole obstacle at this time against the great objective of the Roman Catholic see: a United Roman Catholic Europe.[3]

Links between unionism and Protestantism exist on a more moderate level as well, with the Orange Order, an institution which excludes Catholics, playing a prominent role in the Ulster Unionist Party. One moderate unionist expressed the position of mainstream unionists thus:

> Northern unionists hold the view that the Roman Catholic Church is in such a position of entrenched power because of the control it exercises indirectly through the minds and attitudes of the faithful, as to be able to dictate policy to the state on matters which the Church considers essential to the maintenance of its position.[4]

But the connection between religious affiliation and political viewpoint amongst Protestants is by no means clear. Paisley is much more important as a political figure than as a religious one: Although his Free Presbyterian Church has a high profile, it has a membership of only around thirteen thousand. His Democratic Unionist Party, while drawing some of its support from rural evangelicals, depends for its core vote on urban working-class Protestants where levels of church attendance and religious commitment tend to be relatively weak. And while many unionists are members of the Orange Order, most are not. Some commentators have seen the importance of religion in unionism as stemming from a problem of identity:

> Because they do not have a strong sense of political identity, they fall back on their religion for symbols of identity. And because they take their cohesion in religious matters from an anti-Catholic bias that is common to all their denominations, anti-Catholicism becomes an expression of a shared identity.[5]

Nationalists tend to regard the main issues in the conflict as ones of political and economic injustice rather than religion. The adherence to an Irish nation and the recognition of symbols of that nationality—the Irish flag and the Irish language—have been stressed much more often than the Catholic religion has. Nevertheless, Catholicism has also played a part in nationalism and republicanism, as shown in the Catholic imagery which surrounded the deaths of Bobby Sands and the other hunger strikers. The Catholic Church has taken on the role of advocate for the Catholic community, for example, making protests over internment and police brutality. They also acted as mediators between the IRA and the British government during the hunger strikes and in the early stages of the peace process. Cardinal Tomás O'Fiach was particularly outspoken in his role as head of the Catholic Church in Ireland, causing controversy with his statement in 1978 that the British should withdraw from Northern Ireland and that only a statement of such intent would break the logjam. But it is also the case that, despite a handful of priests who have been implicated in terrorism, the church's most important role has been as a constant critic of violence. In 1979 Bishop Cahal Daly drew a distinction between the modern IRA and the earlier revolutionaries:

> There is no historical continuity whatever between the present, largely faceless, leaders of the self-styled "republican movement" and their honourable forebears; there is no moral continuity between their methods and those of the earlier struggle for independence. One of the aims of the present "republican movement" is to overthrow the very institutions of democracy which earlier republicans sacrificed limb and life to establish.[6]

This stance has contributed to limiting the support for republican paramilitaries. In fact, all the main churches in Northern Ireland have been united in their opposition to violence and their work for peace; ironically, the Troubles have served to bring their leaders more closely together, if not their flocks. The Church of Ireland primate, the Right Reverend Robin Eames, said in 1981: "There is a spiritual dimension to the problems of Northern Ireland. If the churches are part of the problem, they must be part of the solution."[7]

After the partition of Ireland, the main churches retained their all-Ireland organization, making cross-border contacts a normal part of life. Since 1923 the Irish Council of Churches had brought the Protestant denominations together, but suspicion remained between Catholics and Protestants. Indeed, Archbishop McQuaid had been responsible for dissolving Catholic organizations that had sought to promote contacts with Protestants and Jews. The Second Vatican Council's promotion of ecumenism helped to break the ice (see p. 242), and during the 1960s a number of interchurch conferences were held. Meetings of clergy and laity at Glenstal Abbey, near Limerick, and Corrymeela, County Louth, continued to foster understanding and cooperation, and in 1970 the Irish School of Ecumenics was founded in Dublin. Other forces, such as missionary activity overseas and the charismatic renewal movement also helped to bring members of the different denominations together. The Troubles caused an inevitable hardening of attitudes among many, but the main churches remained determined to promote peace. While the withdrawal of the Presbyterian Church of Ireland from the World Council of Churches in 1980 was seen as a setback for ecumenism, that church continued to confront sectarianism, its General Assembly in 1982 welcoming "the overwhelming desire to show love and friendship to Roman Catholics by Presbyterians in Ireland" and encouraging "cooperation with Roman Catholics in matters of mutual interest, provided that the principles of the Reformed Faith are not in any way compromised."

All the main churches have tended to welcome peace initiatives, from the Sunningdale Agreement of 1973 to the Good Friday Agreement of 1998 (see p. 230 and p. 251–53). They have also been unequivocal in their condemnation of violence. In the joint document of 1976, *Violence in Ireland,* their first major statement on the subject, they declared that violent political means had no justification and stated their clear opposition to paramilitaries, while also supporting a bill of rights for Northern Ireland and recognizing the legitimacy of peaceful protest.

The Catholic Church's stance against the paramilitaries has put them at variance with the views of many within their community. In 1972 the prominent republican Rúairí O'Brádaigh criticized Cardinal Conway's peace initiatives:

In his excursion into politics, all the influence he can command is being thrown behind direct rule, just as his predecessors had urged successfully the acceptance of the disastrous treaty of surrender in 1921.[8]

On occasions, Republicans appeared to pose as the true inheritors of the Christian tradition. In 1971 the newspaper *Republican News* criticized a church threat of excommunication for terrorists:

Since August '69 Catholics in the North have been looking to the Hierarchy for some indication of leadership. They looked in vain. As the repression gained in intensity, they found the twisted speeches of their bishops becoming more and more irrelevant....However, the back-stabbing edict issued this week by the Irish Hierarchy's Commission must rank as the greatest act of premeditated treachery against innocent people since Judas betrayed his Saviour with a kiss.[9]

Religion has played an important part in fostering antipathy but has also acted to heal division. Witness, for example, the work for peace of Gordon Wilson, driven by his Christian faith to forgive those who had killed his daughter in the Remembrance Day bombing at Enniskillen in 1987; or the silent vigil led by a West Belfast priest to the place where the IRA had shot two British Army corporals dead in 1988. But despite these efforts and many ordinary, everyday incidents which never make the headlines, the bitterness of history—ancient and recent—and the continued segregation of the population mean that most people still align themselves with those of the same religion. Religious commitment in Northern Ireland has declined in recent years, even if not as dramatically as in the Republic, but identification as Catholic or Protestant looks set to remain the strongest badge of identity.

EVER FAITHFUL?

How long will Catholic Ireland last? That was the question which concerned commentators on Ireland, both ecclesiastical and secular, for much of the last half-century. Its demise was often predicted, by those within the church who saw the modern world as full of danger and by liberals who hoped that secularization and modernization would bring with it a change in the national culture. But Catholic Ireland—a place where a large majority of the population was committed to the faith, where the national culture was shaped by Catholicism and where the state's laws echoed the teaching of the church—proved remarkably resilient. Though cracks in the edifice appeared in the 1950s and deepened over succeeding decades, its collapse did not occur until the last years of the century.

While Catholic ideology loomed large in legislation, its influence was perhaps greater at a more subtle level, in education and health in particular. The church had, until very recently, a remarkably strong control over education, with the manager of a local school usually a Catholic priest and the Christian Brothers running many second-level establishments. Many hospitals, too, were and continue to be run by religious orders, and it was the area of health which proved the ground for the first major clash between church and state.

In the Republic's postwar coalition government, one of the brightest rising stars was the Minister for Health, Dr. Noel Browne. He had witnessed death through tuberculosis in his own family, and in his medical practice had seen how poverty contributed to illness and disease. In 1951 he attempted to introduce free pre- and postnatal care for mothers and free medical care for children under sixteen years of age. However, the "Mother and Child Scheme" ran into strong opposition from the bishops, who were wary of the consequences of health education and gynecological services becoming the responsibility of state authorities. The Taoiseach, John A. Costello, forced Browne to resign and said that he accepted "without qualification and in all respects the social teaching of the church as interpreted by the Roman Catholic hierarchy of Ireland."[10] This controversy illustrated the power of the Catholic

Church over matters which in other societies might have been seen as beyond their remit. Bishop Lucey of Cork reflected in 1955:

> The Church was not just one group among the many groups making up the State, but had a firmer and broader base than any of them....In a word their position was that they were the final arbiters of right and wrong even in political matters. In other spheres the State might for its own good reasons ignore the advice of the experts, but in faith and morals it might not.[11]

But this was not a straightforward matter of the church imposing its will on the state. The controversy showed that the main political parties remained willing to submit to the church's wishes. In doing so, they were reflecting the overwhelming will of the people.

In the early 1960s the Jesuit Father B. F. Biever researched attitudes toward the church. Few agreed with the proposition that the church was "out of date." Typical responses were, "When you've got the truth, lad, you don't worry about keeping up with the times," and:

> I wouldn't change a thing the Church is doing; it keeps the society here in Ireland a God-fearing one, and in the end there is nothing else worth doing. The Church might not be getting us jobs, but it is keeping our people happy and with their feet on the ground.[12]

Ireland remained a very pious society, and a puritanical one. When the writer Brendan Behan enquired after a copy of Plato's *Symposium*, the Dublin bookseller told him:

> We saw a slight run on it, and the same sort of people looking for it, so we just took it out of circulation ourselves. After all we don't have to be made decent minded

by Act of Dáil. We have our own way of detecting smut, however ancient.[13]

As late as 1963 some young Italian tourists were complaining to the Irish press: "If we hold hands in the street, people look askance at us; if we kiss in a public place such as a café, we are immediately put out."[14] Still, the bishops seemed concerned that Catholic Ireland was under siege. In 1962 Archbishop Morris of Cashel described Ireland as "a Christian country surrounded by paganism." In the same year Cardinal d'Alton of Armagh lamented:

> We no longer enjoy our isolation of former days. We are living in a world where many seem to have forgotten God....In this distorted world, through the medium of the press, the radio and the television, we are subject to the impact of views wholly at variance with Catholic teaching.[15]

In the 1960s the Republic of Ireland found a new prosperity, largely thanks to the policies of Seán Lemass's Fianna Fáil government, which, in a reversal of de Valera's isolationism, actively sought investment from abroad. This new prosperity was accompanied by the growth of consumerism, a population shift from the countryside to urban areas and greater participation in second- and third-level education. Ireland began to explore deeper cooperation with other nations, culminating in its entry to the European Economic Community in 1973.

Most important in exposing Ireland to the outside world was the coming of television, with the founding of Telefís Éireann on New Year's Eve 1961. This development was greeted with great trepidation by the church authorities and in its early years attracted frequent denunciations. Especially controversial was *The Late Late Show*, a popular program which discussed matters previously deemed inappropriate in Ireland. As one conservative politician famously complained on that programme, "there was no sex in Ireland before television." Residents on the east coast could also pick up British channels, a contributory factor in the disproportionate growth in liberal attitudes in that region. The church hierarchy continued to be wary of the media, but nevertheless rose to the challenge, training its priests in media studies and using the new medium to its own advantage where possible.

One of the most important changes from abroad came from an unlikely source: Rome. The Second Vatican Council, which met between 1962 and 1965 under the direction of Pope John XXIII and then Pope Paul VI, was treated dismissively by the more conservative amongst the church hierarchy. "Nothing sensational will emerge from this Council," said Bishop Lucey of Cork before his departure to Rome in 1963. "You may have been worried by much talk of changes to come," said Archbishop McQuaid to the faithful on his return from the council in 1965. "Allow me to reassure you. No change will worry the tranquillity of your Christian lives."[16]

They could not have been more wrong. The council radically reformed the church, placing a new emphasis on lay involvement and welcoming enquiry and open discussion. It also helped to stimulate the growth of the ecumenical movement. The transformation was most marked in changes to everyday religious practice: Mass was now widely celebrated in the vernacular (both English and Gaelic), ritual and clerical dress were simplified and some traditional obligations were dispensed with. Though these changes were resisted by such conservatives as McQuaid, others, in particular the new archbishop of Armagh, Cardinal Conway, embraced them with enthusiasm and imagination. Considering the rigid nature of Irish Catholicism, the transition was remarkably smooth and, by adapting to new realities, the process served as a timely reinforcement of the position of the church in Irish life.

The apparent slide toward liberalism within the church was abruptly halted in 1968 when Pope Paul VI reasserted the church's unequivocal opposition to artificial birth control. Though conservatives welcomed this stance, in the long run it probably did more than anything else, in Ireland and elsewhere, to alienate church authorities from their flock. The ban on the sale of contraceptives became the focus for a campaign by women's groups which formed the first real movement to question the church's position in the State. The ban was challenged by judicial review and in 1979 the provision of contraceptives, in very limited circumstances, was legalized. This may have marked the first defeat for Catholic morality in Irish law, but its significance should not be overemphasized. The women's movement was small and divided; at this point there was no evidence of a tide of liberalism. For evidence that Catholic Ireland was still very much alive, one only needed to look at the visit of Pope John Paul II in 1979.

Echoes of the Eucharistic Congress of 1932 were unmistakable as crowds estimated at 2.7 million, more than half the population of the island, witnessed the first appearance of a pope on Irish soil. The extraordinary level of religious enthusiasm that swept the country seemed to prove that even now, surrounded by secular societies, Ireland remained different. John Paul's words as he left the country were: "Ireland: *semper fidelis,* always faithful!" But during his visit he showed himself aware that this was more an aspiration than a certainty. At a Mass in the Phoenix Park, Dublin, attended by more than a million people, he recalled the difficulties which Irish Catholics had faced in the past and warned:

> Ireland, that has overcome so many difficult moments in her history, is being challenged in a new way today, for she is not immune from the influence of ideologies and trends which present-day civilisation and progress carry with them....The challenge that is already with us is the temptation to accept as true freedom what in reality is only a new form of slavery.[17]

Two days later, at Limerick, he reiterated these sentiments, saying: "Your country seems in a sense to be living again the temptations of Christ: Ireland is being asked to prefer the 'kingdoms of the world and their splendour' to the kingdom of God."[18] He went on to make specific references to the dangers of divorce, contraception and abortion, and to the value of the woman's position in the home. Nor did he flinch from urging the faithful to reject any dilution in the Catholic nature of state legislation. As regards divorce, for example, he appealed:

> May Ireland always continue to give witness before the modern world to her traditional commitment, corresponding to the true dignity of man, to the sanctity and the indissolubility of the marriage bond. May the Irish always support marriage, through personal commitment and through positive social and legal action.[19]

The papal visit stimulated a significant, if short-lived, religious revival and prompted conservatives within the church to set about reinforcing the Catholic ethos of the State. But this coincided with a new push toward constitutional pluralism. Many years before, W. B. Yeats had said: "If you show that this country, Southern Ireland, is going to be governed by Catholic ideas and by Catholic ideas alone, you will never get the North."[20] Garret FitzGerald, the son of a southern Catholic and a northern Presbyterian, led a number of short-lived coalition governments during the early and mid-1980s, during which he attempted to make unification more attractive to northern Protestants by removing the Catholic bias from the Constitution. In a radio interview in 1981 he outlined the thinking behind his "crusade":

> We have created here something which the northern Protestants find unacceptable....What I want to do is to lead a crusade—a republican crusade—to make this a genuine

Republic on the principles of Tone and Davis, and, if I can, bring the people of this country on that path and get them to agree down here to the type of state that Tone and Davis looked for. I believe we could have the basis then on which many Protestants in Northern Ireland would be willing to consider a relationship with us, who at present have no reason to do so. If I was an Irish Protestant today, I can't see how I could aspire to getting involved in a State which is itself sectarian in the acutely sectarian way Northern Ireland was in which Catholics were repressed.[21]

By the end of the decade, the conservatives seemed to have won the battle. Taoiseach FitzGerald succeeded in liberalizing the laws on contraception in 1985, but conservatives had clear victories in referendums over the more contentious issues of abortion and divorce. Although abortion was already illegal in Ireland and there were few who sought a change in the law, the Pro-Life Amendment Campaign, founded in 1981, sought to copper-fasten this prohibition by writing it into the Constitution. FitzGerald's government reluctantly submitted to pressure to hold a referendum in 1983. After a victory for the "yes" vote by a two-to-one margin, an amendment to protect the right to life of the unborn child was added to the Constitution. The campaign had been particularly bitter, less about the issues themselves than about two different visions of the future, and showed sharp distinctions between Dublin and the rest of the country, and between the young and the old.

This pattern was mirrored in the 1986 referendum on the provision of divorce, which was defeated by a margin of two to one. Though the referendums showed that a clear majority of the electorate chose a view which coincided with church teaching, these were pyhrric victories. They revealed a cleavage amongst the people of the Republic, most of whom remained Catholics but differed about what that meant to them. The referendum results also showed up splits within the church as to what approach to take to politics.

The Catholic Church hierarchy had, for some time, made attempts to distance itself from matters of state law. In 1973 it had signaled an important departure in its statement that, while artificial contraception was wrong,

> It does not follow, of course, that the State is bound to prohibit the importation and sale of condoms. There are many things which the Catholic Church holds to be morally wrong and no one has ever suggested, least of all the Church herself, that they should be prohibited by the State.[22]

During the abortion and divorce referendums, the hierarchy had reiterated such sentiments while openly supporting one side. In 1983 they stated that they recognized "the right of each person to vote according to their conscience," but called for a "yes" vote which would constitute "a witness before Europe and before the whole world to the dignity and the sacredness of all human life from conception to death."[23] Some of the clergy were more outspoken in their statements, to a degree which even the organizers of the Pro-Life Campaign found unhelpful. During the divorce referendum, Bishop Cassidy encapsulated the difficult position, saying: "We don't dictate to people. We have no right to dictate but we have no option but to teach."[24]

But the question remained: How long would people listen? The 1980s threw up contradictory images of Ireland—both of old certainties and of challenges to the status quo. Two from the middle of the decade were particularly vivid. In the summer of 1985 crowds of more than ten thousand people came every night to pray at the "moving" statue of the Virgin Mary at Balinspittle, County Cork, after claims that it was possessed of miraculous powers. But a year earlier, beside another statue of the Virgin Mary at Clonard, County Longford, a fifteen-year-old girl, Anne Lovett, had died alone in childbirth. She had kept her pregnancy secret from family and friends for fear of the shame it would cause. Catholic Ireland was reassuring and welcoming to many, but as the century neared its end, not everyone was feeling its benefits.

PEACE IN THE NORTH?

In late 1980 and the early 1990s the communist powers of Eastern Europe fell like dominoes. Apartheid rule in South Africa was replaced by the democratically elected government of Nelson Mandela. Everywhere the political map was being reshaped by the changes which swept the globe after the end of the Cold War. But in Northern Ireland, the more things changed, the more they seemed to stay the same. Violence continued, reaching new levels of brutality with the death of ten civilians in the IRA bombing of a fish shop on Belfast's Shankill Road in October 1993 and the shooting dead of seven people in a pub at Greysteel, County Londonderry, a week later. Mainstream politics remained bogged down and peace looked as far away as ever. Yet, behind the headlines, bold moves were afoot which would result in Northern Ireland turning a corner toward peace.

The Troubles entered their third decade with little hope for an end to the war but new energy in its pursuit. In January 1990, as violence continued, talks began involving the British and Irish governments and the main constitutional parties in Northern Ireland. There were three aspects, or "strands," to these discussions: The first concerned the sharing of government between unionist and nationalist parties in Northern Ireland; the second the relationship between North and South; and the third the relationship between the United Kingdom and Ireland. Crucially, it was determined that no aspect of the plan could be implemented without agreement on all three strands. This was the beginning of a long and arduous process that eventually led to the Good Friday Agreement of 1998. The new secretary of state for Northern Ireland, Peter Brooke, signaled a change in the British government's position toward the province by stating that Britain had no "strategic or economic interest" in Ireland and acknowledging "the right of the Irish people to self-determination." While he assured unionists that a change to the position of Northern Ireland required the consent of its people, he added that the British government was neutral on the matter. Brooke also suggested an important shift in thinking toward the Republican movement, saying that he would not rule out talking to Sinn Féin if the IRA renounced violence.

The approach of the British and Irish governments had long been to isolate the extremists and cultivate the middle ground. But, as the Troubles dragged on, some began to consider that no solution could be reached without the participation of all involved. This was the thinking behind John Hume's decision in 1988 to open up secret talks with the Sinn Féin leader Gerry Adams. Although these talks broke down, they were renewed in 1993, resulting in a joint document on progress in Northern Ireland. In the same year it was revealed, to the shock of Unionists, that John Major's Conservative government had itself been conducting secret talks with Sinn Féin. Although Major was reluctant to make concessions to terrorists, he was pressed by the Taoiseach, Albert Reynolds, to take advantage of the Hume-Adams initiative. Reynolds's efforts resulted in the publication of a blueprint for peace in a joint statement by the British and Irish governments, the Downing Street Declaration of December 15, 1993. The British government reiterated that they

> have no selfish strategic or economic interest in Northern Ireland. Their primary interest is to see peace, stability and reconciliation established by agreement among all the people who inhabit the island, and they will work together

with the Irish Government to achieve such an agreement, which will embrace the totality of relationships.[25]

These arrangements could, they added, include a united Ireland if that was the expressed will of the people. The Irish government, for its part, accepted that

> the democratic right of self-determination by the people of Ireland as a whole must be achieved and exercised with and subject to the agreement and consensus of the majority of the people of Northern Ireland and must, consistent with justice and equity, respect the democratic dignity and the civil rights and religious liberties of both communities.[26]

They confirmed that the Irish government would, as part of such an arrangement, work for the removal of the claim to the North from its Constitution. Both governments added:

> The achievement of peace must involve a permanent end to the use of, or support for, paramilitary violence. They confirm that, in these circumstances, democratically mandated parties which establish a commitment to exclusively peaceful methods and which have shown that they abide by the democratic process, are free to participate fully in democratic politics and to join in dialogue in due course between the Governments and the political parties on the way ahead.[27]

In other words, if the paramilitaries renounced violence, they could take part in the process.

The leaders of the republican movement, Gerry Adams and Martin McGuinness, had grown up with the Troubles. They had joined the IRA as young men, had spent time in prison and played a central role in shaping military operations. By the late 1980s they had become convinced that the war was unwinnable and that the future of the Republican movement lay in the promotion of Sinn Féin as a legitimate political force. A similar sentiment was abroad amongst the Loyalist leadership, with such men as David Irvine, formerly a member of the Ulster Volunteer Force, developing strategies for nonviolent loyalism. But both sides found it difficult to take their rank and file with them. In particular, a rejection of the "armed struggle" and the de facto acceptance of partition were too much for many republicans. John Hume and Albert Reynolds, along with prominent Irish Americans, assured Republicans that the British government was genuinely committed to act as impartial facilitators of peace and that real gains were possible for the nationalist community. On August 31, 1994, after an intense period of internal discussion, the IRA announced a "complete cessation of military operations." While insisting that the Downing Street Declaration was not a solution and urging the British government to face up to its responsibilities, the statement said that the Republican movement was committed to peace. Announcements of cease-fires followed shortly afterward by the main loyalist paramilitaries, and new political parties—the *Progressive Unionist Party* and the *Ulster Democratic Party*—emerged from their constituencies.

Sinn Féin soon saw the benefits of its new position, with Adams attending a St. Patrick's Day reception at the White House in March 1995 and engaging in an official meeting with representatives of the British government. However, the IRA cease-fire was put under severe strain by the insistence of the British government—its narrow majority dependent on Unionist support—that the IRA declare its cease-fire "permanent" and prove it by decommissioning weapons. In February 1996 the peace was shattered when a massive IRA bomb exploded at Canary Wharf in London, killing two people. The all-party talks under the chairmanship of United States senator George Mitchell, which began in June, required a total commitment to nonviolence and therefore went ahead without Sinn Féin. However, the new Labour government under Tony Blair, elected in May 1997, made new efforts to break the deadlock and hastened the return of Sinn Féin to discussions. In July 1997 a further cease-fire was called, and within months the representatives of Sinn Féin had entered talks. This new situation, while welcomed by nationalists, made many unionists uneasy. Ian Paisley's DUP refused to take part, and the banning of an Orange Order march through a Catholic residential area of Drumcree became a focus for loyalist resistance.

The efforts of those involved in negotiation bore fruit on Good Friday 1998, when the Anglo-Irish Agreement was signed after an intense period of negotiation. Essential to the success of the Good Friday Agreement, as it has become known, was the fact that it was not intended to be a final settlement, but rather the basis of a process which would ensure peace and establish institutions which all main parties would recognize as legitimate. The agreement reasserted the principle of the consent of the majority of the people of Northern Ireland to any constitutional changes; a subsequent referendum in the Republic removed the state's claim to the six northern counties.

The agreement also envisaged wide-ranging changes, based on the original "three strands." A Northern Ireland Assembly would be set up, with a power-sharing executive. A North-South body would be established to coordinate cross-border cooperation on issues ranging from security to fisheries. Thirdly, a British-Irish Council would form the basis of regular contacts between the two governments, and an assembly of representatives of all regions of the two islands would be established to discuss matters of common interest. The agreement also outlined a program for equality and social justice, a commitment to the reduction of troops, the repeal of emergency powers legislation and the early release of paramilitary prisoners. For their part, the paramilitaries were to work constructively for the decommissioning of weapons. The agreement was put to the northern and southern electorate and was approved by 70 percent of voters—an overwhelming proportion of northern Nationalists and the population of the Republic, and a narrow majority of Unionists. The Executive, led by the UUP leader David Trimble, with Seamus Mallon of the SDLP as deputy, finally became a reality in November 1999. The IRA cease-fire has held since 1997, and in 2001 they began to destroy their weapons collection. The growing respectability of Sinn Féin and the concomitant electoral gains in the North and the South make a return to violence almost unthinkable. The political institutions too, despite many setbacks, have proved resilient.

Still, the Good Friday Agreement has brought neither certain peace nor true reconciliation. Renegade paramilitary groups have continued to commit acts of violence, most appallingly in August 1998 at Omagh, County Tyrone, where twenty-nine people from both communities were killed by a bomb placed by dissident Republicans calling themselves the "Real IRA." Regular tensions around the marching season and bitter conflicts in urban working-class districts where Catholic and Protestant communities sit cheek-by-jowl show no sign of abatement. These ongoing sectarian tensions are reflected in the electoral success of Sinn Féin and the DUP at the expense of the center ground. Nationalists retain grievances, in particular the basic fact of their position within a state to which they owe little or no allegiance. But Unionists now increasingly see themselves as victims of the new dispensation. The release of paramilitary prisoners, the scaling-down of the British military presence, changes to the Northern Ireland police force and the presence of Sinn Féin in the Executive have been perceived by some as concessions to terrorism. As the Church of Ireland primate Archbishop Robin Eames put it in his Easter sermon, 2002:

> Not all can identify with or accept the changes that are taking place; too many feel they are victims of change.

They do not feel they own change. Ownership of change removes suspicion and hatred.[28]

Most of all, the growing proportion of Catholics in Northern Ireland—the present estimate is 46 percent—suggests that a united Ireland will become a reality within the next quarter of a century.

As the communist states of Europe collapsed, some were quick to hail the "end of history." The events of recent years have prompted enthusiastic hopes amongst some that the conflict between the Catholics and Protestants of Northern Ireland will have no place in the world of the twenty-first century. In a society where conflict is not only part of ancient history but also of recent memory this seems too hopeful. Nevertheless, the two communities find themselves, in the new century, in a different position. In an age where the global economy and culture and international institutions such as the European Union and the United Nations play an ever greater part in peoples' lives, there are more opportunities to override the politics of majority and minority. The longer the cease-fires hold and the agreement stands, the more it becomes possible to build on the gains of the 1990s. There will undoubtedly be difficulties ahead, but the abiding image of Good Friday 1998—of the various parties emerging after a long night, blinking in the sunlight—seems an appropriate one.

THE END OF CATHOLIC IRELAND

Precisely when the decline of Catholic Ireland became terminal is unclear, but the election of Mary Robinson as president of the Republic in 1990 seems the defining moment in the birth of a new Ireland. Her résumé read like a catalogue of impediments to electability. First, she was a woman in a state where women had traditionally played a peripheral role in public life. Further, she was a liberal feminist who had led campaigns against the church position on every issue from contraception to divorce. Furthermore, in a country where the invocation of one's nationalist credentials remained a necessary part of any political campaign, this was someone who had left the Labour Party in protest at the imposition of the Anglo-Irish Agreement on Unionists. Yet, she was elected ahead of the nominees of the two largest parties.

Part of her success was undoubtedly due to Robinson's own abilities and the dignified conduct of her campaign, but her election also illustrated the public's willingness to embrace a new direction in Irish life. It demonstrated the voting power of Irish women and a growing challenge to their perception in society. When a Fianna Fáil minister claimed that "none of us who knew Mary Robinson very well in previous incarnations ever heard her claiming to be a great wife and mother," there was outrage, particularly from women.

That same year, there were other signs that the Republic was beginning to embrace a new identity. At the top of the best-seller list was Roddy Doyle, a Dublin novelist who eschewed the traditional themes of Irish literature—the Catholic Church and the Northern Ireland Troubles—in favor of a vision of Ireland which was at home with outside influences, yet remained distinctive. That summer, when Ireland's soccer team reached the quarter-finals of the World Cup, crime ground to a halt, momentarily at least. The last time that had happened was during the papal visit in 1979.

The office of president is a symbolic one, but Robinson went further than any previous incumbent in putting a personal stamp on the office. In her inauguration speech she declared:

> The Ireland that I will be representing is a new Ireland, open, tolerant, inclusive. Many of you who voted for me did so without sharing all my views. This, I believe, is a significant signal of change, a sign, however modest, that we have already passed the threshold to a new, pluralist Ireland.[29]

Robinson's term in office also coincided with a progressive dismantling of the State's overtly Catholic legislation. In 1992 the "X case"—concerning a fourteen-year-old rape victim who was prevented by the courts from traveling to Britain for an abortion—horrified many Irish people and made international news. It led to the modification of the abortion laws. The Supreme Court ruled that the risk of suicide of the mother was a legitimate reason for termination, and a subsequent referendum allowed for freedom to travel and to distribute information on abortion in Ireland. The following year, when the state was challenged in the European Court of Human Rights, homosexual acts between adults were decriminalized. In 1995 a referendum voted—by 51 percent to 49 percent—to remove the constitutional ban on divorce.

These changes did not represent a sudden and overwhelming rejection of Catholic morality. The courts played as much, if not more, of a role than the will of the people, and a large majority outside Dublin opposed the legalization of divorce. Nevertheless, with the exception of the ever controversial issue of abortion, the liberalization of Irish law provoked little public outcry. This was in part because at the same time the church was undergoing an unprecedented crisis.

In 1992 it was revealed that the popular bishop of Galway, Eamonn Casey, had fathered a son by an American woman and had taken no role in the boy's upbringing, except to channel church funds for his support. In 1995 it became known that the well-known, media-friendly priest, Father Michael Cleary, an outspoken opponent of liberal values, had fathered two children in a long-term relationship. These scandals, while relatively trivial in themselves, did much to damage the image of the clergy, making them appear hypocritical or, worse, ridiculous. More serious were the revelations of child abuse. Some were cases of abuse by individual clergy, such as Father Brendan Smyth who, in 1997, was found guilty of seventy-four charges of sexual abuse. Between 1991 and

1999 a total of thirty-five priests, brothers and ex-clergy had been convicted on child-sex-abuse charges. Other verdicts concerned church-maintained institutions, such as the Artane Industrial School, where Christian Brothers were found to have physically and sexually assaulted children in their care in the years before its closure in 1969. What particularly rankled—and this was echoed in the scandals which beset the Catholic Church in the United States at the start of the twenty-first century—was the way in which the church authorities had facilitated such abuse, by moving clergy from parish to parish, rather than turning them over to the authorities. It was the failure to discipline abusers within his diocese which led to the resignation of Bishop Desmond Comisckey of Ferns, County Wexford, in 2002.

It was not that the church became more corrupt in the 1990s—most of the incidents revealed were decades old—but that newspapers were prepared to report on them and people were prepared to listen. The public revulsion at the scandals reflected a general change in attitudes toward authority, coinciding with investigations into corruption against senior politicians which showed up extraordinary levels of fraud and bribery. These scandals also went back to the 1970s and 1980s, but the public focus on them showed a general willingness to question persons in positions of authority. Priests who returned to Ireland in the late 1990s after years abroad at the missions were shocked at the change in attitude from universal respect to widespread suspicion and even hostility.

In the 1990s society in the Republic was turned upside-down. After years of stagnation, the economy took off, thanks to European Union funds, inward investment and adept financial management. The "Celtic Tiger" economy worked the miracle of sharp and sustained growth, combined with low inflation and low unemployment. In short, Ireland became rich. Historically, rises in living standards in Ireland have tended to be accompanied by greater religious piety, and prosperity alone cannot explain a turn away from Catholic values. But the "Celtic Tiger" economy brought with it radical societal changes which could not help but challenge traditional attitudes toward religion.

For more than a century the bedrock of Irish Catholicism had been the close ties of communities, especially in rural areas, and this had been reinforced by a relative insularity. In the 1990s Ireland became a predominantly urban society, where lives were busier and more atomized than before. Consumerism had existed for decades, but at the end of the century materialism appeared rampant. The expansion of the media continued to expose Ireland to global culture, and Irish men and women played an ever more prominent part in that culture. For young people, a large proportion of the population, better educated, wealthier and more open to outside influences than earlier generations had ever been, the ideals on which the state had been founded looked increasingly irrelevant.

The church, while still outspoken on the issue of abortion, has tended to take a less prominent role in the politics of the Republic, often stating its position on current affairs but emphasizing its respect for the conscientious decision of the individual. As well, partly due to the fall in vocations to the priesthood, it has retreated from the management of schools, a position which it had once held on to so tenaciously. The Catholic Church will never regain the hold which it had on the majority of the Irish people from the nineteenth century until recent decades, but there are signs that it may be adapting to a new role. The "Celtic Tiger," while benefiting many, has left others worse off than ever. The work of the Catholic Church in helping the homeless, drug users, and refugees and asylum-seekers points to a new direction, at a time when champions of social justice are more needed than ever.

CONCLUSION

Ireland is no longer a Christian country in the sense that it has been for a millennium and a half. Though a large majority of Irish people call themselves Christian, religion plays a lesser role in peoples' lives, as suggested by falling church attendances and in changing attitudes toward the churches. Religion, which once dominated politics in Ireland, is, if not marginal, no longer central. Irish society, North and South, has changed, everyday life mirroring that found in the secular liberal societies of western Europe. But does this mean that Christianity in Ireland has no future?

One important change that has taken place is that the Irish are now more than ever before a people of many faiths. Other religious traditions have always existed in Ireland, but nowadays, largely because of immigration over the past decade, their communities are much more prevalent than before. Until relatively recently, the only non-Christians who enjoyed any level of visibility in Ireland were the Jews. References to Jews in Ireland go back to the Middle Ages, but most of Ireland's present-day Jews are descended from those who came to Ireland from eastern Europe in the late nineteenth and early twentieth centuries. Over the past century their numbers reached six thousand, and they played a prominent part in business and political life. Dublin and Cork have each had Jewish lord mayors, and though Limerick once witnessed anti-Semitic pogroms, the Jewish tradition was singled out for mention in DeValera's 1937 Constitution. And when James Joyce wrote *Ulysses* he put at its center a Dublin Jew, Leopold Bloom. Nowadays, Ireland has fewer than two thousand Jews, but they continue to play a significant role in Irish life.

Ireland has also, since the early twentieth century, become a home to Hindus, Buddhists and adherents of other Eastern religions, and their numbers have continued to grow. But by far the fastest-growing religion in Ireland is Islam. Muslims have been recorded in Ireland since the nineteenth century; an Islamic Society was established in Dublin in 1959, and a mosque in 1976. But immigration over the past decade, from the Balkan states, North Africa and the Middle East, has accounted for a large increase in numbers of adherents to around twelve thousand. Today the Republic has six mosques and two Muslim schools—the first time the state has funded non-Christian faith schools.

It appears that large numbers of those who were born into Christian families have now abandoned their faith, most dramatically among the Catholics in the Republic. This is most evident in the numbers of those who attend weekly Mass. Between 1973 and 1987 the numbers had declined only from 91 percent to 87 percent, but by 1993 they were down to 77 percent. By the start of the twenty-first century they had plunged to 57 percent, with much lower levels among young people and in urban areas. In some parts of Dublin, attendance was as low as 5 percent. Birth, marriage and death have continued to be marked by church ceremony, but it now plays a much lesser role in everyday life. At the same time, people now appear to take less notice of the church's strictures. A survey in 1998, for example, showed that only 19 percent of Catholics agreed with the church's teaching on contraception.[1] It seems that many have adopted what church leaders have derided as "à la carte Catholicism"—choosing to follow some aspects of church teaching but to reject others.

Though the decline in commitment to the Catholic Church in the South has been spectacular and much commented upon, the churches of Northern Ireland, both Catholic and Protestant, have suffered an equally marked decline in commitment. A survey published in 2002 has shown that while 90 percent of Northern Ireland's residents identify themselves as belonging to a church, all the churches are facing a decline in church attendance, with Protestant churches suffering most. In 1991 47 percent of the population described themselves as members of one of the major Protestant churches, but by 1998 this number had dropped to 39 percent. While 60 percent of Catholics said that they attended weekly Mass, Protestant weekly attendance had dropped from 34 percent to 29 percent between 1991 and 1998. Furthermore, only 20 percent of mainstream Protestants surveyed considered sex before marriage "always wrong." Significantly, both the Protestant and the Catholic churches have an aging population, with much less commitment amongst the young.[2]

There are many reasons why this should have happened. The crises and failure of leadership within the Catholic Church in particular have obviously played a part, but more important are fundamental changes in society. Ireland has never been isolated from the wider world, but for much of the twentieth century it was a more inward-looking place. Mostly due to the conflicts of modern times, the peoples of Ireland tended to stress their communal identities, and these were anchored in their various religious traditions. In more recent years, Ireland has been opened to the world by travel, returning emigrants, the European Union and the media. Most of all, the prosperity which came with the boom of the 1990s in the Republic and the new conditions of post-Troubles Northern Ireland has instilled a confidence which has made older support systems and certainties appear less relevant, especially among young people.

Still, one should not conclude that Christianity in Ireland has collapsed overnight. While the attendance of the Republic's Catholics at Mass has declined drastically, more than half the population still attends regularly, a far greater proportion than in the Catholic countries of continental Europe. Equally, while the commitment to the churches of Northern Ireland has declined, it remains far higher than in the rest of the United Kingdom, where only 20 percent of the population say that they are members of a church.

The defeat of a referendum in 2002 aimed at further restricting the Republic's abortion laws was rightly regarded as a defeat for the Catholic Church which had supported it. But 49 percent of those who cast their vote backed the measure, and the Republic's abortion law remains among the most restrictive in the world. Equally, Britain's liberalizing Abortion Act of 1967 has never been extended to Northern Ireland, due to the opposition of many Catholics and Protestants there. Ireland is a less Christian country than it once was, but Christianity still plays a greater part there than in most of the western world.

To be Irish no longer automatically means to be a Christian. Some Christians have welcomed these developments, arguing that whereas once the Christian faith was something that people were born into and accepted unthinkingly, it is now a conscious decision requiring commitment. Many see the growing range of spiritualities, particularly from the Celtic past, and the growing involvement of the laity, especially women, in church life as positive signs. The challenge appears to be in adapting to the changing nature of society, both North and South. Christianity came to prosper in Ireland over the ages because it interacted with the lives of its people and responded to their needs. If Ireland's present-day Christians can take on board the lessons of the past, Christian Ireland will be ensured a future.

ENDNOTES AND
FURTHER READING

FURTHER READING—GENERAL

Bowen, D., *The History and Shaping of Irish Protestantism* (1995).

Campbell, F., *The Dissenting Voice: Protestant Democracy in Ulster from Plantation to Partition* (1991).

Corish, P., ed., *A History of Irish Catholicism* (1967–71).

Corish, P., *The Irish Catholic Experience* (1985).

de Paor, L., *The Peoples of Ireland: From Prehistory to Modern Times* (1986).

Elliott, M., *The Catholics of Ulster* (2000).

Flaherty, O. P., *Catholicism in Ulster, 1603–1983* (1974).

Foster, R., *Modern Ireland 1600–1972* (1988).

Gill History of Ireland, 12 vols. (1969–75).

Hachey, T. E. et al., *The Irish Experience* (1989).

Helicon History of Ireland, 9 vols. (1981–88).

Holmes, F., *Our Irish Presbyterian Heritage* (1985).

Johnson, T. J. et al., *A History of the Church of Ireland* (1953).

Lang, P., *History and the Shaping of Irish Protestantism* (1995).

Longman History of Ireland, 2 vols. (1995–).

Loughrey, P., *The People of Ireland* (1988).

Lydon, J., *The Making of Ireland* (1998).

Martin, F. X. et al., eds., *A New History of Ireland* (1976–).

Richardson, N., ed., *A Tapestry of Beliefs: Christian Traditions in Northern Ireland* (1988).

Stewart, A. T. Q., *The Narrow Ground: Aspects of Ulster 1609–1969* (1977).

I. BEFORE CHRISTIANITY

1. *Táin Bó Cúalnge*, ed. C. O'Rahilly (1967), p. 158.
2. *Lebor Gabála Erenn*, ed. R.A. S. Macalister, vol. 5 (1956), p. 111.
3. Pope Gregory the Great, Epistle XI, 56, ed. J. Barmby (1898), pp. 84–85.

Further Reading

Green, M., *The Gods of the Celts* (1995).

Harbison, P., *Pre-Christian Ireland: From the First Settlers to the Early Celts* (1988).

Low, M., *Celtic Christianity and Nature* (1996).

O'hOgáin, D., *The Sacred Isle* (1999).

Ross, A., *Everyday Life of the Pagan Celts* (1970).

Sjoestedt, M.-L., *Gods and Heroes of the Celts* (1949).

II. ST. PATRICK AND THE COMING OF CHRISTIANITY

1. L. de Paor, *St. Patrick's World* (1993), p. 99.
2. Ibid., p. 100.
3. Ibid., p. 106.
4. Ibid., p. 108.
5. Ibid., pp. 118–19.

6. The arguments are summarized in D. A. Binchy, "Patrick and his Biographers, Ancient and Modern," in *Studia Hibernica* vol. 2 (1962), pp. 7–173.

7. *St. Patrick's World*, p. 136.

8. Ibid., pp. 137–38.

9. *The Patrician Texts in the Book of Armagh*, ed. L. Bieler (1979), p. 71.

10. Ibid., p. 87.

11. Ibid., pp. 89–99.

12. Ibid., p. 111.

13. Ibid., p. 185.

14. *St. Patrick's World*, p. 160.

Further Reading

Binchy, D. A., "Patrick and His Biographers, Ancient and Modern," *Studia Hibernica*, vol. 2 (1962).

de Paor, L., *St. Patrick's World* (1993).

de Paor, L. and M., *Early Christian Ireland* (1958).

Dumville, D., et al., *St. Patrick, A.D. 449* (1993).

Thompson, E., *Who Was St. Patrick?* (1985).

III. SAINTS AND SCHOLARS

1. L. de Paor, *St. Patrick's World* (1993), p. 104.

2. Ibid., p. 222.

3. Ibid., pp. 223–24.

4. Ibid., p. 207.

5. *The Voyage of St. Brendan*, ed. J. J. O'Meara (1976).

6. T. O'Fiach, *Columbanus In His Own Words* (1974), p. 76.

7. Ibid., p. 80.

8. Ibid., pp. 86, 87, 91.

9. Bede, *A History of the English Church and People,* ed. L. Sherley-Price (1958), iii. 25, p. 188.

10. *An Anthology of Irish Literature*, ed. D. H. Greene (1971), vol. 1, p. 11.

11. Giraldus Cambrensis (Gerald of Wales), *The History and Topography of Ireland*, ed. J. J. O'Meara (1982), p. 71.

12. *Ancient Irish Poetry*, ed. K. Meyer (1913), p. 101.

13. *Annals of Ulster*, pp. 281–83.

14. D. A. Binchy, "The Passing of the Old Order," in *The Impact of the Scandinavian Invasions on the Celtic-Speaking Peoples c. A.D. 800–1100*, ed. B. O'Cuív (1962), pp. 119–32.

15. *Annals of Ulster*, pp. 287–89.

16. Ibid., p. 299.

17. Ibid., p. 301.

Further Reading

Bitel, L. M., *Isle of the Saints: Monastic Settlement and Christian Community in Ireland* (1990).

Herbert, M., *Iona, Kells and Derry* (1996).

Hughes, K., *The Church in Early Irish Society* (1966).

———. *The Modern Traveller to the Early Irish Church* (1977).

Whiteside, L., *In Search of Columba* (1997).

IV. THE ANGLO-NORMAN CHURCH

1. A. Gwynn, "The Twelfth-Century Reform," in *A History of Irish Catholicism*, ed. P. Corish, vol. 2 (1968), p. 3.

2. *The Letters of Lanfranc Archbishop of Canterbury*, eds H. Clover and M. Gibson (1979), no. 9, p. 67.

3. *The Epistolae Vagantes of Pope Gregory VII*, ed. E. J. Cowdrey (1972), no. 57, pp. 139–41.

4. *The Letters of Lanfranc*, no. 10, p. 71.

5. Bernard of Clairvaux, *The Life and Death of St. Malachy the Irishman*, ed. R. T. Meyer (1978), p. 13, para. 16.

6. John of Salisbury, *Metalogicon*, ed. J. Webb (1929), pp. 217–18.

7. *The Historical Works of Giraldus Cambrensis*, ed. T. Wright (1863), pp. 215–16.

8. Stephen of Lexington, *Letters from Ireland 1228–1229*, ed. B. D. O'Dwyer (1922), p. 188.

9. *Irish Historical Documents 1172–1922*, eds. E. Curtis and R. B. Macdowell (1943), p. 43.

10. Cotter, F. J., *The Friars Minor in Ireland* (1994), p. 41.

11. R. Horrox, ed., *The Black Death* (1994), p. 84.

Further Reading

Conlan, P., *Franciscan Ireland* (1988).

Gwynn, A., *The Irish Church in the Eleventh and Twelfth Centuries* (1992).

Henry, F., *Irish Art in the Romanesque Period (1020–1170)* (1970).

Mould, D. Pochin, *The Monasteries of Ireland* (1976).

Stalley, R., *The Cistercian Monasteries of Ireland* (1987).

Watt, J., *The Church and the Two Nations in Medieval Ireland* (1970).

V. REFORMATION AND REVOLUTION

1. *Irish History from Contemporary Sources, 1509–1610*, ed. C. Maxwell (1923), p. 123.

2. Ibid., p. 129.

3. Ibid., p. 135.

4. Ibid., pp. 135–36.

5. Ibid., pp. 146–47.

6. Ibid., p. 150.

7. Ibid., p. 154.

8. C. Lennon, *Sixteenth-Century Ireland* (1994), p. 154.

9. *Irish History*, pp. 137–38.

10. *The Field Day Anthology of Irish Writing*, ed. S. Deane (1991), vol. 1, p. 252.

11. R. Buick Knox, *James Ussher, Archbishop of Armagh* (1967), p. 35.

12. *Irish History*, n.1, p. 151.

13. A. Ford, "The Protestant Reformation," in *Natives and*

Newcomers: The Making of Irish Colonial Society, eds C. Brady and R. Gillespie (1986), p. 73.

14. *Irish History*, pp. 297–98.

15. Thomas Morley, from "A Remonstrance," in *Strangers to That Land: British Perceptions of Ireland from the Reformation to the Famine*, eds A. Hadfield and J. McVeagh (1994), p. 116.

16. Ibid., p. 118.

17. "Letters from Ireland," in *Field Day Anthology*, p. 861.

18. Vincent Gookin, "The Great Case of Transplantation Discussed," in *Strangers to That Land*, p. 127.

Further Reading

Brady, C. and R. Gillespie, eds, *Natives and Newcomers: The Making of Irish Colonial Society 1534–1641* (1986).

Ford, A., *The Protestant Reformation in Ireland, 1590–1641* (1987).

Knox, R. Buick, *James Ussher, Archbishop of Armagh* (1967).

Robinson, P. S., *The Plantation of Ulster* (1984).

VI. CATHOLIC, PROTESTANT AND DISSENTER

1. "Inis Fál," in *The Faber Book of Irish Verse*, ed. J. Montague (1974), p. 145.

2. *English Historical Documents*, vol. 3, ed. A. Browning (1953), p. 765.

3. W. P. Burke, *The Irish Priest in the Penal Times, 1660–1760* (1969), pp. 245–46.

4. Ibid., p. 171.

5. J. Lydon, *The Making of Ireland* (1998), p. 225.

6. *The Field Day Anthology of Irish Writing*, ed. S. Deane (1991), vol. 1, p. 874.

7. Ibid., p. 875.

8. E. M. Johnston, *Ireland in the Eighteenth Century* (1974), p. 17; T. Bartlett, *The Fall and Rise of the Irish Nation* (1992), p. 18.

9. *An Anthology of Irish Literature*, ed. D. H. Greene (1971), vol. 2, p. 250.

10. *Field Day Anthology*, p. 419.

11. Ibid., p. 481.
12. Ibid., p. 388.
13. *The Decade of the United Irishmen: Contemporary Accounts 1791–1801*, ed. T. Killen (1997), p. 21.
14. Ibid., p. 19.
15. P. Corish, *The Irish Catholic Experience* (1985), pp. 143–44.
16. "An Impartial Account…," in *Peep O'Day Boys and Defenders: Selected Documents on the Disturbances in County Armagh, 1784–1796*, ed. D. W. Miller (1990), p. 54.
17. Ibid., pp. 83–84.
18. *The Decade of the United Irishmen*, p. 137.

Further Reading

Bartlett, T., *The Fall and Rise of the Irish Nation* (1992).

Bartlett, T., and Hayton, D., *Penal Era and Golden Age: Essays in Irish History 1690–1800* (1979).

Burke, W. P., *The Irish Priest in the Penal Times, 1660–1760* (1969).

Jackson, R. W., *Jonathan Swift: Dean and Pastor* (1939, repr. 1971).

Kilroy, P., *Protestant Dissent and Controversy in Ireland 1660–1714* (1994).

Landa, L. A., *Swift and the Church of Ireland* (1965).

O'Brien, G., ed., *Christian Ireland in the Eighteenth Century: Collected Essays of Maureen Wall* (1989).

Power, T., and K. Whelan, *Endurance and Emergence: Catholics in Ireland in the Eighteenth Century* (1990).

Williams, T. D., ed., *Secret Societies in Ireland* (1973).

VII. THE MAKING OF MODERN CHRISTIANITY

1. "Description of the…Peasantry of Ireland," in *Strangers to That Land: British Perceptions of Ireland from the Reformation to the Famine*, eds A. Hadfield and J. McVeagh (1994), pp. 212–13.

2. S. Connolly, *Priests and People in Pre-Famine Ireland 1780–1845* (1982), p. 136.

3. "The Irish Sketch Book," in *The Ireland Anthology*, ed. S. Dunne (1997).

4. *Strangers to That Land*, p. 213.

5. *Priests and People*, p. 143.

6. Ibid., p. 139.

7. Ibid., pp. 148–49.

8. Ibid., pp. 152–53.

9. J. G. A. Prim, "An Attempt to Identify the Persons who issued Trademen's Tokens in Kilkenny," *Journal of the Royal Society of Antiquarians of Ireland,* vol. 2 (1852), pp. 323–24.

10. *Priests and People*, p. 193.

11. Ibid., p. 183.

12. R. Uí Ogáin, *Immortal Dan: Daniel O'Connell in Irish Folk Tradition* (1995), p. 104.

13. "The Catholic Rent or Catholic Freedom," in F. O'Ferrall, *Catholic Emancipation: Daniel O'Connell and the Birth of Irish Democracy 1820–1830* (1985), p. 56.

14. Ibid., p. 56.

15. Ibid., p. 107.

16. Ibid., p. 135.

17. *Immortal Dan*, pp. 99–100.

18. *Catholic Emancipation*, p. 142.

19. *The Famine Decade, Contemporary Accounts 1841–51*, ed. J. Killen (1995), p. 21.

20. Ibid., p. 6.

21. D. A. Kerr, *The Catholic Church and the Famine* (1996), p. 26.

22. *Famine Decade*, pp. 206–7.

23. *Catholic Church and Famine*, p. 42.

24. Ibid., pp. 28–29.

25. Ibid., pp. 51–52.

26. Ibid., p. 77.

27. W. D. Griffin, *The Book of Irish Americans* (1990), pp. 118–19.
28. J. White Macauley, "Ireland under an Orange Banner: Reflections on the northern Protestant experiences of emigration," *The Irish Worldwide: History, Heritage, Identity*, vol. 5, ed. P. O'Sullivan (1996).
29. *Book of Irish Americans*, pp. 121–22.
30. C. Wittke, *The Irish in America* (1970), p. 92.
31. *Catholic Church and the Famine*, p. 85.
32. E. Larkin, "The Devotional Revolution in Ireland, 1850–75," *American Historical Review*, vol. 77 (1972), pp. 625–52.
33. R. B. McDowell, *The Church of Ireland 1869–1969* (1975), pp. 28–29.
34. Ibid., p. 29.
35. D. McCartney, "The Churches and Secret Societies," *Secret Societies in Ireland*, ed. T. D. Williams (1973), p. 75.
36. F. S. L. Lyons, *Ireland Since the Famine* (1971), p. 130.
37. J. Lydon, *The Making of Ireland* (1998), p. 314.
38. *The Ireland Anthology*, ed. S. Dunne (1997), p. 256.

Further Reading

Bowen, D., *Paul Cardinal Cullen* (1983).
Connolly, S., *Priests and People in Pre-Famine Ireland 1780–1845* (1982).
———, *Religion and Society in Nineteenth-Century Ireland* (1985).
Hempton, D., and H. Hill, *Evangelical Protestantism in Ulster Society, 1740–1890* (1992).
Kerr, D. A., *The Catholic Church and the Famine* (1996).
Larkin, E., "The Devotional Revolution in Ireland, 1850–75," in *American Historical Review*, vol. 77 (1972).
Lyons, F. S. L., *Ireland Since the Famine* (1971).
McDowell, R. B., *The Church of Ireland 1869–1969* (1975).
O'Ferrall, F., *Catholic Emancipation: Daniel O'Connell and the Birth of Irish Democracy 1820–1830* (1985).

VIII. THE UNION AND THE NATION

1. A. McLelland, "The Later Orange Order," in *Secret Societies in Ireland*, ed. T. D. Williams (1973), p. 127.
2. Ibid., p. 129.
3. F. Campbell, *The Dissenting Voice: Protestant Democracy in Ulster from Plantation to Partition* (1991), pp. 322–23.
4. F. Holmes, *Our Irish Presbyterian Heritage* (1985), p. 134.
5. J. Loughlin, *Ulster Unionism and British National Identity since 1885* (1992), p. 23.
6. D. Hempton and H. Hill, *Evangelical Protestantism in Ulster Society, 1740–1890* (1992), p. 173.
7. D. McCartney, "The Churches and Secret Societies," in *Secret Societies*, p. 76.
8. *Irish Historical Documents 1172–1922*, eds E. Curtis and R. B. McDowell (1943), p. 304.
9. *The Ireland Anthology*, ed. S. Dunne (1997), p. 262.
10. Ibid., pp. 262–63.
11. D. McCartney, *Secret Societies*, p. 76.
12. M. Laffan, "The Sacred Memory: Religion, Revisionists and the Easter Rising," in *Religion and Rebellion*, eds J. Devlin and R. Fanning (1997), p. 176.
13. R. Dudley Edwards, *Patrick Pearse: The Triumph of Failure* (1990), p. 253.
14. Ibid., p. 255.
15. Ibid., pp. 161–62.
16. Ibid., p. 179.
17. Ibid., p. 174.
18. T. Farmar, *Ordinary Lives: Three Generations of Irish Middle Class Experience* (1991), pp. 127–28.
19. J. H. Whyte, *Church and State in Modern Ireland, 1923–79* (1984), p. 27.

20. S. Connolly, *Priests and People in Pre-Famine Ireland 1780–1845* (1982), p. 178.
21. *Church and State*, p. 14.
22. Ibid., p. 37.
23. *Ordinary Lives*, p. 133.
24. J. J. Lee, *Ireland 1912–1985* (1989), p. 163.
25. *Great Irish Speeches of the Twentieth Century*, ed. M. McLoughlin (1996), p. 124.
26. *Ireland 1912–1985*, p. 170.
27. *Great Irish Speeches*, p. 206.
28. *Church and State*, p. 48.
29. Clause 5.1.
30. H. Hyde, *Carson* (1953), p. 449.
31. T. Gray, *The Orange Order* (1972), p. 225.
32. P. Bew, G. Gibbon, and H. Patterson, *Northern Ireland 1921–1994: Political Forces and Social Classes* (1995), p. 15.
33. F. Tobin, *The Best of Decades: Ireland in the Nineteen Sixties* (1984), p. 41.
34. *Great Irish Speeches*, pp. 263, 268.

Further Reading

Edwards, R. Dudley, *Patrick Pearse: The Triumph of Failure* (1990).
Farmar, T., *Ordinary Lives: Three Generations of Irish Middle Class Experience* (1991).
Gray, T., *The Orange Order* (1972).
Hyde, H., *Carson* (1953).
Laffan, M., "The Sacred Memory: Religion, Revisionists and the Easter Rising," in *Religion and Rebellion*, eds J. Devlin and R. Fanning (1997).
Lee, J. J., *Ireland 1912–1985* (1989).
Loughlin, J., *Ulster Unionism and British National Identity since 1885* (1992).
O'Brien, C. Cruise, *States of Ireland* (1972).
Whyte, J. H., *Church and State in Modern Ireland*, 1923–79 (1984).

IX. INTO THE NEW MILLENNIUM

1. P. Bew and G. Gillespie, *Northern Ireland: A Chronology of the Troubles 1968–1999* (1999), p. 18.

2. D. McKitterick, *Endgame: The Search for Peace in Northern Ireland* (1994), p. 43.

3. P. O'Malley, *The Uncivil Wars: Ireland Today* (1997), pp. 178–79.

4. Ibid., p. 135.

5. Ibid., p. 151.

6. G. McElroy, *The Catholic Church and the Northern Ireland Crisis, 1968–86* (1991), pp. 141–42.

7. D. Bowen, *The History and Shaping of Irish Protestantism* (1995), p. 412.

8. *Catholic Church and N.I. Crisis*, p. 43.

9. Ibid., p. 160.

10. J. J. Lee, *Ireland 1912–1985* (1989), p. 317.

11. J. H. Whyte, *Church and State in Modern Ireland 1923–79* (1984), p. 27.

12. T. Farmar, *Ordinary Lives: Three Generations of Irish Middle Class Experience* (1991), p. 154.

13. Ibid., p. 159.

14. Ibid., p. 191.

15. F. Tobin, *Best of Decades: Ireland in the Nineteen Sixties* (1984), p. 41.

16. *History...Irish Protestantism*, p. 427.

17. *The Pope in Ireland: Addresses and Homilies* (1979), pp. 9–10.

18. Ibid., p. 78.

19. Ibid., pp. 78–79.

20. *Great Irish Speeches of the Twentieth Century*, ed. M. McLoughlin (1996).

21. J. Cooney, *The Crozier and the Dáil: Church and State in Ireland 1922–1986* (1986), pp. 7–8.

22. M. Dillon, *Debating Divorce: Moral Conflict in Ireland* (1993), pp. 92–93.

23. Ibid., p. 93.

24. Ibid., pp. 95–96.

25. *Downing Street Declaration*, Clause 4.

26. Ibid.

27. Ibid., Clause 9.

28. *The Irish Times*, January 4, 2002.

29. *Great Irish Speeches*, p. 369.

Further Reading

Cassidy, E. G., *Faith and Culture in the Irish Context* (1996).

Cooney, J., *The Crozier and the Dáil: Church and State in Ireland 1922–1986* (1986).

Dillon, M., *Debating Divorce: Moral Conflict in Ireland* (1993).

Dunne, S., *Facets of the Conflict in Northern Ireland* (1995).

Gallagher, E., and S. Worrall, *Christians in Ulster, 1968–1980* (1982).

Irvine, M., *Northern Ireland—faith and faction* (1991).

McElroy, G., *The Catholic Church and the Northern Ireland Crisis, 1968–86* (1991).

McKitterick, D., *Endgame: The Search for Peace in Northern Ireland* (1994).

O'Malley, P., *The Uncivil Wars: Ireland Today* (1997).

O'Toole, F., *The Lie of the Land: Irish Identities* (1998).

Taylor, L.J., *Occasions of Faith: An Anthropology of Irish Catholicism* (1995).

Tobin, F., *The Best of Decades: Ireland in the Nineteen Sixties* (1984).

CONCLUSION

1. *The Irish Times*, February 5, 1998; December 17, 1999; and December 27, 2000.

2. Professor John Bower, "Are There Any Christians in Northern Ireland?" *Irish Times,* January 10, 2002. Based on *Irish Times* survey.

PICTURE CREDITS

Permission to use copyright material is gratefully acknowledged to the following. While every effort has been made to trace all copyright holders, the publisher apologizes to any holders possibly not acknowledged.

Art Resource: page 44

Bord Failte—Irish Tourist Board: pages 23, 46

Christian Charisius: page 152

Duchas, The Heritage Service: pages viii, 4, 13, 20, 31, 33, 40, 48, 51, 67, 68, 70, 80, 81, 86, 96, 137, 190

Selga Medenieks: page 34

National Gallery of Ireland: pages 126, 136, 145, 166

Courtesy of the National Library of Ireland: pages 72, 93, 109, 121, 154, 202

National Museum of Ireland: pages 18, 59, 64

Bill Rolston, from *Drawing Support: Murals of War and Peace*, Belfast, 1995: pages 226, 229

Michael Staunton: page 224

INDEX